GEORGE

# INDIAN REMINISCENCES

OR

## THE BENGAL MOOFUSSUL MISCELLANY

Elibron Classics
www.elibron.com

Elibron Classics series.



ISBN 1-4021-5445-3 (paperback)
ISBN 1-4021-1984-4 (hardcover)

This Elibron Classics Replica Edition is an unabridged facsimile of the edition published in 1837 by Edward Bull, London.

# INDIAN REMINISCENCES.

## TO THE PUBLIC.

THE profits arising from the sale of this publication will be devoted to a charitable purpose. It is not, however, intended to propitiate, on this account alone, the good feelings and patronage of the public in its favour; for, by so doing, the editor of the volume feels it would be an injustice to the literary merits and memory of the young and accomplished author of its principal contents.

# INDIAN REMINISCENCES

OR

# THE BENGAL MOOFUSSUL MISCELLANY

CHIEFLY WRITTEN

BY THE LATE

G.A. ADDISON, ESQ.

LONDON:

EDWARD BULL, 19, HOLLES STREET.

MDCCCXXXVII.

LONDON:
C. RICHARDS, ST. MARTIN'S LANE, CHARING CROSS.

# CONTENTS.

# INTRODUCTION.

To perpetuate the existence of thoughts and feelings recorded in by-gone days, and in distant lands, is surely not an unworthy or useless task; for by it the memory of early friendships and youthful associations, is often revived, the mind carried back, through vicissitudes of fortune, through the rain and sunshine of chequered existence, to that bright portion of it, when "gay hope was hers by fancy fed:"—to many readers, therefore, it is hoped, that this volume will prove acceptable, from recalling to mind scenes and friends of the olden time.

As by far the greater portion of the following papers was composed by the late G. A. Addison, Esq., the Editor considers it but a fair meed, and honourable tribute of praise to the deceased, as well as a debt of justice to the public, to preface the work with a faithful and succinct memoir of their young and accomplished author.

George Augustus Addison was born at Calcutta, in 1792,—and at an early age, sent to England for his education. His father, the late John Addison, Esq., was in the Civil Service of the Honourable East India Company. He held the situation of Judge of Nattore, at the period of his son's birth, and subsequently, other situations high in the Service: and, at the time of his death, was President of Bauleah.

Mr. Addison senior, as the nearest collateral descendant, was heir-at-law to the celebrated moralist,—that great man having a daughter only in the direct line, who died unmarried.

Although no hereditary claim to the intellectual powers of the poet can be maintained, it is impossible to deny the existence of an affinity in ability and talent that would not have disgraced a nearer tie.

In his fifth year, George was entered at Hackney school, at that period a celebrated place of education for youth, enrolling in its academic list the scions of various illustrious houses, and producing many promising students,—who, under the auspices of Dr. Newcomb, rose, in after life, to eminence.

Illustrative of our author's great abilities in this early stage, may be quoted an anecdote, exemplifying his capacity, quick apprehension, and extraordinary retention of memory. Dr. Newcomb having established an exhibition of the talents of his pupils, under the familiar term of "Speeches," was, on the eve of one of these trying and anxious scenes, mortified by the sudden illness of the young gentleman who was to have taken a prominent part in the proceedings of the day, by the delivery of a Greek oration, of great length, and requiring superior powers of elocution. Announcing the fact to his scholars, the learned doctor enlarged on the embarrassment he felt, to meet the nobility and gentry formally invited to assemble and judge of his abilities as a teacher, by the proficiency and talents of those confided to his care.

In this dilemma, George Addison, modestly, but firmly, presented himself to supply the invalid's place,—a task, that the worthy doctor, coupling the few hours left for its performance with the knowledge of its concomitant difficulties, (even under the advantage of time and study,) confessed himself sceptical of the success of,—but, nevertheless, as an only alternative, he embraced it, from confidence in the young aspirant. Nor were the nervous feelings of the master diminished in the morning, by the many heads of schools and colleges collected to witness the examination.

Every thing went on however as was expected, till George Addison mounted the rostrum to deliver the oration,—when the master's agitation betrayed itself palpably, and was reciprocated by all who were in the secret. As, however, the speaker warmed in his subject, the applause became general;—and when he concluded, so great was the burst of approbation that sealed his triumph, as to overcome the phlegmatic character of the excellent doctor, who, yielding to the impulse of feelings, rarely excited, ran down and embraced the youthful orator, thanking him publicly, in terms of the highest encomium, for maintaining the credit of the school.

George's name remains engraved in characters of gold in the school, with those of others, who similarly distinguished themselves at different times.

At the period in question, he was only fourteen years of age,—and this promise of talent, his after life did not belie.

Shortly after, he embarked for India. Without entering into the subordinate details of his useful career,—suffice it that he ultimately became Private Secretary to J. S. Raffles, Esq. (afterwards Sir Stamford Raffles) then Governor of Java.

In the enlarged sphere thus presented for the exercise of those qualities which distinguished him, whether as the polished gentleman—the accomplished scholar—the indefatigable man of business —or the affable and kind friend of all who deserved advancement, his popularity rose to a height rarely attained; and his appointment to the post of Secretary to the Government, subsequently was made the occasion of an address from the mercantile body at Batavia. At a later period, the thanks of the Governor in Council, were accorded to his services: and the official report of their nature and extent, furnishes a document of inestimable value to his family.

George Addison died, beloved and lamented, at Java, in the twenty-second year of his age, of a fever, that carried him off in a few days. The subjoined extracts of letters from Sir Stamford Raffles, attest his high sense of the worth of this excellent and able young man: and few could better judge of, or appreciate his character and acquirements, than that talented individual.

EXTRACT OF A LETTER FROM SIR STAMFORD RAFFLES, GOVERNOR OF JAVA, TO MR. E——.

*Buitenzorg, 28th Feb.* 1814.

"I have had the opportunity of meeting your wishes fully with regard to Mr. Addison, who has in every way proved himself deserving of the high encomiums you passed upon him, and of the confidence which I immediately placed in his ability and character. He arrived very opportunely at a moment when I required an able assistant in the superintendence and direction of the Revenue arrangements, and has been appointed Assistant Secretary to

Government in this department; an office which I hope the Supreme Government will sanction, under the recent change of system.

"It is probable that he will write to you himself, expressive of the satisfaction he feels in his present situation. He lives with us at Government House, and forms one of our family in every respect, and it is due to his amiable character that I should return you my sincere thanks for having introduced so much virtue and ability to my acquaintance.

(Signed) "J. S. RAFFLES."

EXTRACT OF A LETTER FROM THE GOVERNOR OF JAVA TO THE SECRETARY OF THE SUPREME GOVERNMENT OF BENGAL.

"SIR,—

"I am directed by the Honourable the Lieutenant Governor in Council, to report to you the death of Mr. G. A. Addison, Assistant Secretary to the Revenue and Judicial Departments.

"In communicating this lamented occurrence, the Lieutenant Governor in Council is anxious to take the opportunity of expressing the high sense he entertains of the talents, merits, and services, of Mr. Addison. His abilities and acquirements were remarkably great, his application and exertions unwearied, and his personal conduct as amiable as his public services were eminent.

"The Lieutenant Governor in Council therefore sincerely regrets his loss in every point of view.

(Signed) "CHARLES ASSEY."
*Secretary to Government.*

*Batavia, 21st Jan.* 1815.

No higher praise than the above can well be bestowed. By his scientific acquirements, Mr. Addison was enabled to methodise the arrangement of his duties, and to make his adaptation of the principles of political economy beneficial to the interests of the colony. Yet he found time to keep up a sportive acquaintance with the Muses, and indulge in pursuits of a less grave character.

The papers and poems he has left, speak the cultivation of his mind; and his correspondence with friends he valued, on literary topics, and very varied subjects, evince a playfulness of fancy, delicacy of feeling, and soundness of judgment, remarkable in one so young;—in a word, he was master of six languages—a first-rate mathematician, an admitted classic, a firm and zealous friend, a devoted son, an affectionate brother, and an unostentatious Christian.

We feel inclined to repine at the early removal of such men. Natural reason understands not why death alights on one so youthful and serviceable, just at a period when his usefulness becomes valuable to his country, and his virtues begin to exert an influence on the society in which he moves; but it is the Divine Will, so to order events: and this recollection should satisfy the repiner.

> "Health, is at best, a vain precarious thing,
> And fair-faced youth is ever on the wing:"

These lines are part of a version of Pope's melancholy letter to Mr. Steele, (vol. vii. p. 187, 1st edit.) by Mr. West, another of those whose early promise, like G. A. Addison's, was blighted in its prime.

Truly poetical (but nothing more) are the thoughts of Pope upon the subject;—they would indeed come admirably from an unenlightened heathen moralist: The reader shall judge for himself, and will doubtless consider their beauty and appropriateness to the present topic, as a sufficient apology for inserting them.

"Youth, at the very best, is but the betrayer of human life in a gentler and smoother manner than age: 'tis like the stream that nourishes a plant upon a bank, and causes it to flourish and blossom to the sight, but at the same time is undermining it at the root in secret. * * * * The morning after my exit, the sun will rise as bright as ever, the flowers smell as sweet, the plants spring as green: people will laugh as heartily, and marry as fast as they used to do.—'The memory of man' (as it is elegantly expressed in the Book of Wisdom) 'passeth away as the remembrance of a guest, that tarrieth but one day.' There are reasons enough in the fourth chapter of the same book to make any young man contented with the prospect of death.—'For honourable age is not that which standeth in length of time, or is measured by number of years; but wisdom is the grey hair to man, and an unspotted life is old age: he was taken away speedily, lest wickedness should alter his understanding, or deceit beguile his soul."

Much of the above quotation is, indeed, equally applicable to the lamented George Addison.

His short career was adorned by every virtue of domestic life. His unaffected manliness of character, integrity of spirit, and benevolent disposition, won the esteem and affection of all who came into communion with him.

Thus much may be permitted to one who sincerely regarded the subject of this brief memoir, and who would fain snatch from oblivion a few memorials of his worth and talents, by this feeble tribute to his name.

The remainder of the papers in this collection are from the pens of persons (chiefly now no more) who held civil and military appointments, and of various other British residents in Bengal.

*December*, 1836.

" Fuge, quo descendere gestis :
Non erit emisso reditus tibi. Quid miser egi ?
Quid volui ?"

HOR. *Lib.* I. *Ep.* xx. *v.* 5, 6,7.

## ADDRESS TO THE READER.

---

Dr. Johnson commences a periodical work with observing, that every one must have felt the difficulty of the first address on any new occasion. At this moment, alas! I experience how wofully true is his remark, and gladly would I waive altogether such previous ceremony, but that custom—imperious custom—forbids;—she has pronounced a Preface to be an indispensable preliminary, and to her dictates I must with submission bow. Yet, by the way, in all works, except those that resemble the present, there is somewhat of a blunder in giving them this denomination, for they seldom contain any prefatory observations, and should rather be styled, and take the usual place of Postscripts, serving, as they do, to extenuate, or more fully explain, matter that ought previously to have been read. So sensible of this was Mr. Plowden, that he termed his a "postliminous preface;" rather a strange term it is true, but perfectly appropriate when we remember that it was attached to a history of Ireland.

In periodical publications, however, a preface has to perform the functions that its name implies—to explain what is intended *to be*, not what *is* done: and we accordingly find, that this part of the work generally bears marks of the writer's most sedulous attention. Example, nevertheless, instead of instigating me, as perhaps it ought, has here, I must confess, a very opposite deterring effect. For when I view the various, excellently-laid projects, the large and flourishing promises, which usher in so many brilliant commencements—and remark afterwards, in so many continuances, so sad, so unfortunate an oblivion of all execution and fulfilment—I fear, I own, to incur the danger of falling into a similar error, and of meriting with them the being stigmatized from the ever-sensible Horace with "Parturiunt montes." I know but of one mode of easily and certainly obviating this—it is by pledging myself to no schemes, and by not holding out any promises whatsoever. However little may, then, be done, that little will still exceed aught to be claimed as matter of right. I cannot, then, in any event, be said to have falsified my reader's hopes, for I shall not have incited him to entertain any: and if I do, subsequently, prove better than my word, and "pay the debt I never promised," my first offence of omission will at least be compensated for by "making that offence a skill."

But still there may be some who condemn me

for having troubled myself to write at all, and more, for having presumed to trouble them, who may *good-naturedly* cite to me—

> "Let such teach others, who themselves excel,
> And censure freely who have written well,"—

and then ask how I have had the rashness to think myself competent to give them either advice or information? To these I must observe, that my own *trouble* I shall consider but as in the light of pleasure, as I write myself, and invite others to do so —only for amusement. With respect to themselves, I disclaim any responsibility, for if they encounter trouble, to them be it imputed, for now that we are but in the vestibule, every one has of course a full liberty to enter in or go no farther, as he may choose. As to the presumption of thinking myself competent to give advice or information, the latter charge I deny—I do not expect from any writing of my own to add to the stock of ideas that my readers may possess: but I do hope—perhaps too sanguinely—that some kind correspondents may start up to please and instruct both them and myself. On the former charge—if it be a crime—I at once plead guilty. I will not say that such is my intention, but I certainly consider myself able to give *advice*; and I challenge my accuser to produce any person who thinks otherwise: for himself, his hints to me at least implicate him in the charge. Some sage philosopher—though I cannot just now recollect his name

—very finely observes, that "there are three things we can all do, viz. prescribe medicine, give advice, and poke the fire." Why then should I be denied a privilege which is thus declared common?

The quotation from Pope I will not heed, it is indeed somewhat unfair, and Johnson has observed, that it resembles the sentiment "Who drives fat oxen should himself be fat;" I prefer the more liberal one of Horace, of which I trust my readers will excuse the following rough translation:—

> "I, though I scribble in Apollo's spite,
> Can teach to others what is just and right;
> And thus the whetstones on the steel bestow
> An edge with which themselves can never glow."

But I have now said enough, and must not forget another excellent hint of his—

> "Non fumum ex fulgore, sed ex fumo dare lucem"—

not to let my brightness sink into smoke, but, (like the patent gas-light society) to elicit from smoke a brilliant light. I will at least endeavour to keep this in mind, and even should I not succeed, will remember the "magnis tamen excidit ausis"—"though he has fallen, he dared greatly," with many other such pertinent observations, and thus, like Hudibras,—

> "Console myself with ends of verse,
> And sayings of philosophers."

## NOTICE TO CORRESPONDENTS.

THE Editor of "The Moofossul Miscellany" will consider himself extremely obliged to any persons who may aid him in his undertaking, and honour him with their correspondence. He pledges himself that the greatest attention shall be paid to their favours. At the same time, it will of course rest with him, as with all other editors, to insert or reject what may be offered, as he shall deem good:—and he begs that it may be farther understood that he intends to exercise this prerogative in silence. He is aware that, in giving up the "notices to correspondents," he deprives himself of excellent opportunities for displaying keen and witty remarks,—such as,—

"A. B.'s lines to Delia" contain much more *affection* than poetry:

"C. D. in his Essay on Conscience," seems to think it not requisite to shew any to his readers:

"E. F.'s Epigram on the Comet" wants, unfortunately, what its subject so eminently possesses—a brilliant tail, &c. &c.

This, at the best, is taking an *ex parte* advantage,—striking a blow without giving your adversary an opportunity of parrying or retaliating it; and in renouncing it, therefore, he flatters himself he shall be thought to have deviated from a custom "more honoured in the breach than the observance."

## ON CHARACTERISTICAL PARTIALITIES.

---

Sir,—I offer you a few thoughts, loosely thrown together, on a subject which must have frequently presented itself to the observation of every one of your readers, viz.—Characteristical Partialities.

Nothing is more commonly met with than these, yet there is nothing which a wise man should more strenuously strive to avoid, for though the entertaining a love for any particular object or science is, in itself, by no means reprehensible, yet, when this love becomes so inordinate, as to exclude from the mind the power of duly admiring aught besides, there is nothing which serves more to weaken the reasoning faculties, or narrow the understanding.

Yet the minds of most men have naturally a bent towards this failing; and it is against the approaches to it, therefore, that our attention should chiefly be directed. "Il n'y a que le premier pas qui coute,"—habits of thinking upon only one subject are very soon acquired, and this too quickly becomes, as it were, an unalterable part of the constitution of the mind. A violent and unequal partiality is contracted, and so devoted, in a short time, is every faculty to it, that attention cannot but be excluded from other pursuits, whose importance, only a want of understanding, or this habitual infatuation, could conceal from the mind, or banish from the thoughts. We should, therefore, with the greatest sedulity, guard against such an infatuation, since, as is seen, it reduces us to a level with men of the weakest understandings.

Our minds were not formed to be restricted to one object—to one pursuit; but have received from the hand of Nature a fineness of tact, that can apprehend every thing, from the grossness of mere matter, to the most intellectual visions of the soul,—and a capacity, that can comprehend whatever hath existed, or may at any future time exist —either in the regions of fancy or of reality!—

> "The expanded mind
> Pluming her wings, may take her airy way
> Through yonder worlds of light!"—

and as it "glances from heaven to earth, from earth to heaven," may seize the universe itself, and "all which it inherit." Like the divinity of Lucan,—

> "Estne animi sedes, nisi terra, et pontus, et aer,
> Et cælum, et virtus!"

"Has not the mind its seat in the earth, the sea, the air, the heavens, and virtue?"—Yes: "quodcunque vides, quocunque moveris,"—"whatever you see, wherever you move," that is subjugated to its command, and there its power extends!

To turn it, then, from such noble and vast uses, —to contract it to one small sphere of action,—is indeed to abuse the noblest gift we possess. It should range free as air. The river that flows over many soils, carries sweetness and health wherever it goes; but the spring that bubbles but from a metallic bed, cannot but acquire the corrosive qualities of its channel: and it is in overflowing its banks only that the Nile bestows fertility on Egypt. But now for some instances of this power, which partialities, or, to use a stronger and harsher term, prejudices, have assumed over the minds of even the wisest men. I shall confine myself, however, to those that occur in the literary world,—in the love for particular studies; and even with these, many volumes might be filled.

I know of no one species of reading that more takes hold of the whole mind than mathematics; even Plato was so enraptured with its beauties, and convinced of its universal utility, that he had inscribed over his door, "Nemo huc pedem inferat, nisi Geometres,"—"Let no man enter here that is not a mathematician." And, considering, indeed, how essentially necessary it is in every branch of science, from the most common and simple, to the sublimest speculations of the mind, and how much it serves to expand the thoughts, and correct the judgment, such a partiality may, if not carried to an extreme length, be excused, and even deserve applause. But when all the mind is given up to mathematical deductions, merely for their own sake, without considering them as valuable only as they relate to other branches of science,—then, indeed, we can only pity the enthusiast who wastes his time in such fruitless labours,—even though he be employed at the quadrature of the circle!

Who can with patience hear the learned Dr. Free, when his blind attachment to this study makes him declare, that the proper *definition* of a man is, "a being who can prove the three angles of a triangle to be equal to two right ones!!" This is almost as bad as Boswell's famous definition of man being "a cooking animal;" or Plato's, that he is "bipes, implumis,"—"two footed, without feathers!" It is, moreover, unjust; for if, as is fair, we invert his proposition, and say that the being, who cannot prove the three angles, &c. is *no* man, then how many two-footed, unfeathered animals must we exclude from the class of the lords of the creation! (This demonstration is the thirty-second problem of Euclid, and as his problems are arranged in the synthetic order, or by reasoning *a priori,* it follows, that the proving of this one involves the proving of all which precede it; and to demonstrate the thirty-second, therefore, a person must be able to demonstrate the fifth, or to prove that the angles at the base of an isosceles triangle are equal to one another, &c.—and yet how many have we known who have forfeited their claims to manhood, by not being able to cross this "bridge of asses.") The witty author of the "Loves of the Triangles," however, seems to agree with Dr. Free, and thus thunders forth his anathemas against all poor unmathematical wights:—

"Debased, corrupted, grovelling, and confined,
No definitions touch your senseless mind:
To you no postulates prefer their claim,
Nor ardent axioms your dull souls inflame;
For you no tangents touch, no angles meet,
Nor circles join in osculation sweet."

The next that offer themselves are the Naturalists,—who hold, of course, that mathematics, and every other branch of knowledge but their own, are totally unworthy the serious attention of man. On the thorough acquaintance of all the minutiæ of beasts, birds, insects, fishes, shells, petrifactions, and vegetables, they make depend all that is valuable, and even virtuous in the world;—to the ascertaining that "*fleas* are not *lobsters*," (as the witty Peter observes) they sacrifice their whole time: and to these men, the ark of Noah, or Egypt in the time of Pharaoh's plagues, would have been a seventh paradise! I, of course, here speak of the *madmen*, if I may so call them, of the science. Linnæus, Buffon, and other such great investigators of the phenomena of the creation, I hold in due veneration, for than these, every one must own, none have laboured more usefully. But we cannot but despise persons, so enthusiastically rapt up in admiration of the elegant formation of grubs, worms, and caterpillars, as, like the celebrated and *voluminous* Dr. Hill, to declare, that the knowledge of natural phenomena is the *only source and support of morality!* (on this occasion, the wags of his time facetiously observed, that, if ever the Doctor went to heaven, it must be on the back of a beetle.) La Bruyère, in his ever happy manner, thus presents to us one of the naturalists, suffering under the severest stroke the fates could inflict on him:—"Il est plongé dans une amère douleur, il a l'humeur noire, chagrine, et dont toute sa famille souffre,—aussi a-t-il fait une perte irréparable: approchez, regardez ce qu'il vous montre sur son doigt, qui n'a plus de vie,—et qui vient d'expirer; c'est une *chenille*,—et quelle *chenille*." "'Tis a caterpillar, and what a caterpillar!"

The experimental philosopher holds in utter contempt, however, these "disturbers of the peace of insects," and at once boldly asserts, that all useful knowledge and morality is to be deduced only from *philosophical experiment!* Thus Dr. Beddoes, by inflating a man with pure *oxygen*, inspires in him an assemblage of blissful sensations, which are attended with three concomitant propellants to virtuous actions;—he asserts, that a man, thus *blown* up, feels himself, as it were, a god,—that he treads on air,—his faculties are brightened,—and that he is every way lifted above himself: but I fear the Doctor will not be able to deny that *champagne* produces effects precisely similar to his vaunted *gaseous inhalations.*

Next comes the Poet, who, "with his eyes in a fine frenzy rolling," is convinced that virtue is more lovely in elegant, poetic drapery, floating by like one of the Graces, than when dressed in the "antique ruff and bonnet" of musty dull prose: his only study are the works of Homer, Virgil, Milton, Pope, and others of the Parnassian fraternity,—these "Nocturnâ versat manu, versatque diurnâ,"—"he reads by day and meditates by night,"—nor does he feel such diffidence of his own powers, as not to be conscious that he could himself, if not *excel,* at least *equal* the mightiest masters of the poetic art. Revelling in such fine day-dreams as these, of course nothing more excites his wonder, than to hear how reasonable men can pore over such stupid things as trapeziums, dodecahedrons, or parallelopipeds,—dissect an overgrown maggot,—convert their lungs into a pair of bellows, —make a dead frog cast a somerset,—or, in short, amuse themselves with any of the other *flim-flams* of science. But poets have long been considered in their proper light—as all worthy of lodgings in Bedlam or St. Lukes,—"aut insanit, aut versus facit,"—"the man is mad, or making verses;" here there is scarce a hair's breadth between the two ideas. Boileau, too, would bestow on them places in "les petites maisons;" and it has so generally, in all ages, been decided that "every poet is a fool," that it can scarcely be necessary, at this time of day, to enter into a demonstration of what is declared to be so obvious,—and yet, "entre nous," I do think it would puzzle even the *learned* Dr. Free, to prove it, rather more than to prove his problem about the triangles. J. J. Rousseau is almost the only writer who stands forward in their defence, and even he but indirectly; he says —"il n-y-a qu'un géomètre et un sot, qui puissent parler sans figures." Now, if figurative speaking be the *Shibboleth* of fools, how very far removed from them must be poets, who scarcely ever speak but in figures.

The violent attachment of novelists and dramatists to their particular lines of reading, is well known, and has already been commented on, and censured, by far abler pens than mine. Nor will I speak of the weaknesses of politicians, which are of all others the most outrageous; so much so, indeed, as to have acquired a distinct *specific name*, the *generic* one being "*partiality;*" but for politicians, the word "*party*" is given, and every one is acquainted with the violence of this. Thomson very justly observes—

> "With what impartial care
> Ought we to watch o'er prejudice and passion,
> Nor trust too much the jaundiced eye of party!"

for to this eye, "all seems yellow," and yet on its delusive optics depends entirely the light in which every matter is viewed by its adherents; the same thing is not only considered as different, by people of opposite principles, but even, by the *same* persons, it is held as differing from *itself*, as the *times* of viewing it differ; what is distorted often seems straight, and the most beautiful things, through this medium, frequently appear deformed. But the very subject is *odious*, and I will only dwell on it one moment longer, to recall to your memory the well-known saying of the democratic and violent Mrs. Macauley; she observed, "that it was not Milton the *poet*, but Milton the *politician*, that she valued!" Now, as I admire just as vehemently *only* Milton the *poet*, I deem such a confession to be little short of impiety.

Some men are so *devoted* to particular *amusements*, as to completely incapacitate themselves for every thing else; of this, Prince Bathiani may be adduced as an example. A late writer, (Mr. Cox, if I recollect rightly,) in speaking of him, says,— "he seems to possess no ambition beyond a desire to analyze the whole composition of the game of chess. Could Addison's ideas be followed up, in the dissection of the brain of this man, nothing would be found in it but various models of all the various pieces made use of in this game, from the pawn to the king. He sees, he hears, he thinks of nothing but chess. It is the first thought of his waking hours, and the last of his nocturnal slumbers. I endeavoured, in vain, to detach him but for a moment from the precious continuity of his ideas, by introducing some observations upon the situation of his country; to these he made no reply, but, pulling a small chess-board out of his pocket, he assured me that he had it made in London, by one of the ablest artists of which Great Britain had to boast!"

Hogarth, in his "Analysis of Beauty," gives us an entertaining anecdote of a dancing-master, who told him, "that though the *minuet* had been the study of his *whole life*, he could only say, with Socrates, that he knew nothing;" and added, "that he thought Hogarth happy in his profession, because some bounds might be set to the study of it." The above is somewhat like an observation made by an old gentleman of seventy, who was complimented on his perfect knowledge of the art of hunting;—"O, Sir," said he, "life is too short!" The relator of this, a sportsman himself, and a writer on the subject, very gravely adds,—"that he has found this to be *a serious truth!*"

But some of your readers may exclaim, "Ohe, jam satis," and I am very much of this opinion myself. I think I have written quite sufficient to weary any common patience, and will, therefore, prepare to conclude.

By all the above instances, it has been, I hope, made evident, that what I set out with advancing is true, viz. that nothing serves more to narrow the mind, than the confining its studies to one particular object or science. And as no one would wish to acquire the character of a *prejudiced* man,—from which nothing is more distant than that of a *wise* one,—we ought, while we *can*, to preserve our minds clear of any bias. And though we should sometimes see such examples of unequal partiality, as I have before mentioned, defended, or seemingly sanctioned, by the names of great and learned men, yet, this ought only more strongly to impress on us the wisdom of avoiding those rocks on which *even they* have split. For if the most wise can be so led astray by their power, what trust can we place in our frailty? I will not, with the French philosopher, bid you rejoice in the misfortunes of others, but I certainly recommend the availing ourselves of them;—we should use them as the beacons on wrecks, and, taught by their failure, let us not *dare* these dangers, but rather avoid than resist—for *prevention* hath ever been esteemed superior to *cure*.

MENTOR.

## GENERAL SOLUTION OF THE KNIGHT'S TRICK AT CHESS.

---

Sir,—What has engaged the attention of such mathematicians as Ozanam, De Moivre, and Euler, may not be thought undeserving of a place in your work :—I send you, therefore, the following general solution of what is called "the Knight's Trick at Chess."

The conditions of this celebrated puzzle are, that the knight shall, according to his manner of moving, cover the sixty-four squares of the chess-board in as many moves. It is evident that the trick can be performed in a great variety of ways; any one, by repeated trials on paper, may discover a method, but this is only chance. The difficulty is, to find some general rule for always solving it with certainty and regularity,—which has, as yet, baffled the endeavours of all who have attempted it.

Ozanam says, "this problem can be effected many ways; it is considerable enough to have merited the attention of several great geometricians. It is true, they have not given us any general solution of it, which shews the difficulty there is in finding it."

In a work, entitled "Essai sur le jeu des Echecs," it is observed of this trick, that it is supposed one may succeed at it, beginning from any of the squares, by taking care that the last move, into the sixty-fourth square, be just a single knight's move distant from the first. Mr. Twiss observes, that this is the only attempt that has been made towards a general solution of the puzzle, though he deems it far from being satisfactory. In fact, there is nothing new in the above observation—the conditions first laid down imply precisely the same, and it is impossible to perform the trick otherwise; as, unless the first and sixty-fourth numbers are exactly a knight's move distant from each other, there will, in reality, have been but sixty-three moves, and the first number will never have been covered,—for setting out from it cannot be considered as covering it: and, consequently, what the conditions require will not have been performed. This, however, has escaped the attention of most who have endeavoured to solve the problem; and the ways they have proposed of performing it have, accordingly, been imperfect. Such is the case with the method given by the celebrated De Moivre; it is the most regular of any in appearance, but the first and sixty-fourth squares being more than a knight's move distant from each other, the conditions laid down are not fulfilled, and the problem of course is not effected.

Ozanam, in 1722, published two other methods.

Guzot, in his "Récréations Mathématiques," gave one, and Mr. Twiss also, in his work on chess, (8vo. 1777) inserted two ways, which he had discovered by repeated trials on a slate. Several others were printed on cards, and sold at what was formerly the great chess rendezvous, the Café de la Régence in Paris: and, to speak from my own experience, any one, who may choose to try, may discover numerous other manners of performing it. But most of those already published have been imperfect, in containing, in the way I have shewn, really but sixty-three moves; and the others, which were merely found by accident, are neither regular nor certain, and afford nothing like a general solution.

The author of the "Eulogium on Euler," pronounced before the French Academy, observes of this great mathematician, that the knight's movement in the game of Chess, and different other problems of situation, had excited his curiosity, and exercised his genius. As, however, I have never seen these papers, I am ignorant whether the above has any reference to a *solution* of this puzzle, or merely to Euler's having, like De Moivre and others, found out by trials a *way* of doing it. I am inclined to think only the latter, as Mr. Twiss, who has made every possible research on the question, does not at all notice it in his first work, which was published subsequently to those of

Euler;—and in a late one, entitled "Miscellanies," he no farther speaks of it than to copy the moves from a German pamphlet describing the celebrated chess-playing image of M. de Kempeler:—had it been a *solution,* he would certainly have done more than this, and have diligently examined into and explained it. Instead of this, he sums up his enquiry by observing, that no one had been successful in finding a rule, and expressed it as his opinion that the trick is not capable of a general solution. I am happy to prove him mistaken in this,—having myself discovered one which is general and complete. This I shall describe as briefly as I can.

Setting off from one of the corner squares of the board, form a re-entering scheme of four knights' moves;—that is, let the fourth figure be precisely a knight's move distant from the first. Do the same with the other three corners, and then with other twelve squares on the border of the board. There will then be formed sixteen re-entering schemes, of four knight's moves each, which will exactly fill the sixty-four squares of the board. These schemes I shall distinguish, in the following diagram, by marking them with different letters, as, A 1, 2, 3, 4, B 1, 2, 3, 4, &c.

| | | | | | | | |
|---|---|---|---|---|---|---|---|
| A 1 | M 1 | I 1 | E 1 | G 1 | K 1 | O 1 | B 1 |
| I 2 | E 2 | A 2 | M 2 | O 2 | B 2 | G 2 | K 2 |
| M 4 | A 4 | E 4 | I 4 | K 4 | G 4 | B 4 | O 4 |
| E 3 | I 3 | M 3 | A 3 | B 3 | O 3 | K 3 | G 3 |
| F 3 | J 3 | N 3 | D 3 | C 3 | P 3 | L 3 | H 3 |
| N 4 | D 4 | F 4 | J 4 | L 4 | H 4 | C 4 | P 4 |
| J 2 | F 2 | D 2 | N 2 | P 2 | C 2 | H 2 | L 2 |
| D 1 | N 1 | J 1 | F 1 | H 1 | L 1 | P 1 | C 1 |

Of this Figure the squares marked

| | | | | | | |
|---|---|---|---|---|---|---|
| A 2 | and | A 3 | let into | G 1 | and | G 4. |
| B 2 | ... | B 3 | ...... | E 1 | ... | E 4. |
| C 2 | ... | C 3 | ...... | F 1 | ... | F 4. |
| D 2 | ... | D 3 | ...... | H 1 | ... | H 4. |
| M 2 | ... | M 3 | ...... | K 1 | ... | K 4. |
| N 2 | ... | N 3 | ...... | L 4 | ... | L 1. |
| O 1 | ... | O 3 | ...... | I 1 | ... | I 4. |
| P 1 | ... | P 3 | ...... | J 1 | ... | J 4. |

Observe then what two schemes can be so blended into each other, by knights' moves, as to form a new one, of eight figures, possessing, like the former, the property of having its first and last figures exactly a knight's move asunder. The schemes can be so blended or interlaced, when any two adjoining figures of one, form with any two adjoining figures of any other, a re-entering scheme of four knights' moves, thus:

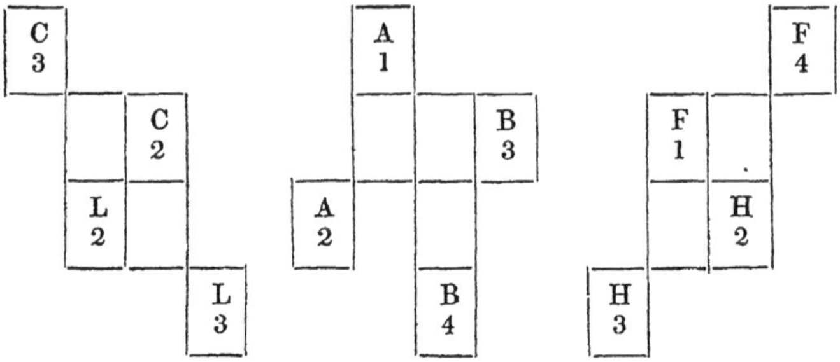


Form in this manner the sixteen schemes into eight, each of eight figures:

| | | | | | | | |
|---|---|---|---|---|---|---|---|
| A G<br>1 | M K<br>1 | O I<br>3 | B E<br>3 | A G<br>3 | M K<br>3 | O I<br>1 | B E<br>1 |
| O I<br>4 | B E<br>4 | A G<br>2 | M K<br>2 | O I<br>2 | B E<br>2 | A G<br>4 | M K<br>4 |
| M K<br>8 | A G<br>8 | B E<br>6 | O I<br>6 | M K<br>6 | A G<br>6 | B E<br>8 | O I<br>8 |
| B E<br>5 | O I<br>5 | M K<br>7 | A G<br>7 | B E<br>7 | O I<br>7 | M K<br>5 | A G<br>5 |
| C F<br>5 | P J<br>5 | N L<br>7 | D H<br>7 | C F<br>7 | P J<br>7 | N L<br>5 | D H<br>5 |
| N L<br>8 | D H<br>8 | C F<br>6 | P J<br>6 | N L<br>6 | D H<br>6 | C F<br>8 | P J<br>5 |
| P J<br>4 | C F<br>4 | D H<br>2 | N L<br>2 | P J<br>2 | C F<br>2 | D H<br>4 | N L<br>4 |
| D H<br>1 | N L<br>1 | P J<br>3 | C F<br>3 | D H<br>3 | N L<br>3 | P J<br>1 | C F<br>1 |

Each of these Eight schemes is marked with the letters of the two schemes, of the first figure which enters into its construction.

Of this Figure the square, marked

| | | | | | | | |
|---|---|---|---|---|---|---|---|
| AG 2 | and | AG 3 | let into | OI 5 | and | OI 6. |
| BE 2 | ... | BE 3 | ...... | MK 5 | ... | MK 6. |
| DH 2 | ... | DH 3 | ...... | PJ 5 | ... | PJ 6. |
| CF 2 | ... | CF 3 | ...... | NL 5 | ... | NL 6. |

In the same manner blend these eight schemes into pairs or fours:

| | | | | | | | |
|---|---|---|---|---|---|---|---|
| A O 1 | B M 7 | A O 5 | B M 11 | A O 11 | B M 5 | A O 7 | B M 1 |
| A O 4 | B M 12 | A O 2 | B M 6 | A O 6 | B M 2 | A O 12 | B M 4 |
| B M 8 | A O 16 | B M 14 | A O 10 | B M 10 | A O 14 | B M 16 | A O 8 |
| B M 13 | A O 3 | B M 9 | A O 15 | B M 15 | A O 9 | B M 3 | A O 13 |
| C N 13 | D P 3 | C N 9 | D P 15 | C N 15 | D P 9 | C N 3 | D P 13 |
| C N 8 | D P 16 | C N 14 | D P 10 | C N 10 | D P 14 | C N 16 | D P 8 |
| D P 4 | C N 12 | D P 2 | C N 6 | D P 6 | C N 2 | D P 12 | C N 4 |
| D P 1 | C N 7 | D P 5 | C N 11 | D P 11 | C N 5 | D P 7 | C N 1 |

In each of these four schemes, instead of taking all the letters of the two of the last figure, which compose it, I have, for want of room, inserted only the initial ones.

Of this Figure the squares marked

| | | | | | | |
|---|---|---|---|---|---|---|
| AO 9 | and | AO 10 | let into | CN 10 | and | CN 9. |
| BM 9 | ... | BM 10 | ...... | DP 10 | ... | DP 9. |

Proceed similarly with these four schemes, interlacing them into *two*, each of thirty-two figures, which re-enter or circulate:—

| | | | | | | | |
|---|---|---|---|---|---|---|---|
| A C 1 | B D 7 | A C 5 | B D 27 | A C 27 | B D 5 | A C 7 | B D 1 |
| A C 4 | B D 28 | A C 2 | B D 6 | A C 6 | B D 2 | A C 28 | B D 4 |
| B D 8 | A C 32 | B D 30 | A C 26 | B D 26 | A C 30 | B D 32 | A C 8 |
| B D 29 | A C 3 | B D 9 | A C 31 | B D 31 | A C 9 | B D 3 | A C 29 |
| A C 13 | B D 19 | A C 25 | B D 15 | A C 15 | B D 25 | A C 19 | B D 13 |
| A C 24 | B D 16 | A C 14 | B D 10 | A C 10 | B D 14 | A C 16 | B D 24 |
| B D 20 | A C 12 | B D 18 | A C 22 | B D 22 | A C 18 | B D 12 | A C 20 |
| B D 17 | A C 23 | B D 21 | A C 11 | B D 11 | A C 21 | B D 23 | A C 17 |

Again, for want of room, I take only the Initial Letters of the former Schemes.

Of this Figure the Squares marked,
AC 9 and AC 10, let into BD 13 and BD 12.

And, lastly, in the same manner blend them into *one* :—

| | | | | | | | |
|---|---|---|---|---|---|---|---|
| 1 | 36 | 5 | 24 | 59 | 34 | 7 | 30 |
| 4 | 25 | 2 | 35 | 6 | 31 | 60 | 33 |
| 37 | 64 | 27 | 58 | 23 | 62 | 29 | 8 |
| 26 | 3 | 38 | 63 | 28 | 9 | 32 | 61 |
| 45 | 16 | 57 | 12 | 47 | 22 | 51 | 10 |
| 56 | 13 | 46 | 39 | 42 | 11 | 48 | 21 |
| 17 | 44 | 15 | 54 | 19 | 50 | 41 | 52 |
| 14 | 55 | 18 | 43 | 40 | 53 | 20 | 49 |

As there is no farther distinction necessary, I drop the Letters altogether in this last Diagram.

This, as it covers the sixty-four squares in as many moves, and is so arranged that the first and sixty-fourth numbers are precisely a knight's move distant from each other,—fulfils the conditions and solves the problem.

Yours, &c.

PHILO-PHILLIDOR.

## ON VARIOUS MODES OF DIVINATION.

MEN, ever since the creation, have endeavoured to pry into the secrets of futurity:—this desire is inherent in us, and has been by many philosophers adduced as one of the strongest proofs of the immortality of the soul, that, indignant at its confinement, is ever attempting to release itself, and soar beyond present time and circumstances.

Finding, however, all their efforts to discover them, by the force of reason, vain, they have naturally resorted to the aid of the blind god Chance,—and hence, omens from the flight of birds—from the entrails of sacrifices—in short, from every thing around,—oracles and divination by *lots* have arisen.

Of this last alone I propose now to write to you. When a choice between two equal things was to be made, the referring it to chance, by the casting of *lots,* would obviously present itself as a fair mode of deciding, where the judgment was unequal to do so: and we find, therefore, this among the most ancient of usages recorded in the Bible;—thus Aaron cast *lots* for the scape-goat. The direction of these lots would, of course, be soon imputed to the divine pleasure of the Almighty observer and guider of all things, and it would then occur to the inquisitive, that this mode might be adopted for looking into futurity. Accordingly, we see that this superstitious practice was very quickly applied to such purposes, an instance of which is given in Esther, c. iii. v. 7, where, when Haman desired to find out the most proper time in which to slay all the Jews, he ordered the "pur" to be cast—that is, *the lots,* from day to day, and from month to month, and discovered that the thirteenth day of the twelfth month was most favourable for his designs; but he was deceived, and the event proved the vanity of relying on such divination. This mode, however, was too *simple* for the generality of men, and the custom next adopted was the mixing together a number of *letters* in an urn, throwing them out, and examining the arrangement into which they might fall; but, as frequently, no sense could be discovered from these, in lieu of letters, whole words were adopted: and even here the answer was very often not to be understood. To obviate this, Cicero tells us, that a variety of predictions were inscribed on pieces of wood, which were kept in a box, shaken, and one drawn out by a child. He informs us how these were first discovered, but observes, "tota res est inventa fallaciis, aut ad quæstum, aut ad superstitionem"—"the whole matter is, however, fallacious every way:" and again, in speaking of it, he says, "quibus in rebus temeritas et casus, non ratio, nec consilium valet"—"chance, not reason, presides over these things." This mode of divination is continually spoken of by the writers of that age; thus Lucretius—

"Necquicquam Divûm numen, sortesque fatigant"—

"In vain they implore the Gods, and search the *lots;*" and Ovid, "auxilium per sacras quærere sortes"—"to seek for aid in the sacred *lots;*" numberless other instances might be given of the frequency of the practice. But as the urn and heaven-descended mystical pieces of wood were not always at hand, another mode was invented throughout Greece and Italy, which superseded their use.

This was to take the works of some celebrated poet, as Homer, Euripides, or Virgil, to open the book at hazard, and to receive as an oracle the first passage that met the eye. This, in Greek, as

Homer was principally consulted, was termed rhapsadomoncy (Ραψωδομαντεια); and by the Romans, the "sortes Homericæ," or "Virgilianæ." The resorting to them was very frequent: thus Severus founded his hopes of the Roman Empire on a Virgilian consultation, which had declared to him—

"Tu regere imperio populos, Romane, memento.
ÆN. lib. vi. v. 852.

Roman, 'tis thine to hold imperial sway,
The world itself shall thee its lord obey.

And Gordianus, whose reign was extremely short, was dismayed by another in the same page, which said—

"Ostendunt terris hunc tantum fata, neque ultra
Esse sinent." IBID. v. 870.

Him just on earth the rigorous Fates shall show,
Then snatch him early to the shades below.

Brutus is likewise said to have looked into Homer the night before the battle of Philippi, and most ominously fell on the passage where Patroclus is lamenting his defeat and death.

Among the Hebrews, too, there was a divination called the *Bath-Kol* (בת קול), which was, taking as a prediction the first words they heard anybody pronounce; and, as superstitions have ever been contagious, we find something similar to this in the Grecian records, for when Socrates was in prison, a person there happened to quote from Homer the following line—

Ἤματί κεν τριτάτῳ φθίην ἐρίβωλον ἱκοίμην.

I Phthia's shores the third day hence shall reach.

Socrates immediately cried to Æschinus, "from this I learn that I shall die in three days."

He formed this opinion from the double sense of the word *Phthia,* it being in Greek not only the name of a place, but also signifies *death.* Conformably to this prediction, Socrates was put to death three days after.

All these various modes have descended to our times. The first Christians, in adopting them, rejected the searching in profane writers, and looked for these—as they termed them, divine ordinances, in the Scripture. They termed them the "sortes sanctorum," and even attempted to justify the practice from the authority of Proverbs, c. xvi. v. 33:—"The *lot* is cast into the lap, but the disposing thereof is of the Lord;" and again of this text—"search, and ye shall find; but, on the other hand, they omitted to pay due attention to such verses as these—"thou shalt not tempt the Lord thy God;" and Deut. c. xviii. v. 10, "there shall not be found among you any that useth divination, &c.; for all that do these things are an abomination unto the Lord:" and their sentence, according to Leviticus, c. xx. v. 27, was to be stoned to death.

St. Augustine, in his Epistles, tells us that he does not disapprove of this practice, provided it be not for worldly purposes. So common was once the custom, that every bishop, on coming to his see, examined the "sortes sanctorum," to discover the future success of his episcopate.

The choice itself of bishops sometimes depended on it; thus when Aignan was proposed for the see of Orleans, the people first demanded a biblical confirmation, and on opening, the following verse in the Psalms appeared:—"Blessed is the man whom thou choosest; he shall dwell in thy holy temple." It was usual, however, to go previously through many ceremonies, among others, the Bible was first laid on the altar.

When Heraclius, in his war against Cosroes, wished to learn in what place he should take up his winter-quarters, he purified his army for three days, opened the Gospels, and found "*Arabia!*" a thousand other instances might be given, to prove its prevalency; and many learned divines have *seriously* argued in its favour in many grave and ponderous folio volumes!!

Nor is it less amusing now-a-days to remember, that the Council of Agda, at which were assembled all the chief dignitaries of the Church, and all the learned men of that age, thought it worth their while to take the matter into their serious consideration, and after discussing with due solemnity all the pros and cons of the question, they, in the year 506, condemned the practice as *superstitious, heretical*, and *abominable;* and denounced the severest ecclesiastical vengeance on all who should resort to it!!

The Virgilian lots, in the meantime, did not languish, though the "holy" ones so much flourished; there were still found many admirers of the classics, who preferred consulting Virgil to Scripture,—not the less so, perhaps, from the then generally received opinion of Virgil's having been a great *conjuror*, (some entertaining proofs of which are given, by the by, in Walter Scott's "Lay of the Last Minstrel.")

In the reign of Charles the First, when implicit credence was placed in *lots, anagrams*, &c. we meet with several accounts of this divination having been had recourse to. Howell, in his entertaining letters, frequently mentions it; and Cowley, in writing of the Scotch treaty, makes use of the following curious words:—"The Scotch will moderate something of the rigour of their demands; the mutual necessity of an accord is visible; the King is persuaded of it, and, to tell you the truth, (which I take to be an argument above all the rest) *Virgil* has told the same thing to that purpose." Charles the First himself, and Lord Falkland, being in the Bodleian Library, were shewn a magnificently bound Virgil, and the latter, to amuse the King, proposed that they should try to discover, in the "Virgilian *lots*," their future fortunes: they did so, and met with passages equally ominous to each. That of the King was the following:—

"At bello audacis populi vexatus et armis,
Finibus extorris, complexu avulsus Iuli,
Auxilium imploret, videatque indigna suorum
Funera: nec, quum se sub leges pacis iniquæ
Tradiderit, regno aut optatâ luce fruatur:
Sed cadat ante diem, mediâque inhumatus arenâ."

ÆNEID, lib. iv. v. 615.

"Harrassed by wars that wage th' audacious race,
Torn from his home, and much loved son's embrace;
Let him around in vain for succour call,
See unrevenged his dearest subjects fall;
Nor, when at length disgraceful peace he gain,
May he enjoy or life or peaceful reign;—
But by some murderous hand untimely die,
And on the weltering shore unburied lie!"

To Lord Falkland, whose son, it must be remembered, fell at the battle of Newbury, the following passage presented itself:—

"Non hæc, ô Palla, dederas promissa parenti.
Cautiùs ut sævo velles te credere Marti!
Haud ignarus eram, quantum nova gloria in armis,
Et prædulce decus primo certamine posset.
Primitiæ juvenis miseræ! bellique propinqui
Dura rudimenta! et nulli exaudita deorum
Vota, precesque meæ!"

ÆNEID, lib. xi. v. 152.

"Not thus, O Pallas! thou thy promise gave,
Thy word was pledged with caution to be brave;
Too well I knew—where youthful ardour leads,
Joyous it glows, nor aught of peril heeds.—

O curst essay!—O blighted unripe age!
Of wars to come, the dire, the sad presage!
O cruel gods!—all, all relentless were,
Vain every vow—nor heard one fervent prayer!*

Nor has this superstition been confined to Europe, or the borders of the Mediterranean; it is equally to be met with in Arabia and Persia—for "Credula mens hominis, et fabulis erectæ aures,"—the mind of man is every where equally credulous, and the ears equally open, in all parts of the world, to receive fables. Superstitious practices are therefore never lost: but where the slightest intercourse exists, the first things bartered for are these.

We need not, then, be surprised to find, that a precisely similar custom prevails in the East, where this sortilege is termed تفأل—"tefau-ōol." Hafiz is the chief poet whom they consult. So great is the veneration the Persians entertain for him, that they have given him the title of "*divine*," and on every remarkable occasion, his book of odes is opened for oracular information. When Hafiz himself died, several of the Ulemas violently objected to granting him the usual rites of sepulture, on account of the licentiousness of his poetry: but, at length, after much dispute, it was agreed that the matter should be decided by the words of

* The reader will, I hope, excuse the above hastily-written translations.

Hafiz himself. For this purpose, his Deewan (or collection of poems) was brought, and being opened at random, the first passage that presented itself was read,—it proved to be the following :—

قدم دریغ مدار از جنازهٔ حافظ
اگرچه غرق گناه هست میرود بهشت

"Turn not thy steps from Hafiz' mournful grave,
Him, plunged in sin, shall heavenly mercy save!"

Of course every funeral honour was immediately ordered to be paid him; he was buried at his favourite Mosella: a magnificent tomb was raised over his almost adored remains, shadowed (as Capt. Franklin tells us) by the poets beloved cypresses: in this, a remarkably fine copy of his odes was continually placed, for the purpose of being used in divinations of this kind.

This old tomb is to be seen in a sketch of Kæmpfer's. A new one, of white marble, has since been raised to his memory by Kerim Khan, a prince of most elegant taste, the Augustus, indeed, of Shiraz; having adorned it with numerous beautiful public buildings, and being still celebrated in Persia for his munificence in rewarding merit of every kind. The epitaph is a very singular one, and I propose communicating it to you in a future letter, on another subject. When the great Nadir Shah and his officers were passing by this tomb, near Shiraz, they were shewn the copy of the poet's works, and one of the company opening it, the first passage that met their eyes was the following—which of course they immediately applied to the conqueror:—" It is but just that thou shouldst receive a tribute from all fair youths, since thou art the sovereign of all the beauties in the universe: thy two piercing eyes have thrown Khater (Scythia) and Khoten (Tartary) into confusion; India and China pay homage to thy curled locks: thy graceful mouth gave the 'streams of life' to *Khezr*,—thy sugared lip renders the sweet reeds of Misr (Egypt) contemptible." Of the hero, sage, or prophet Khezr, above-mentioned, the Persian romances give a very strange account. He was the vizier of Secunder, or Caicobad, (not the Macedonian) and is said to have gained immortality by drinking the *(Aubi-Hyaut)* fountain of life. He is generally confounded with the prophet Elias, and, what is more singular, with our *St. George of England*, whom they call *Khezr Elias*, imagining that the same soul animated both, by transmigration.

Nadir Shah again visited the place when he was about to set out on his expedition against Tauris; and recollecting how favourably the poet had before addressed him, he again consulted his poems. Upon opening the volume he found this couplet—

عراق وپارص گرفتي بشعر خويش حافظ
بيا كه نوبت بغداد ووقت تبريز است

" Irak and Pars already own thy sway,
'Tis Bagdad's turn,—to Tauris lead the way."

The celebrated Haroun Alraschid is also said to have once opened a book of poetry, and to have read the following passage—"Where are the Kings, and where the rest of the world? They are gone the way which thou shalt go. O thou, who choosest a perishable world, and callest him happy whom it glorifies,—take all the world can give thee,—but death is at the end!" At these words, he, who had murdered Yahia and the virtuous Barmecides, was so much affected, that he wept aloud.

This subject is by no means exhausted: I doubt not but many of your readers, who are well skilled in Arabic and Persian lore, can communicate to you numerous other similar anecdotes; and as I think the subject is really curious, they would by so doing oblige—Yours, &c.

NUGARUM AMATOR.

## CRITICISM ON A PASSAGE IN THOMSON.

SIR,—In Thomson's beautiful and well-known episode of Palemon and Lavinia, there is a passage which I am much surprised no critic has observed on,—I must, however, confess, that I have read it myself an hundred times without perceiving that there was a fault, and I am even now rather angry at myself for having detected it; my enthusiastic admiration of its beauties ought never to have so far subsided, as to have allowed me to read but, as it were, with dazzled eyes, for true poetry should not only be written, but read, with a "furor mentis,"—with the "eyes in a fine phrenzy rolling," —and with the mind—"filled with fury, rapt, inspired," and who, in such a state, can stop to cavil at any petty fault?

Johnson, in speaking of Dryden's celebrated "Ode to St. Cecilia," says—"some of the lines are without correspondent rhymes, a defect which I never detected but after an acquaintance of *many years*, and which the enthusiasm of the writer might hinder him from perceiving." This might also have been the case with Thomson:—the passage to which I allude is the following:

> "He saw her charming, but he saw not *half*
> The charms her downcast modesty concealed."

This, to me, savours very much of an Hibernicism: that "he saw her charming," is very well, —but that "he saw not *half*" the charms her downcast modesty concealed," implies evidently that he did see a *part* of them;—but how could he see that which was concealed? Here is certainly a contradiction in terms. The meaning, however, is obvious, and though there is a slight confusion in the expressing it, yet, as Cowley says,

> "'Tis so like *sense* 'twill serve the turn as well."

ZOILUS

## SINGULAR MODE OF TAKING BEES' NESTS.

Sir,—I lately witnessed an operation of this kind, which appeared to me so extraordinary, that I have thought the communication of it might not prove unwelcome to you.

A large swarm of bees had fixed their abode on the ceiling of a verandah, and, in due time, when their honey was deposited, we wished to collect it, but were for some time at a loss for means. Hearing, however, that there was a gardener, who possessed a peculiar art of doing it unhurt, he was sent for, and desired to bring down the honey. I watched him closely through the whole process, and was told by him, and believe, that he used no other precaution than the following. He took some of the plant called *toolsy*, and rubbed it over his body, face, arms, and hands, he then chewed a little, and held a sprig of it in his mouth. With no other than this, apparently slight, defence, he mounted a ladder, a large dish in one hand, and a sharp knife in the other; and though as thinly clad as his class usually are,—with thousands of bees swarming about his naked body,—he, with the greatest *sang froid*, cut immediately through the upper part of the comb, where it was suspended to the roof, and, receiving the whole of it in his dish, brought it down, without having suffered from a single sting!!

This appeared to me so singular and novel a manner of proceeding, that, I assure you, had I been the sole spectator, I should have hesitated to have written it to you, but two other gentlemen of this station were also witnesses of the fact, and will confirm my statement, if necessary, by their testimony.

I know not how to account for this phenomenon, though, if experiment prove it to be constant, it cannot but be ascribed, I should think, to the bees being deceived by the strong odour of the plant, and, misled by instinct, deeming it useless to attack with their stings what they suppose to be a vegetable. The courage displayed by the man, though it may aid, is surely of itself not sufficient to produce this effect; for the stings of bees have never been considered as of a similar nature with those of nettles, of which latter it is said—"grasp them like a man of metal, and they soft as silk remain." But, whatever may be the cause, if such shall always be found to be the result, it is a process which ought to be known and practised in Europe. The present mode of taking hives, by destroying all the bees with smoke, is certainly both cruel and ungrateful, and every owner of an apiary would rejoice at being enabled to spare the lives of his useful and highly-valued insects. On the score of profit, too, he would be glad to adopt such an innocent measure,—for then, instead of losing them entirely, as he at present does, at every gathering of the honey, he might, with the greatest ease, again swarm them, and place them in new hives, there to recommence their operations.

The plant which I have above mentioned, is the *black ocymum* of botanists. Its aromatic odour is, perhaps, the strongest there is. I know that some of the species of this genus are cultivated with success in England; this, therefore, might be, in all probability, if it is not so already.

Sir William Jones addresses it in one of his poems—" Hail! *sacred* toolsy, pride of plains!" This epithet he has given to it from its particular prevalent use in the Brahminical rites; indeed, the extraordinary sanctity attached to it, is evinced, by its forming, with Ganges' water, the basis of the Hindoos' most solemn oath:—his mode of swearing is the touching these. The legend respecting it in the Sanscrit records is, that it was once a most beautiful nymph of the same name, passionately beloved by Chrisna, who, to perpetuate her memory, transformed her into this plant, and ordained that no worship to him should be availing or complete, which was not graced by her presence; hence it is invariably used in all *Poojahs* made by the followers of Vishnu.

On such a metamorphosis, with the circumstance added of the bees still paying so deep a respect to her charms, how elegant an Ovidian tale might be formed!

A GATHERER.

## MOONLIGHT THOUGHTS.

How oft, as I've roved by the moon's trembling light,
When slumber'd all Nature around,
Have I thought of those joys with a chasten'd delight,
Which I felt on a far-distant ground.

First the form of my mother arose in my mind,—
That mother who loved me so true!
And casting a look of repentance behind,
I've wept that I bade her adieu.

Next my sisters, my brother, each friend I hold dear,
In turn hath oppress'd me with woe,—
Ah! little once deem'd I that ever a tear
In thinking of you should thus flow!

Yet not long on my mind has this gloominess prey'd,
For sooth'd by all Nature's deep calm,
Kind fancy has come to afford me her aid,
And has pour'd on my soul her sweet balm.

Then forgetting the realms and the oceans between,
I have thought each companion was nigh,—
Their figures air-drawn in the moon's rays I've seen,
Their voices I've heard in the sky.

Yes, my mother! your accents my ear loves to drink,
And my cheek often glows with your kiss!
In such rapture dissolved, can I snatch time to think
That I've bade a farewell to the bliss?

Now delighted, my soul, borne on memory's wings,
Hasts to roam where I wander'd a boy;
Away from each care it indignantly flings,
And basks in the rays of pure joy.

Thus an eagle, who sits where the hurricane roars,
Nobly bursts from the region of storms,
And spurns them away, as sublimely he soars
Where no cloud the sun's disk e'er deforms.

## INVOCATION TO SLEEP.

Come, gentle Sleep, and shed thy liquid balm,
On eyes that oft have painful vigils known;
Shield me from terror,—visionary harm,
And make me some few hours of grief disown.

Blest pow'r! that gives the soul, though steeped in care,
A transient bliss—oblivion of its woes,
Fain would I have thee blunt my keen despair,
And grant soft mitigation to my throes.

Yet canst thou not retrieve the broken heart,
  Too weak, alas! t'extract the hidden pain;
Tho' soft the balm thou gently dost impart,
  More sweet to grief than Philomel's sad strain.

But ah! for sorrows such as wring my breast,
Death's night alone can yield a perfect rest!

## ODE TO ENTHUSIASM.

I.

Yes—it is thine—that magic lyre
Whose every chord a ray of fire
    Can thrill the inmost soul;
The kindling votary drinks the sound—
A thousand visions wake around—
And see!—in madd'ning raptures drown'd—
    His frenzied eye-balls roll!
But ah! what mortal hand shall dare
  From yonder bough that shell to seize?
Whose notes can give to storms the air,
  Or lull entranc'd the list'ning breeze.—
Say—for thou canst—what mortal eye
  Has favour'd seen its radiant frame?
What hand has swell'd its notes on high?
  What voice inspired its song of flame?

II.

Yes, first on Scotia's barren, bleakest rocks,
Where the hoarse surge in foam incessant breaks,
The night-winds rustling through his hoary locks,—
Its song sublime the mighty Ossian wakes!—
His eyes which glow'd with warlike fire,
Or melted once with soft desire,
Are now deep set in gloom;
But like the solar ray confin'd,
The sparks concentre on his mind,
And bright his soul illume.
Bending o'er his harp he sits,
Lost in musing, pleasing fits.
Every varying theme he tries,
Each with melody replies;—

III.

Now on softest numbers dwelling,
Love alone his lays prolong,
And now to notes tumultuous swelling,
Hark! the battle bursts along!
Lo—at his call—a thousand forms
Quick mount the midnight gale,
The hero comes on the wings of the storms,—
Now flits the lover pale,
The Ghosts are these of chiefs who fell
Where loud the battle's clangours swell.
Who dying scorn'd their foes;—
Of youths—who loved with latest breath,
Of maidens—sunk in early death—
Too true the outline of their woes!

IV.

Dim through them gleams the moon-light ray,
As quitting each his clay-cold cell,
They listening hang around;
Entranced—as by a magic spell—
They eager drink each heav'nly sound,
And as their souls suck in the rapturous lay,—
In joys ecstatic drown'd,—their silent homage pay.
He sings how heroes' bosoms glow,
He sings how heaves the breast of snow;
Death no more can fears impart,
Warriors smiling meet the dart;
Lovers with new ardours burn,
Maidens feel the wish'd return;
Thus from death to pleasure straying,
Stern—terrific—gentle—bland,
Every passion fond obeying,
Owns the mighty master's hand.

## ON DEATH.

مرگ اگر مردست گو که پیشم بیا    تا در آغوشش بیگیرم تنگ تنگ
من از او ستانم عمر جاودان    او از من بیگیرد این دلق رنگ رنگ

TRANSLATION.

Should death intrepid meet me face to face,
Gladly I'd grasp him in a firm embrace;
This motley form, the garb of sin, resign,
And take th' immortal gift of life divine.

## EPIGRAM OF BUCHANAN'S.

Illa mihi semper præsenti dura Neæra,
  Me quoties absum semper abesse dolet;
Non desiderio nostri, non mæret amore,
  Sed se non nostro posse dolore frui.

TRANSLATION.

Though at her feet my offer'd vows
  With scorn Neæra hears,
No sooner do I quit her house
  Than she dissolves in tears.

'Tis not through love Neæra grieves,
  Though she with truth complain—
My absence her of joy bereaves—
  The joy of giving pain.

## ON THE CLOSE OF DAY.

See the bright orb of parting day—
  Its last faint beam now quiv'ring glows,
And gently fading to decay,
  Shews wearied nature hast'ning to repose.

The soft'ning twilight overspreads,
  And dims the landscape's power;
The flow'rets droop their dewy heads,
  As deep'ning shadows lower.

The straggling herds have left the plain,
  And Philomel now chaunts her strain,
    To melancholy dear:
Ah! much this silent hour I prize,
  When thoughts of those we love arise,
    And claim the grateful tear!

---

## En voyant le portrait de Madame ———, qui se servait d'un peu de fard.

L'artiste qui a peint ce Portrait,
  N'a que copié l'ouvrage d'un autre:
Vous en doutez, Madame ——, mais c'est vrai,
  La première peinture fut la vôtre.

---

## ANECDOTES.

One of the first English vessels that visited the Indian Seas, fell in, when off the Coromandel coast, with a catamaran; there were two natives on it, whose bodies of course seemed to be rising out of the water, and they were paddling in their usual manner, that is, with quick strokes alternately to the right and left. The crew of the ship, as may well be imagined, were greatly surprised and alarmed at this strange and unheard of phenomenon; and the report of it entered in their log-book, ran as follows:—"Good ship. The trades increase. August 15th, 1615—Lat. —, Long. —, at 2 P.M.—beheld distinctly two black devils in the water, playing at single-stick!!! They were within twenty fathom of the ship, and the whole crew saw, and can vouch for the truth of this statement: these infernal imps remained visible for at least an hour, and were then lost in the distance. 'They who go down to the sea in ships shall see the wonders of the deep,'—and from this, learn, ye incredulous, how vain be the hardness of your hearts! (N.B. Certes this matter should portend a great storm,—or some revolution in the states of Europe,—or, peradventure, somewhat relating to the Pope of Rome!! Heaven send no ill betide us!")

---

At a dinner, where a fine English ham was the chief sufferer, puns happened to be the order of the day, and they flew about very abundantly on all sides. One gentleman, however, was much the most successful, and grew, at length, himself so pleased with his 'ben trovatos,' that, in a little fit of vanity, he challenged any present to give him words on which he could not make puns:—"We will try that," cried one,—"Shem, Ham, and Japhet:" to which he instantly replied, assuming an Irish accent, "*Shem* on me if this is n't as good a *Ham* as ever entered my *Jaw—fait!*"

"Ah! spare yon emmet, rich in hoarded grain,
He lives with pleasure, and he dies with pain."

SIR WM. JONES' TRANSLATION FROM "SADI."

"Mea nec Falernæ
Temperant vites, neque Formiani
Pocula colles."

HOR. *Cam. lib.* I. *od.* XX.

## ON ANAGRAMS.

"But with still more disorder'd step advance,
(Nor march it seem'd, but wild fantastic dance)
The uncouth anagram's distorted train,
Shifting, in double mazes, o'er the plain."
CAMBRIDGE'S SCRIBLERIAD.

SIR,—A minor branch of this very scientific and ingenious art, viz. the "Game of Letters," having lately formed the evening's amusement of the fashionable circles of Moorshedabad, it may not be thought uninteresting to give you some short account of the rise and progress of Ana,—or, as some will have it, meta-grammatism. To tread in the steps of the great Addison, may be justly deemed a presumptuous attempt; to obviate which imputation of rashness, I will pursue an opposite course to that taken by our illustrious moralist, and, instead of reasoning on its unworthiness to enter into serious composition, I will merely give instances of its prevalency.

The "Spectator" ascribes its origin to the monkish age of barbarism; but it may certainly claim a much higher antiquity, for not only in the East (where every luxuriance flourishes) has it prevailed from time immemorial, but even among the chaster Grecians, instances of it may be found. That it tortured the brains, too, of many a Roman, I have no doubt, though I am not prepared to prove the fact. Unfortunately, no copious *ana* of the Roman, as of the French beaux-esprits, have come down to us, or, very probably, Cicero's claims to wit had been strengthened as much by anagrams as by miserable puns and rebusses.

An instance in the Greek is the following compliment, which was paid to one of the Ptolemies :— Πτολεμᾶιος, ἀπὸ μέλιτος, that is,—Ptolemy — anagrammatically—" formed of honey." Among the Arabians and Persians this art is held in high esteem ; it is considered as one of the chief graces of composition : indeed, every *alliterative* beauty is to be found in profusion in their writings : scarcely a line but salutes you with some harmonious jingle, some recondite quibble, or some very elegant conceit, which is carried through all its moods and tenses, without the slightest mercy on the poor reader. Cowley, in spinning out a prettiness, is nothing to one of these poets ; they will give you a whole epic on the charms of one maid. I have, indeed, in my possession a musnuvee, or long elegiac poem, the entire subject of which is a panegyrical description of a young lady : it is divided into regular sections, each of which is on some particular charm, and is headed thus :—

"Chap. 1st.—Her Hair. Chap. 2nd.—Her Forehead," and so descends gradually from top to toe! The praises, too, are sometimes beautifully imagined; in one place, for example, the poet says,—his mistress perspires rose-water; what a very charming and delicate idea! But, by the bye, I am digressing sadly!

The anagram is termed تحريف—"tuhreef," but as a figure of rhetoric, where it holds a distinguished place, it is named مقلوب—"mukloob, and a great variety of rules are laid down by the grammarians for its introduction into poetry. Sometimes it is necessary that words, which are co-anagrams, should commence and end a couplet; sometimes that they should be thrown in promiscuously,—suffice one example of the latter from "Gladwin's Dissertations:"

راي تو يار صوات داد تو محض وداد فتح تو حتف حسود ضيف
تو فيض مراد

"Your wisdom is a meritorious friend, your justice is friendship in the extreme, your victory is the death of the envious man, your being host gratifies desire." In a translation it is impossible to preserve *beauties* of this nature, but the anagrams of the original, are راي and يار—فتح and حتف—ضيف and فيض. So that when you see a poet of Persia with his "eyes glancing from heaven to earth, from earth to heaven," it is fair to consider him not as searching for "the thoughts that breathe, and words that burn," but as deeply pondering—

> "Where buds an L, and where a B,
> Where sprouts a V, and where a T.—COWLEY.

In England, too, especially in the time of that inveterate punster, James the First, anagrams were in great repute, and there was no species of composition into which they did not enter. No man wrote a dedication but it was accompanied by an anagram; thus—"to the ryght worthy Thomas Nevyle,—'*most heavenly*.'" Nor did any one, who wished to gain his fair lady's love, forget first to twist her name into some elegant anagrammatic motto or epithet.

The "Spectator" gives an admirable description of one of these ingenious beaux-esprits, which I cannot forbear quoting here:—"I have heard of a gentleman who, when this kind of wit was in fashion, endeavoured to gain his mistress's heart by it; she was one of the finest women of her age, and was known by the name of the Lady Mary Boon. The lover not being able to make any thing of Mary, by certain liberties indulged to this kind of writing, converted it into *Moll*, and after having shut himself up for half-a-year, with indefatigable industry, produced an anagram. Upon his presenting it to his mistress, who was a little vexed in her heart to see herself degraded to *Moll Boon*, she told him, to his infinite surprise, that he had mistaken her sirname, for that it was not *Boon*, but *Bohun*.

> "—— —— Ibi omnis
> Effusus labor."

The lover was thunderstruck with his misfortune, insomuch, that, in a little time after, he lost his senses, which, indeed, had been very much impaired by that continual application he had given to his anagram."

This art continued long in vogue, and sometimes a considerable stress was laid on the accidental resemblances the name anagrammatized might bear:—so much so indeed as to call for the cognizance of the Ecclesiastical Court; as may be seen in the following anecdote—"In the reign of Charles the First,—Lady Eleanor Davies, widow of the Attorney-General of Ireland, happened to utter a kind of prediction about the Duke of Buckingham, which appeared to be verified by his death, and, in consequence, she acquired a very high fame among the vulgar as a prophetess. She even herself believed that she was endowed with this miraculous power, and was confirmed in this belief by her name, *Eleanor Davies*—forming (very nearly) the anagram of '*Reveal O Daniel.*'—The High Court of Commission hearing of this lady's enthusiasm, cited her to appear before them, and there, in all the pomp and formality of Church dignity, began to reason with and reprehend her from the authority of Scripture;—but Dr. Lamb, who was present, with the most happy wit, took up a pen and wrote—'*Dame Eleanor Davies*'—the exact anagram of 'never soe mad a ladie'—'Here Madam'—said he—'is an anagram according to the strictest rules of art, and which I hope will fit you as well as the other.'—This admirable stroke convulsed the whole Court with laughter, and the poor prophetess retired overwhelmed with confusion, leave being given her to comfort herself with the inspiration of any *spirit* she pleased."

Many other instances may be given from the annals of this age, but I will confine myself to the following one:—Howel, in his very entertaining letters, in speaking of William Noy, who was Attorney General to Charles the First, and advised him to that odious measure, Ship Money, says—"with infinite pains and indefatigable study he came to his knowledge in the Law, but I never heard a more pertinent anagram than was made upon his name, William Noy—'*I moyl in Law.*'"

The French have not been behind us in this art: The oldest I recollect to have seen of theirs is one, which assigns a reason for the House of Lorrain wearing eaglets in their arms, namely, because *alerion* is the anagram of *Loraine:* and the best I have met with is the one, which stigmatizes the monster *Frère Jacques Clément,* (who so cruelly murdered Henry III, of France) by making him pronounce, in the letters of his own name,—" c'est l'enfer qui m'a créé."

In Queen Anne's Augustan age, this *science* still kept its ground, and Addison tells us that Whig and Tory anagrams were to be met with in the greatest abundance. About that time too, they prevailed much on the Continent. One of them for its singularity and beauty, really deserves to be preserved. When young Stanislaus, afterwards King of Poland, returned home from his travels, all the illustrious family of Leczinski assembled at Lissa to congratulate him on his arrival. Festivals, shows, and rejoicing of every kind took place,—but the most ingenious compliment that graced the occasion, was the one paid by the College of Lissa. There appeared on the stage thirteen dancers, dressed as youthful warriors; each held in his hand a shield, on which was engraved, in characters of gold, one of the thirteen letters, which compose the two words—Domus Lescinia. They then commenced their dance, and so arranged it, that at each turn their row of bucklers formed different anagrams. At the first pause they presented them in the natural order, or

————————Domus Lescinia ... House of Leczinski.
At the Second ...Ades Incolumis ... Thou art present safe.
At the Third......Omnis es Lucida ... All bright art thou.
At the Fourth ...Mane Sidus Loci... Remain the star of the place.
At the Fifth......Sis Columna Dei... Mayst thou be a pillar of God
And the Last ...I, scande Solium... Go, ascend the Throne.

This last is the more remarkable, as it was a prophecy which proved true.

In the present day we have not degenerated—our elaborate compositions may fully vie with any antiquity can shew: indeed the well known one on Horatio Nelson—"*Honor est à Nilo*," may be considered as the very ne plus ultra of the art, as the king of anagrams. The following one is also excellent—"*Bona rapta pone Leno*"—"lay down the stolen goods, you rascal;"—how exquisitely applicable to "*Napoleon Bonaparte.*" By the bye, would not one think that the Emperor had been sitting for his portrait, when Seneca,—"with a master's hand, and prophet's fire," thus emphatically describes Corsica?

"Prima est ulcisci lex, altera vivere rapto,
"Tertia mentiri, quarta negare Deos."

Thirst of revenge first warms the Corsic breast,
And next the love of plunder is imprest;—
Each fraud prevails—'tis virtuous deem'd to lie,
And last, e'en God th' impious race deny.

After the above excellent anagrams, I ought in no small degree to resemble Friar Bacon's famous Head, when I attempt to slide in a couple of my own; however "coute qui coute" les voici—"Mors! Ii honore!"—"O Death, I have gone with honour," and "The War yells, rule!"—As I can hardly expect any of my readers to condescend to take the trouble of finding these out, I must tell them that they are the names of two of Britain's

Heroes,—*Sir John Moore*, and Sir *Arthur Wellesley*. Some will perhaps say, I have written this letter only with the view of sporting my own witticism, but this is slander; and even were it true, I ought to be excused, for, like the Irishman, I have passed my bad half-penny between two good shillings.

It must be remembered that I do not, by any means, attempt to defend this art, as it relates to composition, for it is undoubtedly a species of *false wit*, and will not undergo the fair test of translation which the Spectator proposes;—but, nevertheless, as being an innocent and entertaining mode of killing time, I see no reason why it should be banished from our polite circles. The bow must not always be bent, and to preserve a proper tone, it is necessary sometimes to descend "from grave to gay." We have instances of heroes who have amused themselves by jumping over chairs,—of others who have whiled away the lingering time by catching flies, or by forming the flexile mass of iron into graceful bars;—why, then, should it be forbidden to the more elegant minds of the Moorshedabadites to recreate themselves with the very classical and literary amusement of the "Game of Letters?" And as all sciences should have Greek appellations, I propose that this be henceforth called the "Grammatikepaidia," (*γραμματίκη παιδια.*) This manner of passing an evening is certainly inferior to the "feast of reason, and the flow of soul,"—but where is that to be met with? The "concordance of sweet sounds," may also be ranked higher,—but it ought, I think, in point of general festivity, to take precedence of cards or dice,—in point of interest, to sitting silent,—and, in point of ingenuity, it should win the day, in my opinion, against even that delightful and very fashionable amusement, "puss in the corner,"—but Martinus Scriblerus, let me beg thy pardon,—I should have called it "*Apodidiascinda.*" Yours, &c.

NUGARUM AMATOR.

P.S.—For the satisfaction of the curious, I have calculated the changes that it is possible to produce on any number of letters up to twelve.

| | | | | | | | |
|---|---|---|---|---|---|---|---|
| 2 | Letters produce | 2 | changes. | 7 | Letters produce | 5,040 | changes. |
| 3 | —— | 6 | — | 8 | —— | 40,320 | — |
| 4 | —— | 24 | — | 9 | —— | .362,880 | — |
| 5 | —— | 120 | — | 10 | —— | 3,628,800 | — |
| 6 | —— | 720 | — | 11 | —— | 39,916,800 | — |
| | | | | 12 | —— | 479,001,600 | — |

Allowing that twenty words, of twelve letters each, can be written in one minute, then to write the full extent of changes out that a twelve-lettered word may produce, would require exactly forty-five years and two hundred and seven days!

# EXTRACT OF A JOURNAL FROM MANGALORE TO SERINGAPATAM, THROUGH THE COORGA TERRITORY.

---

The climate of Mangalore is temperate throughout the year, the extremes of heat and cold not being felt here in so great a degree as in most other parts of India. The land and sea breezes are generally fresher, and the time of their setting-in more regular than at other places. In December and January the mercury in the thermometer never fell below sixty-six degrees.

The strong hill fort of Jumalabad is thirty-six miles inland from Mangalore. I accompanied my friend R—— and his family on an excursion to this place, which occupied us about a week. The third day, on reaching an eminence, we obtained a view of the rock of Jumalabad, which at the distance of a few miles, wears the appearance of a small peak of land, rising to an inconsiderable height; this may be owing to the proximity of the neighbouring Ghauts, called by Rennell the Indian Apennines, which occasion the former to appear comparatively diminutive.

Approaching the fort on the southern side, it gradually enlarges to the eye, and by its magnitude excites the greatest surprise, since the base of the hill is several miles in circumference; and the stupendous rock itself juts out perpendicularly from the latter, to the height of several hundred yards. The lower and middle forts are small works situated on the top of the first hill, and are intended to serve as a cover to the upper fort or citadel. At the time of investing the place, our troops formed a lodgment in the middle fort, and were effectually sheltered by part of the most craggy rock that overhangs the gateway. From the latter place, a passage of nine or ten feet in breadth, (and flanked on the exterior side with a stone parapet) winds along the south-east quarter to the summit of the rock. This communication, which forms the only possible entrance into the upper fort, was made at a considerable expense, by cutting and blowing away the hard rock, to the perpendicular height, I should suppose, of at least nine or ten hundred feet.

The prospect from the summit of this lofty and airy site, is the most pleasing possible; it commands an extensive view over the whole country, except on the eastern side, where the Ghauts form, at the distance of four or five miles, a barrier between this province and the table-land of Mysore. The southern and western landscape is diversified by fields of corn, and others laying fallow, by villages scarcely perceptible, forests extending over the wavy hills, and such a variety of other objects, that it would be very difficult to describe or give the faintest idea of the beauty and grandeur of the original.

The upper fort has five batteries, and contains some fine pieces of cannon: there are, also, several magazines, with an abundance of military stores, and grain sufficient for the supply of several years; and as water enough is collected in tanks, during the periodical rains, for the consumption of the year, the inaccessible rock might not only deride the efforts of the most powerful army, but hold out against the strictest blockade: indeed, the saying of Louis XIV. respecting the fortress of Namur, would be far more appropriate if applied to Jumalabad:—"It may be surrendered, but cannot be conquered."

This hill fort fell into our possession on the demise of Tippoo; the garrison made a slight resistance, with the intention of gaining terms for the payment of their arrears.

1801. The 20th January.—To *Feringypete* nine miles. This village is so denominated from having been the residence of many Portuguese families. Tippoo gave some encouragement to the settlement, by granting them a spot of ground to build upon, as well as the privilege of a church: some time afterwards he seized their persons and property, and obliged them (it is reported) to conform to the Mussulman creed.

21st.—To Pany Mangalore, a small village opposite to Buntwal, and in the afternoon I proceeded on to Kurry-swally, nine miles farther. At Buntwal I crossed a small river, which has its rise among the Ghauts, near Jumalabad, and falls into the sea by Mangalore, a little to the southward of the old fort. Kurry-swally is in so ruinous a state, as to render it difficult to obtain any kind of provision or grain.

A short time prior to the fall of Seringapatam, the Coorgs made an irruption into the Malabar province, and by way of retaliating on their old enemy the miseries of war, plundered every part of the country, and carried off several thousand families: the remaining ryots fled to the jungles, the tradesmen for protection elsewhere; and from these losses, it will require a considerable time before the province can again be brought into any settled state. Distance marched this day, eighteen miles.

22nd.—By Putone, to the small village of Surwy, or Perdoty,—sixteen miles. The road leading through a hilly and woody tract of country. Among the different species of lofty trees that rise on every side, the sindee is one of the most beautiful; its flowers branch out from the top, and fall in the form of a luxuriant tress down the trunk of the tree.

23rd.—To Bellary, nine miles. This place, within the last two years, was a considerable town, but at present, little remains of its former population. As we approach the Ghauts, the country assumes a wilder and more romantic appearance, the whole surface is hill and dale, and the intervening valleys are covered with plantations of rice, divided regularly into square beds; a small bank of earth divides each bed or field, and being set on each side with a number of cocoa-nut and plantain trees, the whole wears rather the appearance of a garden, than plantations of grain.

24th.—To Soolia, twelve miles. To-day we passed the barrier, separating the Coorga and Company's territories by one *sooltany-coss* (equal to four miles.) Very heavy dews fall during the night, and the weather is much colder than usual.

25th.—To Tory Khan, at the foot of the Coorga Pass, fourteen miles. At this place the Rajah has established a small *chokey* (picquet guard) of six or eight men. The districts round Soolia and Tory Khan, were many years a subject of dispute between the Mysoreans and Coorgs.

26th.—After a toilsome march of three hours, I ascended the pass of the first mountain, and then halted. Afterwards, I proceeded on over a less difficult road, winding up two smaller hills, and, at noon, gained the highest part of the ascent. On the northern and southern sides, this chain of the Indian Apennines is continued as far as the eye can reach; many of the ridges rear their heads abruptly above the clouds, while their base remains enveloped in the mists and exhalations of the low country. To the west, two distinct ranges branch off towards the sea, and are separated by a shelving valley, until lost in the bounds of the horizon. On every side the mountains appear covered with majestic woods, and Nature sways the wide domain, with an air of primeval grandeur and varied magnificence; indeed, the very elevated situation of the summit of these Ghauts, and extensive prospect from them, may not unaptly be compared to that spot from whence Scipio, in his dream, viewed the whole surface of the earth, and could scarcely discern that speck of dirt—*the Roman Empire!*

The sandal, teak, sissoo, and other forest trees, grow in great abundance over this mountainous tract. After descending by a gradual declivity for two hours, I went on, two miles farther, to Baugmundel, and reached the village at three o'clock in the afternoon—distance about sixteen miles. Baugmundel is an inconsiderable village, with a large pagoda: the Brahmins here were very civil and attentive. From the little information I could obtain of them, there appears to be a schism among the Hindoos, in regard to the power and pre-eminence of the Maha Deo and Vishnoo,—the Deccannees esteem the former as having the greater rank and authority; while the followers of Brahma, at Benares, give the precedence to Vishnoo, or Bishun.

27th.—To Nauknar, the Coorga Rajah's residence, sixteen miles. Nauknar, situated at the foot of a mountain, that surrounds the place on every side except the north, is the Rajah's residence during the dry season. On my arrival, I sent a message, with Mr. U——'s letter of introduction, to the Rajah; and, in the course of the afternoon, I waited on him in person: on this occasion I presented Dr. C—'s letter, to whom, as well as to Mr. U——, he seemed to me much attached. His manners and address are very easy, frank, and affable. The Rajah has a small, but good stud of horses, and among these are some excellent mares, which formerly belonged to Tippoo's stable, and had been presented by General S—— (commanding the Bombay army) to the Coorga chief.

29th.—This afternoon the Rajah set off on a hunting excursion, on which I accompanied him. We proceeded ten miles in a north-west direction, and pitched our tents in the centre of a small plain, surrounded on all sides by

> " Majestic woods of every vig'rous green,
> Stage above stage high waving o'er the hills."

The whole of this district appears mountainous and woody, but the land, although good, is not much cultivated. This may be attributed to the invasion of the country, about fifteen years ago, by the Mysore prince: the severe losses sustained by the Coorgas on this occasion, have not yet been repaired.

Passing by several villages, I observed, on the

Rajah's approach, that the men and women who belonged to them came out; the men, who carried arms, drew up in one rank, to pay their homage and make their salam,—while the women, each with a lighted *cheragh* in her hand, stood in a modest, respectful attitude on one side of the road. The marks of attention and respect appear to originate in the affection and gratitude of the inhabitants to their chieftain, who, by his courage and address, delivered them from the severest persecution, and the most cruel bondage. This evening, a number of Coorgas, armed with a *kuttee*, (a kind of hatchet) and matchlock, came and paid their respects to the Maharaj.

The 30th and 31st.—We made excursions into the adjacent jungles—there was plenty of game, but neither tiger nor wild elephant could be found. The first day our party killed six buffaloes, and twenty sombre or large deer. The second day, seven or eight more of the former, and thirty of the latter, besides smaller game. The wild buffalo of this country is of an uncommon size, and very powerful; he is called by the natives, the "*Junglee Coorga.*"

The mode of hunting the larger game is as follows:—A body of ten, twelve, or fifteen hundred men are sent off early in the morning to the place of rendezvous; about one half of them surround a wood of several miles in extent, forming a chain of sentries at the distance of twenty-five or thirty paces from each other;—on a given signal, the remaining party entered the jungle, with arms and long sticks to beat about, and drove every thing before them, toward the centre of the enclosed space, where we had taken our seats among the branches of the trees, cut and prepared for this purpose. The game being thus surrounded and fired on from all quarters, has little chance of escaping. The matchlock-men on the flank keep up a continued fire on those animals that endeavour to escape; and they do not quit their post until the thickets have been several times beaten. In the evening the heads of all the principal game are brought to the tents.

(*To be continued.*)

## ON THE ELOQUENCE OF SILENCE.

"HAIL! gracious silence!" says the inimitable Shakspeare; and when we reflect on all its extensive powers and various beauties, we cannot but join in the exclamation.

It is not, however, to the silence of *discretion*, which declares the man to be wise who speaks little, or to that of secrecy, I allude,—but to the mute enunciation—the eloquence without words—

which surpasses all language in power, and is attended often with the most beautiful and sublime effects!

In rhetoric there is no name to express this—if I may so Hibernically call it—figure of speech; yet there is none which more deserves the serious attention of the orator. The President Hénault justly remarks, "that it would have been impossible to have given it a name, and laid down rules for its application, as with prosopopœia, metaphor, metonomy, &c. it being an incident entirely dependent on taste—and taste admits of no precept." "It is," he observes, "an *instinct* of reason, which, like an instinct of nature, never deceives itself." Burke, in his admirable Essay, has placed it as one of the chief sources of sublimity; and if Longinus's definition be just, it deserves this rank, for it possesses all the characters which he gives to the true sublime:—its effect is instantaneous,—striking as the flash of lightning—and can only be felt—not understood.

Marmontel observes, "quelquefois même le sublime se passe de paroles;" and had he added, "il aime s'en passer," he would, in my opinion, have been right; for of this beautiful manner of expression I agree perfectly with Rousseau, "l'impression de la parole est toujours foible, et l'on parle au cœur par les yeux bien mieux que par les oreilles."

No lover at least will attempt to deny the truth

of this; for who of them ever complained of the want of words? So far from it, Quinhault has said, "Jusques à la silence toute parle en elle." Tasso, in his Aminta,

"Et silenzio ancor suole
Aver prieghi e parole."

and Congreve—"Even silence may be eloquent in love." But it is not of its more soft, though eloquent, effects that I mean to speak, but of those grand and sublime results that we see frequently produced by it.

The great poets, in describing a scene of horror, or in impressing on us the ideas of night and solitude, have not failed to introduce the striking image of all nature being at rest, and a profound silence reigning around. Virgil seems to have been particularly aware of the effect it would have in heightening his pictures; and in his accounts of the regions below, instead of dwelling on the tortures there suffered, or any of the other incidents usually recounted, he, at one stroke, gives us a full idea of their vastness, horror, and hopelessness, by saying that they were "loca nocte tacentia latè," and inhabited by "umbræ silentes." This deep silence impresses an awe and mournful despair, by no means equalled by Popc's "shrieks of woe."

But the sublimest and most wonderfully poetical instance of this nature that can be adduced, is from the Book of Job. "In thoughts from the visions of the night, when deep sleep falleth on man, fear came upon me and trembling, which made all my bones to shake. Then a spirit passed before my face; the hair of my flesh stood up;—it stood still, but I could not discern the form thereof: an image was before mine eyes:—*there was silence.* And I heard a voice, saying, 'shall mortal man be more just than God?—Shall a man be more pure than his Maker?'" What can be more exquisite, more happily finished than this whole passage! Here is a "silence more dreadful than severest sounds." One feels a thrill of awe in reading it; and, independently of the sacredness of the subject, as merely a grand and masterly stroke of poetry, in my opinion, it excels every thing that classical antiquity can produce. There is a sensation of sublimity which resembles the above, in the deep calm and awful stillness that precedes a storm;—this has a more impressive effect than even the subsequent raging of the tempest itself; and were it possible to give adequate expressions to such feelings, the description of them would rank with the above passage from Job, among the finest and grandest flights of poetry.

This kind of silence is frequently felt, too, in a strong and awful degree, when about to enter on any very solemn or momentous undertaking. What can be more imposing than the stillness preparatory to a battle?

Campbell admirably describes it, when speaking of two hostile fleets approaching each other to engage. He says—

> " As they drifted on their path,
> There was silence deep as death,
> And the boldest held his breath
> For a time."

The ancient Druids, who well knew how to raise the feelings of their votaries to the most exquisite pitch of superstitious reverence, availed themselves of a similar sensation; and choosing the gloomy solitude of deep primeval woods, added to the horrors of the dreadful human sacrifices they there performed, by preserving a solemn and overwhelming silence. Nay, even in simple stillness itself, unaccompanied with any other circumstance, who has not often felt a strange mysterious thrill of awe creep over the mind, till he has become so enwrapped by it, so unaccountably appalled, that he has even suspended his breath, fearing almost that life itself depended on not awaking the deep silence around! or has not—

> "Back recoiled—he knew not why,
> E'en at the sound himself had made.

Of to how high a degree this is sometimes carried, an occurrence mentioned by travellers through the Alps, offers a singular instance. The guides caution you, previous to passing through certain particularly wild and dreary spots, surrounded with fearful overhanging rocks, and vast loose pieces of ice, to be careful not to speak a word, lest the unaccustomed sound should draw destruction on you, by bringing the cliffs down headlong.

Two very beautiful instances of silence that "eloquently speaks," are to be met with in Homer and Virgil. The first is that of Ajax. When Ulysses meets him in the shades below, he finds him alone, apart from all others, and still brooding over his disappointment respecting the arms of Achilles, which had been adjudged to his rival Ulysses, who now, in his most blandishing manner, addresses him, recalls to him his former glory, and attempts to soothe his wounded pride; but what was the answer of Ajax? What words could indeed have done justice to the mingled emotions of his soul? Homer, the grand master of this art, who knew passion's every key, felt conscious that all expression must despair to reach it; and at once therefore, in rejecting words, bade language labour after him in vain. Ajax did not deign to give an answer, but stalked away in sullen silence.

"Alone, apart, in discontented mood,
A gloomy shade, the sullen Ajax stood.
Touch'd at the sight, from tears I scarce refrain,
And tender sorrow thrills through every vein;
Pensive and sad I stood,—at length accost,
With accents mild, th' inexorable ghost.
'Still burns thy rage? and can brave souls resent,
E'en after death? Relent, great shade, relent:
Turn then, oh! peaceful turn: thy wrath control,
And calm the raging tempest of thy soul!'
While yet I speak, the shade disdains to stay,
In silence turns, and sullen stalks away."

POPE'S HOMER, *b.* xi. *l.* 665.

Virgil has imitated this in the sixth book of his Æneid, in his interview of Dido and Æneas in the regions below.

"Inter quas Phœnissa recens à vulnere Dido."—etc. *l.* 450.

"Amongst the rest Phœnician Dido strayed,
Her wounds still bleeding, in the pensive glade;
Her beauteous form the wondering Trojan viewed,
And knew, tho' doubting, thro' the gloomy wood.
(Uncertain thus, when new-born Dian gleams,
'Mid clouds we view, or seem to view, her beams)
First for her woes some pitying tears he shed,
Then, warm with love, in sweetest accents said,—
'Unhappy Queen! then true the message came,
You fell untimely by this hapless flame;
And I the cause! Yet by the stars I swear,
By every god whom heaven or hell revere,
Unwilling, Dido, was I forced from thee;
Torn from thy shore by Jove's unwished decree—
O stay thy steps, nor cruel turn away;
'Tis thy fond lover, Dido, bids thee stay.
Whom would you fly? And can'st thou fly me now,
In these last moments that the Fates allow?'
With words so soft in vain Æneas strove:
Her sullen mood nor prayers nor tears can move.
Fixt on the earth she kept her beauteous eyes,
In silence heard, with silence sad replies.
No more his words effect her settled soul,
Than move the rock the waves that round it roll.
She deign'd not look, but sullen flung away,
To deepest shades impervious to the day:
There, with her lord, her loved Sicheus strayed,
Who shared her every care, and love for love repaid."

The above is certainly a beautiful passage, and

the "Illa solo," &c. has a felicity of expression not to be equalled,—but it does not, I think, come up to the corresponding scene in Homer. I will not enter into all the arguments that have been advanced in favour of either poet, but I cannot but differ from Hénault, who decidedly gives the preference to Virgil:—to me, the conduct of Ajax is most admirable, and perfectly in unison with his general character; but it is not equally natural in Dido to vent her's by *silence;* an enraged woman adopts a far different mode; this expresses only a profound *contempt,* which, though Æneas certainly richly deserved, yet Virgil could not have wished us to entertain for his hero; and, in this one place only, I think it may be said to him—"tetigit, et non ornavit." He has touched without adding ornament.

Another fine example of this forcible mode of expression is the conduct of Mark Anthony at the death of Cæsar. He rose to make his funeral oration, and every one expected a speech replete with pathos: but no—Anthony was more truly eloquent; he said nothing; but he displayed before them Cæsar's robe covered with blood! and what words could have produced an equal effect with such pathetic, though mute oratory?

In Sophocles, too, there is an admirable stroke of eloquence without words. Œdipus, when his children are brought to him that he had by his own mother, stretches out his arms to them, and exclaims, "Come and embrace your . . . . . . ," but he cannot finish, for in what words could he express to them his relationship, and how sublime an effect has his silence. It is like the veil which Timanthes threw over the face of Agamemnon, when he despaired to express, by his painting, the profoundness of his grief at the sacrifice of his daughter Iphigenia.

How noble was Scipio's behaviour when accused before the Senate of peculation. He could at once have done away the slanderous imputation; but this would have been beneath him;—to have granted the justice of even a suspicion would have been degrading. When he therefore rose, he spoke not a word in reply to the charges, but said—"Come, my countrymen, it is years since I conquered Carthage,—let us go to the Temple to thank the Gods;" and at the instant every one rose and followed him, for such is ever the imposing power of sublimity!

There is nothing that more emphatically expresses contempt or indignation than silence. Thus, in the time of our Henry V., when Paris was the British capital in France, a party of English entered the city, and were ordered to march under the windows of the detested Isabella of Bavaria, who sat there in great state, surrounded by her courtiers, to receive their salutations. But what was her rage and disappointment!—not a voice uttered her name; not a prayer was heard for her safety;

they passed in gloomy silence, with eyes fixed on the ground, nor did one of them deign to cast a single glance at her windows! Could language have expressed an equal contempt?

Something resembling the above was the triumph of Cæsar. When he entered Rome, surrounded with all the pageants of victory, the skies were rent with applauses; every voice resounded his name, and implored blessings on his head. But no sooner did the statue of the god-like Cato appear in the procession, than "the day was overcast;" the triumph ceased; a deep and expressive silence reigned around, and "the world's great conqueror passed unheeded by."

In short, this is the most forcible manner possible of expressing the strongest feelings of the mind. Silent contempt strikes a thousand times more acutely than the most bitter invective; and so sensible to this mute mode of attack was a certain French writer, that he published a furious reply to a person who had thus offended him. The book was entitled, "Réponse à la silence de Monsieur D——."

Neither is there any way in which greater respect or veneration can be shown. Thus, when Virgil entered the theatre, the house did not thunder with applause; all was in a moment hushed, and every person, by a simultaneous impulse, respectfully stood up.

With what respect, too, did Aaron receive the

commands of the Lord, when his two sons had been slain for violating their duty as priests. "Moses said unto him, this is what Jehovah spake, saying, I will be sanctified in them that come nigh me; and before all the people I will be glorified: and Aaron held his peace." How natural would it have been to have burst out with exclamations expressive of the lacerated feelings of the father;—but such was his piety and religious resignation, that Aaron was silent, and kissed the chastening rod.

A thousand examples might be given from the sacred writings of a similar nature. When Abraham is about to sacrifice Isaac, he preserves a profound and most respectful silence; not a murmur, not an expression of grief escapes him! M. Rollin, in commenting on this passage, expresses his admiration of its beauty. He contrasts the account of Moses with that given by Josephus, where an eloquent and affecting speech is made by Abraham, and gives of course a decided preference to the former. The one, he observes, wrote as a man influenced by his own spirit; the other as holding the pen of the Divinity, who dictated to him what he should write.

When it is necessary to give us an idea of the vast power of Cyrus, how beautifully does the sacred writ say, "the earth is *silent* at his presence." There is a similar image very happily introduced by Milton in his 7th Book, where, when the Almighty is entering Chaos in his way to create new worlds, even Discord is immediately hushed at the sound of his voice, and the vast abyss receives him in respectful stillness:

> "Silence, ye troubled waves, and thou deep, peace—
> Said then th' omnific Word, your discord end!
> Nor stay'd—but on the wings of Cherubim
> Uplifted, in paternal glory rode
> Far into Chaos, and the world unborn;
> For Chaos heard his voice."

But by far the most beautiful passage of this kind, is that with which Thomson concludes his Hymn on the Seasons. He first calls on all nature to "sound the stupendous praise" of Nature's God; but when he rises towards him through the beauties of his works, he feels conscious that this mode is inadequate to express the sensations that such a view inspires, and he most sublimely concludes with exclaiming—

> "I cannot go
> Where universal love not smiles around,
> Sustaining all yon orbs, and all their suns;
> From seeming evil still educing good,
> And better thence again, and better still,
> In infinite progression. But I lose
> Myself in him, in light ineffable;
> Come then, *expressive Silence,* muse His praise."

In short, every feeling of the heart, whether joyous or otherwise, which is extreme, defies the power of language to express it. Thus Shakspeare says—

> "Silence is the perfectest herald of joy:
> I were but little happy, if I could say how much."

Otway—

> "Silent as th' extatic bliss
> Of souls, that by intelligence converse."

and we all know how common is the being unable to speak when affected with emotions of excessive joy or gratitude.

As to *grief*, silence may be said to be its proper language; and the "erravit sine voce dolor," ("grief wandered silent") of Lacon, has ever been esteemed a most beautiful and sublime passage. Tacitus, speaking of Agrippina returning with the ashes of Germanicus, says of the multitude that had flocked to meet her on her landing, that they were "mœrentium turba, et rogitantium inter se, silentione, an voce aliquâ, egredientem exciperent, neque satis constabat, quid pro tempore foret." "A croud of mourners, who were asking each other, whether they should receive her, on landing, in *silence*, or with loud expressions of grief, for they were undecided in their opinion which mode was most suitable to the occasion."

But Sterne, who was a better judge of feeling, does not hesitate a moment,—"My uncle Toby sat down by the bedside of his distressed friend, and *said nothing.*" Southey, in his Thalaba, equally shows his intimate acquaintance with the best emotions of the soul. He writes—

> " Pitying, and silently he heard,—
> Not with the busy hand
> Of consolation, fretting the sore wound
> He could not hope to heal."

Æschylus, whose vivid imagination, and enthusiastic fire, though they frequently forced him (like our own Shakspeare) into great faults, yet, more often obtained for him beauties of the sublimest nature, has a stroke of feeling very similar to the foregoing one. He describes the wretched Niobe sitting disconsolately at the tomb of her children for three days, covered with a veil, and observing a profound silence. Thus, too, Sophocles, when her son informs Deianira of the mistake by which she has poisoned her husband Hercules, represents at once how unspeakable are her sorrow and despair, by making her retire in silence from the stage. Equally noble and beautiful is a passage in Job, where, when his friends, who come to mourn with him, and to comfort him, see to how miserable a state he is reduced,—tormented, destitute, afflicted with disease, bereft of every solace,—of every blessing ; and so worn down, so altered by his sorrows, that they scarcely knew him,—they are thus represented as offering their condolement :—" They sat down with him upon the ground seven days and seven nights, and none spake a word unto him, for they saw that his grief was great." Dr. Warton justly observes on this passage,—"Were ever sorrow, and misery, and compassion expressed, more forcibly and feelingly?" and adds,—"such silences are more affecting, and more strikingly expressive of passion, than the most artful speeches."

It is now time to conclude: the above instances will suffice to show how exquisitely beautiful this manner of expression may sometimes be. In a word, (as Marmontel observes) true sublimity does not consist in words, but things,—and the only merit of *style*, is not to weaken these,—not to injure the effect they would produce, could souls communicate together without the intervention of speech; and this direct communication is attained by the "*eloquence of silence*,"—which may, therefore, be considered as the most proper channel of the true sublime.

## CURIOUS ERROR OF DR. ASH'S.

Sir,—Allow me to offer, for the amusement of your readers, the following instance of as curious and gross a literary blunder as I think it is possible to meet with; it well deserves a place in that very entertaining work of D'Israeli's—"the Curiosities of Literature," and even there it would not be eclipsed.

As I was lately turning over the leaves of Dr. Ash's Dictionary for some word or other, my eye glanced on "*curmudgeon*," and curious to see its etymology, I stopped at it, and read as follows: "Curmudgeon, from the French 'cœur,' *unknown*, and 'méchant,' *a correspondent*. This naturally surprised me in no small degree; for first, that "cœur," signified *unknown*, and "méchant" *a correspondent*, was perfectly new to me! and next, had such been their signification, I was still at a loss to conjecture in what manner the idea of a "*curmudgeon*," and "*an unknown correspondent*" could be assimilated.

In this difficulty, I thought it would be best to apply to Dr. Johnson for aid, and accordingly turned over to the word in him, where I at once found a clue to the mystery.

The article in Dr. Johnson ran thus: "Curmudgeon, a vicious manner of pronouncing 'cœur-méchant.' (*Fr*: An unknown correspondent.)"

This was perfectly plain. "Curmudgeon" he asserts to be a corruption of the French words "cœur-méchant," which, as every body knows, mean a bad-hearted person, or a sorry fellow; and for this etymology, he gives, as an authority—an unknown correspondent;—but Dr. Ash must evidently have taken this *authority* as a *transla-*

*tion*, and as each consists of two words, he very sagaciously divides them into the proper couples, and wisely informs us that *cœur méchant* is the etymon of Curmudgeon—that is, "cœur," *unknown*, and "méchant," a *correspondent!* Profound lexicographer! Sage etymologist!!!

To suppose, however, that the learned author of Grammatical Institutes, could really have been guilty of such vile and gross stupidity, would, in my opinion, be nearly as absurd as the blunder itself. Dr. Ash certainly never could have been so egregiously dull; and I think, without being too extenuating, the mistake may fairly be imputed to one of the underling drudges, whom Dr. Ash, or rather more probably the bookseller, employed. This palliation, however, is paying a compliment to his talents, at the expense of what is infinitely more important—his principles; and he had better have been stupid as the above would declare him, than so fraudulent, (which in the other case we are forced to conclude) as to let pass and be circulated under his name, what is really not his production. Such kinds of literary impositions are not uncommon; and a name once acquired, has often, by booksellers' gold, been made to shield words of dullness which its possessor not only did not write, but perhaps never read.

I know of no *fraud* that deserves severer reprehension;—and were I a member of Apollo's Parliament, there is none for which I would propose a more signal punishment. Perhaps, however, some of your readers may differ from me here, and consider the crime of *prosing* as still more heinous. Not to offend them, therefore, I conclude,

Your humble Servant,

COMMON-PLACE-BOOK.

*Note.* The above error is only to be found in the earlier edition of Ash's Dictionary.

## REPLY TO THE CRITICISM ON THOMSON.

SIR,—I cannot coincide with your correspondent, 'Zoilus,' in his "Criticism on Thomson's Episode of Palemon and Lavinia." The introductory remarks are fair and candid, but, in citing the lines, I think the passage should have been quoted at greater length: otherwise, the sense becomes altered or lost, and the poet becomes guilty of what may be termed an Hibernicism.—

> "He then, his fancy with autumnal scenes
> Amusing, chanced beside his reaper train
> To walk, when poor Lavinia drew his eye;
> Unconscious of her power, and turning quick,
> With unaffected blushes, from his gaze:
> He saw her charming, but he saw not half
> Her charms, by downcast modesty concealed."

The critic asks, how could he see that which was concealed? For my part, I see no contradiction; "The charms her downcast modesty concealed," were not merely personal, although, as in the following lines, I am willing to allow the latter their due share:—

> "Her form was fresher than the morning rose,
> When the dew wets its leaves, unstain'd and pure
> As is the lily, or the mountain snow."

This is an enchanting description, and even here, it appears to me, the poet was right in saying, "he saw not half the charms," &c.—they were concealed, or, if the critic prefers the term, "veiled," by modesty, diffidence, and humility. But the superior, the more fascinating beauties of the mind,—"the modest virtues mingled in her eyes,"—"th'enlivening sense,"—"the smiling patience in her looks,"—these, in a great measure, lie hid from common observation; the rustic, although he may be alive to the more palpable, the grosser objects of our sense, observes them not—nor would he find himself, like Palemon—

> "With conscious virtue, gratitude, and love,
> Above the vulgar joy divinely raised."

The fair Lavinia, sheltered from the world by virtuous poverty,—"but more by bashful modesty concealed,"—shrinks abashed before the fond and ardent gaze of a stranger, the young, generous, rich Palemon. It is true, those charms, the poet contemplates, those softened beauties, modest virtues, were in part revealed to Palemon, at his first interview; but the artless innocence, the bashful reserve and timidity of an unprotected orphan, concealed the rest. If thus much is granted, I may add, the preceding part of my quotation fully explains the latter, and that the discovery or concealment alluded to, chiefly depended on the judgment of the lover.

In arguing this point so strenuously, I can only plead the attachment I feel to the author of the "Seasons;"—probably the critic may recollect, that many of the Roman ladies wore a slight veil, solely for the purpose of concealing their beauty, and, by leaving something to the imagination, enhanced the idea. The modern belles will probably dispute the policy of this conduct, and deem it one of those antiquated notions, which have been long ago exploded: whatever they may determine, I shall not venture to anticipate their opinion, or to trouble you any further with mine.

Yours, LYSANDER.

## A PERSIAN REPARTEE.

SIR,—There is no place more appropriate for Persian bon-mots than an Indian Miscellany—allow me then to beg your insertion of the following.

There was a Jester named Rubbee, who was a very profligate character, but possessed of considerable keenness and readiness of wit; the flashes of which he darted most unsparingly on all around. Among others he once chose to attack a Poet who was in company; and, after sporting his wit in various shapes at his expense, ended with turning his name into several ridiculous forms:—and then triumphantly challenged him to retort. The Poet immediately wrote

د م خر بر سر مقلوب عیب است

that is—" it is the tail of an ass at the head of an inversion of (the word) عیب"* (*ayb*).—To understand this, an explanation is necessary: the tail or *end* of خر (*khur*) is the letter ر (*r*)—and عیب inverted, is بیع—now ر (*r*) being put at the head of this, gives Rubbee ربیع, the jester's name; who, it scarcely need be added, was severely discomfited by the repartee, and made as speedy an exit as possible, amid the hootings and hissings of all present.

* Ayb, an Arabic word, signifying, blemish, defect, vice, &c.

## TRANSLATION OF A SONNET FROM THE FRENCH OF SCARRON.

---

VAST monuments! that human pride hath raised,
  Ye tombs and pyramids, of structure vain!
Where high-triumphant toil we view amazed,
  And see o'er Nature Art assume the reign!

Ye ancient temples, now in ruins laid,
  Where Roman skill her utmost pow'rs bestowed;
Chief, Coloseum—once, which crowds displayed,
  That o'er the dying gladiator glowed.

All, all have felt the hand of ruthless Time;
  Thrown from your height, ye bite the yellow sand;
In vain ye lifted once your heads sublime,—
  Not e'en your marble could Time's force withstand!

Why weep I then—that more than two years worn,
My old black coat should be at elbows torn!

---

## TO THE MEMORY OF AN INFANT.

---

Refreshed with dew, the morning rose
  Peers from it's bed at break of day;
Beset with pearls its beams disclose,
  In beauteous folds, mild Spring's array.

With innocence and beauty blest
  Thus bloom'd Eliza's darling boy;
In smiles array'd, the lovely guest
  Diffused around a tender joy.

Fled are those halcyon days before
  The blast, that rends the vernal glades;
The roseate hue of health no more,
  The garden's transient glory fades.

Corroding sorrows intervene,
  Frail hope and evanescent fear;
With partial views, distract the scene,
  Till sad regret bedews the bier.

Sweet child of Spring! thy blossoms shorn,
  The muse laments thy early tomb.
Eliza weeps her infant torn
  From life, by fate's resistless doom.

Ardent the cherub wings his flight
  To heaven;—from earthly sorrows free,
He gains the blissful realms of light
  To dwell in immortality.

---

## TO SUSPENSE.

SUSPENSE! Thou sad tormentor of the mind,
Oh! do not thus upon my spirits press;
Most painful bonds thine influence I find,
When ev'ry thought is wrung with deep distress.

Why wilt thou then with keenest feelings play?
Throw every wish and hope in wild alarm?
Fain would I fling each pallid fear away,
But thou, sad power, dost soon destroy the calm.

How oft a heavy cloud with gloom o'erspread,
Mars the fair prospect of a summer's day;
Thus clothed in doubts—Suspense, with horror's dread,
Kills trembling Hope, and curses with delay!

Much rather let the direst truth be known,
The mind elastic, gains new force to ply;
The long-tried heart can bear Fate's darkest frown,
But dread Suspense makes every effort die.

## IMITATION OF ANACREON.—ODE XXIX.

"And call'd the thing—a beau."
MERRICK.

PAINTER, now thy power show,
Deck the canvass with the beau,—
Every gaudy tint prepare—
Mark the fashion—catch the air:

Draw his snowy, powder'd tresses,
Which the soft pomatum dresses;
Dangling in black-riband tail,
Thick as those that comets trail;
Or gently tuck his matted hair
'Neath a bag and solitaire.
Let his charcoal'd eyebrows swell
On a forehead varnished well.
Let his eyes for real pass—
One though form'd of painted glass.
Borrow next a bully's look,
Though a deer his heart partook.
This from real harm will save,
That will make him cowards brave.
Next his cheeks with carmine spread,
Or the rouge's beauteous red.
With such art describe the flush,
Let them take it for a blush.
Ill description points the way
On his lips the salve to lay:
Through them let soft nonsense glide
Simp'ring screw'd from side to side;
Purse them till they seem to speak
In a shrill falsetto squeak.
Now the face's features told,
Draw his cravat's triple fold;
Made of Indian muslin fair,
Such as Munny Beegums wear.
Next to frill and shirt-pin haste,
And the finger's ring of paste.
But I'll not presume to tell
You, who know each fashion well,
How the Spanish pumps are made;
How the glitt'ring buckle laid.

I the price you ask will give—
'Tis so dull it seems to live.
View this case—for gold I've none—
'Tis an Indian stuff'd baboon.
Take it—and dress'd up, 'twill show
How to model out a beau.
When to London you repair,
Look for Billy Fribble there.
If the travell'd ape you'd hit—
Billy Fribble ask to sit.

## TRANSLATION OF GRAY'S ODE WRITTEN AT THE GRAND CHARTREUSE, "OH TU, SEVERI RELIGIO LOCI," &C.

OH ! thou, the genius of this awful place !
Whatever name delighteth most thine ear ;
(For sure yon flood—these woods—primeval race—
Proclaim no common deity is here.

The pathless rocks, the dreary, savage steeps,
Wild roaring torrents—rushing down amain ;
The frowning graves where night eternal sleeps,
And cliffs abrupt—declare a Godhead's reign.

A God far greater these sublimely show
Than ever deck'd a temple's gorgeous shrine ;
Though Phidias there his utmost power bestow,
Though Citron beams with gold profusely shine.)

Hear then, dread Genius! now invoked with truth,
Benignant grant thy suppliant's warm request;
In soft repose, oh lull my wearied youth!
And let me taste the joys of placid rest.

But if stern fortune ev'ry hope should blight,
Forbid the bliss of Silence, hallow'd reign!—
If she should tear me from each fond delight,
And plunge me 'mid the angry waves again;

At least, O Father! to my closing life
Grant some retreat—where I my age may bear;
There place me far remote from vulgar strife,
And shelter'd safe from every human care.

## SONG.

Tune—"Begone dull Care."

Behold! where Spain
Lifts her glittering turrets on high,—
Behold! where Spain
Spreads her lap to the azure blue sky.

Ah, why do her hills, and sweet vallies between,
Seem brighter and brighter, I pray?
'Tis the breath of fair Liberty blows o'er the scene,
And drives the dull clouds away.

Arise! bold Spain,—
 Spread thy glittering banner on high,—
Arise! bold Spain,
 Thy day of redemption is nigh.

The blood that warm'd thy sons of old,
 Shall fire thy sons to day;
And the spirit that chased the valiant Moor,
 Shall drive the proud Gaul away.

## ANECDOTES.

It is with no small degree of pleasure I enter on the most grateful office an Editor of a work like the present has to perform, that of arresting sometimes in their flight the erratic productions of Genius, and of gracing my pages by giving in them a local habitation to the scattered gems that have escaped the industry and research of more regular collectors. For presenting to them the following very elegant effusion from the pen of the celebrated David Garrick, I challenge the thanks of every reader of taste, and I here gratefully offer mine to the friend who so obligingly favoured me with it.

### To Miss Ann Wilton, by D. Garrick.

---

O Nanny! why when ardent love
  Beats in each trembling pulse of mine,
Dost thou the generous flame reprove,
  By ev'ry killing look of thine?

But Nanny, thou wilt nothing stake,
  No little trifling danger run
For him, who freely for thy sake,
  A thousand ways would be undone.

The above was set to music by Dr. Burney, but it has never yet, I believe, appeared in print. It certainly is not in Kearsley's collection of Garrick's poetical works, though nothing can be more beautiful.

Of the lady to whom these lines were addressed, I will only observe that this is not the only tribute paid to her by Garrick; nor was he the only poet that broke a lance in her honour. Of her beauty and accomplishments what testimony can be given superior to the verses themselves?

---

## ANECDOTE OF ACBAR SANEE.

In a conversation I some time since had the honour of holding with the present Emperor of Hindostan, Acbar Sanee, His Majesty recited to me an anecdote of his royal and ill-starred father Shaw Allum; which at once displayed his own manly and nervous appreciation of character, and fineness of tact, in seizing on that happy minuteness which marked, more than the most elaborate description could have done, the form and measure of his illustrious father's mind;—and displayed both the deepest sensations of respect and veneration for that great and much suffering descendant of Timour.—" My Father"—said His Majesty to me, " was a great man, he possessed an exalted mind, and a firmness of character perhaps unequalled,—of this, I will adduce a strong proof. He was affected, Sir, with a disease, which I believe, is vulgarly termed the *Bengal Itch;* it was represented to him by the most learned of his physicians, that nothing would more exasperate, and consequently retard longer his case, than scratching himself, and at the same time it is known, that in this disease, the desire of scratching most violently predominates, and is indeed considered invincible. Yet what was my father's conduct on this occasion? He perceived that to scratch would be unwise—and this was for him sufficient; strong as the inclination must naturally have been, he determined to repress it; and I now assure you on my royal word, that what I am about to tell you is a solemn truth: Shaw Allum had the magnanimity, Sir, not to scratch himself once!!!"

"Magnanimous indeed!"—said I, in a rapture of enthusiasm—"thus greatly to deny himself a luxury which one of our kings (James the First) has declared to be too exquisite for any but Sovereigns to enjoy!"

---

"'Tis best sometimes your censure to restrain,
And charitably let the dull be vain."

Pope's Essay on Criticism.

" Floriferis ut apes in saltibus omnia libant,
Omnia nos."

LUCRETIUS.

## ON CHRONOGRAMS.

---

" Not thus the looser Chronograms prepare,
Careless their troops, undisciplined to war;
With ranks irregular, confused, they stand,
The chieftains mingled with the vulgar band."

CAMBRIDGE'S SCRIBLERIAD.

---

THE Chronogram seems now to have gone entirely out of fashion,—yet the day has been when it held a highly distinguished rank among the various species of composition. We have, indeed, Addison's authority for saying, that there were formerly foreign universities, where, as you praise a man in England for being an excellent philosopher or poet, it was an ordinary character to be a great chronogrammatist: and if fame and reward were to be proportioned to *toil*, there would be nothing deserving of more praise, because nothing is more difficult in the construction, than this elaborate kind of wit. We hear, from the above author, that one of your laborious German beaux-esprits would turn over a whole dictionary for an ingenious device of this nature, and when one would have thought he was searching for an apt classical term, he was only looking for a word that had an

L, an M, or a D, in it. But, alas! labour is not generally considered as the test of genius, and where the only beauty consists in overcoming a difficulty, the ill-natured world is too often apt to term such studies—"stultus labor ineptiarum." But, waiving the pretensions the chronogram has to rank and fame, let us merely lay down the rules for its construction, and give a few examples, that future candidates in this art may not be without guides to its attainment.

In Europe, the chronogram is generally used for medals, marking in the inscription the year in which they were struck; but in Asia (for there it is equally, if not more, prevalent than with us) it is chiefly applied to epitaphs, and serves to denote the year in which the persons died. Generally speaking, the Asiatic is much more ingeniously composed than the European chronogram, as our following examples will shew,—with us it is necessary that all the letters which represent the Roman numerals, being picked out of the inscription, should together form the date required, as in this one,—"ChrIstVs DuX ergo trIVMphVs;" which being placed in due order, gives MDCXXVII, or 1627, the year in which this medal of Gustavus Adolphus was stamped. (The occasion was of course a victory,—and, for this—"Christ was our leader, therefore we triumphed"—is sufficiently appropriate.)

The following one, according to the above rules, is somewhat incorrect.

"Gloria Lausque Deo sæC'loruM in sæcVla sUnt."

"Glory and praise to God throughout all ages."

Here, if we reckon only those letters which overtop the others, we have 1660; but Howel justly observes, that this is not a fair chronogrammatical verse, for it not only includes the date, 1660, but contains numerical letters enough for several hundred years farther.

One of the best chronograms that was ever made, was composed on the birth of Louis XIV, at which time there happened to be a conjunction of the constellations of the Eagle and Lion's-heart,—it was as follows:—

"eXorIens DeLphIn aqVILæ CorDIsqVe LeonIs
CongressV gaLLas spe LætItIaqVe refeCit."

"The Dauphin, rising in the conjunction of the Eagle and Lion's-heart, hath inspired the Gauls with new hope and joy." The numerical letters being added together, give the year 1638. It must be remembered, that the birth of the great Louis was hailed by the French with peculiar demonstrations of joy; for his mother, Ann of Austria, had been then childless twenty-two years; and he was on this account surnamed "Dieu-donné," or the gift of Heaven to the prayers of the people. Chronogrammatism at that time was in very high repute in France, so much so, that it is on record, that one of the professors of this art, Thomas

Billor, was allowed a pension of 1200 livres from Louis XIII. and was called the Chronogrammatist Royal!!

The nearer the sense of the inscription comes to the occasion for which it was written, of course the better,—but, as the witty Spectator observes, it is not so much for the sense, as the year of our Lord, that we are to look; and, indeed, it would be very hard if this double task were to be imposed on these ingenious writers: it is sufficient for them to puzzle their brains in fixing the date, and following Dryden's advice of torturing one poor word a thousand ways; as Bayes says of his rhyme—it may be a very fine chronogram, though absolute nonsense.

The Asiatics, however, who, in all studies of this kind, spare no labour, are not contented to forego *sense* in their compositions, and are always at the very unnecessary trouble of giving us both date and meaning. The name for chronogram is with them simply "tareekh," or date. One grand advantage it has over the European one is, that all the letters which compose the word or sentence, are numerals, by which the incongruous appearance of some of the letters overtopping each other is avoided, and, at the same time, the being restricted from using a single one which does not enter into the account, makes the composition very much more terse and ingenious.

In our loose straggling manner, where, to one

numeral, fifty non-effective letters may be inserted, it is evident, that not only every one may form a chronogram, but that, when formed, it will have an inelegant appearance. The only merit is, when it at once comprises an appropriate sense, and no more letters than are absolutely necessary to represent the date with. This is the object in view in the Arabic and Persian compositions of this nature, and sometimes it is attained with a wonderful degree of success.

As I before observed, every letter with the Asiatics has a numeral power :—these are enumerated in an arithmetical verse, which, from the first word in it, is termed the "abjed."

| ضظغ | ثخذ | قرشت | سعفص | كلمن | حطي | هوز | ابجد |
| --- | --- | --- | --- | --- | --- | --- | --- |
| 1000 900 800 | 700 600 500 | 400 300 200 100 | 90 80 70 60 | 50 40 30 20 | 10 9 8 | 7 6 5 | 4 3 2 1 |

The Persian letters, which are not to be found in the Arabic alphabet, denote the same as those to which they most nearly approach, "pé" and "bé," having the same power, or *two*.

The following is a very beautiful, if I may so term it, chronogram, and is strictly conformable to the above rules.

When Sumbha, the Mahratta chief, with his wife and children, were taken prisoners by the troops of Aurungzebe, a person expressed the date thereof in the following hemistich :—

با زن و فرزند سنبها شد اسیر

"Sumbha was made prisoner, with his wife and children."

The letters which compose this line, being added together, according to the rules of the "abjed," the sum of them gives the year 1104 of the Hegira, which was the date of the circumstance. The following is also a very curious composition of this kind, for the poet, Mobâruk, has not only contrived to include in it the date of writing the book, but has, moreover, given us an acrostic of his name,—as following:—

ما که میگوئیم توحید خدا
باد مقبول جناب کبریا
احمد واصحاب وآلش‌را مدام
رحمت حق باد از ما والسلام
کرده.شد این نسخه تاریخ ونام
جمله در ابواب منظومه تمام

"I declare the Unity of God; may it be acceptable to the divine threshold; Ahmed and his companions and family for ever! May the mercy of God, I pray, be upon them, and peace! The title of this book expresses also the date when it was written." This is the literal translation given by Gladwin, but of course it is impossible to preserve either the acrostic or the chronogram of the original. The latter is comprised in the words ابواب منظومه—which contain the year 1053 A.H.

But, as I before remarked, the most common use of the chronagram in the east is to denote the date in epitaphs, and as the most celebrated instance that can be given, I subjoin the inscription on the tomb of the Anacreon of Shiraz:—

هفت ونود ويك بحكم لم يزلي
جهان فضل وهنر در جواز يافت
يگانه سعدي ثاني محمد حافظ
ازين سراچه فاني بباغ جنت رفت
چراغ اهل معني خواجه حافظ
كه شعي بود از نور تجلي
چو در خاك مصلا ساخت منزل
بجو تاريخش از خاك مصلي

"In the year seven hundred ninety and one,
A world of excellence and genius departed to the residence of mercy:
The incomparable, second Sadi, Mahomed Hafiz,
Quitted this perishable region, and went to the garden of Paradise.
Khojeh Hafiz was the camp of the learned:
A luminary was he of a brilliant lustre;
As Mosella was his chosen residence,
Search in Mosella for the time of his decease."

Here it must be observed, that the single letters which form the words khak خاك and Mosella مصلي being added together, according to their numerical value, are equivalent to the year of the Hejira, 791, or A. D. 1340, which was the period of the death of Hafiz,—of which admirable bard only thus much farther, may the earth lie lightly on his breast!

I must give my reader one more example, which has I believe never yet been published, and will I think, be considered as remarkably singular and interesting, so much so, that in my opinion, it deserves to be inscribed in a Persian couplet on the tomb of the illustrious character to whom it relates. Lord Cornwallis died, as every one must remember, in October, 1805, at Ghazeepoor:—some ingenious wit has discovered that the name of this place represents, by the rules of the "abjed," the period of his decease, thus, غازيپر or,

$$1000 + 1 + 7 + 10 + 2 + 200 = 1220,$$

which is the year of the Hejira corresponding to A.D. 1805. The above was communicated to me by a learned native friend of mine; but with the name of the author, or rather the discoverer, of the Chronogram, I am unacquainted.—The coincidence in it is very remarkable, and it surprizes me much that it has not before been offered to the public.

Sir William Jones very justly observes, that every Asiatic subject partakes of infinity, and indeed it may be said of them—"facilis descensus, sed revocare gradum—hoc opus, hic labor est;" or as La Fontaine makes Renard remark of the Lion's den, "je vois fort bien comme l'on entre, et ne le vois pas comme on en sort,"—I will not therefore venture farther in, lest I be unable to extricate myself.

Addison has condemned this kind of composition as a species of false wit, and to controvert any of his decisions, is neither in my inclination or power;—yet like its fellow-sufferers, puns, anagrams, &c. it has been much more abused, I think, than it has deserved to be. Of its illegitimacy there is no doubt, and to waste on its composition, as much time and toil as would produce a folio of Theology, would certainly be ridiculous;—yet when an unstudied Chronogram is offered to us, which contains a happy coincidence or allusion, a smile for the ingenious discoverer can hardly be said to be thrown away.

Yours, &c.

NUGARUM AMATOR.

## JOURNAL FROM MANGALORE TO SERINGAPATAM.

(*Concluded from page* 73.)

1ST FEBRUARY.—We scoured one or two other woods on our return, and towards evening reached Nauknar.

2d.—Halted this day at Nauknar. The Coorgs are a hardy race of mountaineers, and somewhat similar, in their manners and martial appearance, to the Rajpoots of Hindostan. They go always armed with a *kuttee*, or Coorga hatchet; and being on every occasion accustomed to wear this singular weapon, use it with the greatest dexterity. It is also an established custom among the natives, to clothe every male child, when only three years old, with a *kumberbund* ; at the age of seven they assume the *kuttee*, and at twelve carry a match-lock. From twenty until the age of fifty, they yield, whenever required, an alternate personal attendance of fifteen days on the Rajah. Part of the men are thus employed on the public service, and the rest remain with their families, attending to the cultivation of their lands.

This custom resembles the feudal system of the ancient Germans, and other nations who invaded the Roman Empire, in the decline of its power; every vassal being obliged to perform military service for the lands he held of his liege lord.

This territory was subject, several centuries ago, to the same family that at present possess the government. From the strength of the country, and the character of the inhabitants, I am inclined to think, the small but mountainous district of Coorga was at all times independent, until Hyder Ali obtained a footing in the country, by interfering in the family disputes of former Rajahs. The Mysorean Regent subjugated the neighbouring districts belonging to the Rajahs of Bednore, Soondoor, and other petty chieftains of Malabar; and, in consequence of some dispute concerning the right of inheritance, he afterwards invaded Coorga. Hyder, having espoused the cause of Singa Rajah, and his adherents, reinstated him, in opposition to another branch of the family in authority; obtained the cession of several districts above and below the Ghauts, and imposed a tribute on the country: among the districts ceded are those of Soolia and Bellary.

Veer Rajander Warriar (or Warrior,) the present Rajah, succeeded about twenty-one years ago to his paternal inheritance. Being left a minor, Hyder, in the name of the young Prince, assumed the government of the country, and shortly after, put him into confinement. Against this usurpation the inhabitants continually revolted, and gained many advantages over the Mysorean troops, until Tippoo, by an insidious peace, contrived to cut off, or carry into bondage, many thousands of the unfortunate Coorgs; part of the prisoners were sent to Seringapatam, circumcised, and formed into slave battalions; the remainder having been distributed among the villages and towns of Mysore.

In 1787, the Rajah escaped from confinement, collected an inconsiderable number of his subjects, defeated the enemy in several engagements, and, by his own gallantry and good conduct, regained the patrimony of his ancestors. Veer Rajander, however, never obtained the entire or undisturbed possession of his country, until the conclusion of the war, in 1792: at this time it was guaranteed to him by the English, very much against the inclination of the revengeful Mysorean.

It is worthy of remark, that, at a time when the Rajah was besieging one of the principal forts, or strong-holds, in this country, a Mussulman, who, in adverse days, had been the young Rajah's friend, advanced with a convoy to the relief of the place: being unable to effect it by force, he applied, in this dilemma, to the Rajah, and acquainted him, that a failure of the duty he had been ordered upon, would prove fatal to himself and family, since it was the constant policy of his master to detain the latter at Seringapatam, to answer for any misbehaviour or misconduct in his servants. Veer Rajander admitted the convoy, to save his benefactor.

The Rajah has always shewn the greatest attachment and fidelity to the English, as the following orders, by Generals Floyd and Stuart, will evince: —" Major-General Floyd desires to inform the troops he has the honour to command, that the Coorga Rajah, who this day received them in the field, expressed the highest approbation at the appearance of the corps, composing the division of the Grand Army.

" Major-General Floyd thinks it necessary, for the public information, to state, that the army under General Stuart, has lately received the same ample assistance, as that under Sir Ralph Abercrombie experienced during the late war, from this faithful ally of the British Government in India."

It was Sir Ralph Abercrombie who first engaged the Rajah's friendship, and formed an alliance between him and the Honorable Company.

During my stay at Nauknar, I spent the evenings mostly with the Rajah, and was amused with the performance of some dancing girls, who sang Canarese songs and Hindostanee geets. Whether these are the same fascinating damsels, of whom the Abbé Raynal, in his history of the East Indies, gives such an enchanting description, I cannot take upon me to say; but their dress, consisting of a small tight jacket, loose pyjamma, and kumber-bund, appears better calculated to show off the attitudes, and various graceful motions of the body and limbs, than that worn by the same class of people in Hindostan.

At Nauknar, the thermometer generally stood, early in the morning, at fifty-five or fifty-six degrees, and very heavy dews fell during the night; at our encampment, ten miles to the north-west, the mercury, exposed to the open air, sank sometimes to within ten degrees of the freezing point.

3rd February.—To Veer Rajander Pete, sixteen miles. When I took my leave of the Coorga chief, yesterday evening, he shook me very heartily by the hand, and desired that I would sometimes remember him as a friend. This village derives its name from the present Rajah, by whom it was built, to serve as an asylum for a number of Portuguese families, which fled from Mysore to avoid the persecution and tyranny of its ruler. The inhabitants of this denomination amount to about a thousand, and have the privilege of a church; a number of Hindoos are also settled here.

4th.—To Sedaseer, nineteen miles. This morning I passed over the ground, at Sedapoor, where the Bombay army was encamped, in February 1799, waiting the arrival of the grand army, under General Harris, before Seringapatam. From Sedapoor to Sedaseer, the road is plain and good, although leading through a continued jungle; neither house, inhabitant, or plantation, are to be seen, in any part of this route; and the only residents in this inhospitable frontier, are elephants and tigers, which frequent in great numbers the bamboo thickets.

In the evening, I went to the spot where Tippoo, with eleven or twelve thousand of his best troops, attacked Colonel Montresor's detachment of three battalions; the assailants, in their approach to the post on Sedaseer hill, were favoured by the intricacy of the adjacent country, and the thickness of the underwood; in repelling the attack, our men had expended all their ammunition, when General Stuart, with a detachment from the 75th and 77th regiments, arrived, and put the enemy to flight at the point of the bayonet. A small chokey, near Sedaseer, is the boundary between Mysore and Coorga.

5th.—By Perriaputtun, (or, as it is called in the

maps, Periapatam) to Chilcoonder, fourteen miles. Perriaputtun has been a very large fortified town. In Lord Cornwallis's campaigns in Mysore, as the Bombay army advanced towards the capital, the enemy, in retiring, plundered and laid waste the whole country: among the rest, this unfortunate city was dismantled and burnt, in order to prevent its being tenable to any troops hereafter. To-day we entered a more campaign country. Walking out at Chilcoonder, a few minutes before sunset, I received an inexpressible satisfaction in viewing the distant mountains I had so lately passed over, and which, rising from the level surface of the plain, have a similar appearance to a high tract of land emerging out of the sea.

Six or seven miles to the north, is the peak of a large and lofty hill, jutting out in the form of a cone, and so insulated, if I may use the expression, by the low and level plain of Mysore, as to form, with the adjacent Ghauts, a beautiful and striking contrast. The following little tribute to Coorga, is expressive of my feelings on this occasion:—

FAREWELL! ye distant mounts and vales,
  Where memory loves to trace
Thy hills embower'd, and green-clad vales,
  The bourn, the woodland chase.

What tho' thy groves and bowers among,
  No muse e'er deign'd to stray,
To lisp sweet pleasure's airy song,
  Or raise the heav'nly lay.

Yet oft thy tuneful feath'ry throngs,
Make grove and hill resound,
Whilst Echo's voice the notes prolongs,
And gladdens all around.

Ye tow'ring hills, once more Adieu,—
Where Nature decks with simplest grace,
Each winding dell and chequer'd view,
That charms the Coorgan warrior race.

6th.—To Hassenpore, twenty miles. At Malibary, there is an old fort in a very ruinous state. Every village or town in this neighbourhood, has been destroyed three times by fire within the last thirty years: by the Mahrattas in the year 1771, and again, in Lord Cornwallis's, and General Harris's campaigns.

7th.—To Seringapatam, sixteen miles. On the road I saw some magnificent, and even beautiful, ruins of Pagodas, which had been defaced and broken down, by order of the late bigoted prince, to repair the walls of his capital.

VIATOR.

## AN INFALLIBLE CURE FOR NOSE-BLEEDING.

MR. EDITOR,—I am an inglorious mortal, and prefer the civic to the laurel wreath; let others gain applause by spilling the blood of our enemies, but suffice it for me to lessen, if I can, the effusion of our own. I hate your dark-lanthorn gentry, who keep all their wonderful knowledge to themselves; when I find a treasure, I am only happy as I can share it with my friends; and at present, I have, I think, a real one to offer you,—a communication that ought to place my name in the same rank with Æsculapius and Hippocrates:—it is, in short, no less than an infallible cure for nose-bleeding!

But, as my friend Horace says, let us keep in mind the "lucidus ordo:"—pay, then, due attention to the following brief directions:—When the nose begins to bleed, observe at which nostril it does so, whether right or left, and, with a piece of pack-thread, tie up very tightly the middle joint of the corresponding little finger: do not loosen this until the bleeding has stopped, which will be almost instantaneously!!!

Of this recipe, it may really be said—"simplex munditiis,"—it is at once simple and neat. "But the proof of the pudding," very elegantly and acutely observes an old English writer, "is in the eating,"—and even by this rule, I can conscientiously recommend the above process, for a frequent practice has perfectly convinced me of its efficacy.

The knowledge of it came to me among a large mass of other very valuable and curious information of a similar nature, from a worthy, and, by me, much venerated old lady in England; and I have since, found reason to admire her veracity and accuracy, for in a very valuable treatise, I have, entitled "The way to get Wealth—or a list of noble dishes, containing two hundred fit for an Emperor, the which shall not cost more than three halfpence a piece"—dated 1701,—I met with this remedy, (of course as one of the dishes) given in precisely the same terms, or as Elias Ashmole would say—"in syllables."

Some of your fastidious readers may perhaps *insist* upon having a reason given, before they lend me their belief of its miraculous powers:—to these I reply with Falstaff,—"That if reasons were as plenty as blackberries, I would not give one on compulsion;"—however, if they ask me civilly, I will relax, and tell them that a report goes, that there be certain nerves, or veins, (I am not sure which) that run from the little finger to the nostril: and in that case, the mode of cure is precisely on the principle of Sir William Blizzard's *tourniquet*.

If your readers choose to deny this communication of nerves or veins, I must intrench myself behind authority; not however the authority of modern anatomists, for these fellows are so precise in their experiments, and adhere so closely to dull matter of fact, that they would ruin the most beautiful hypothesis in the world.—No; I will defend myself analogically by what the ancients have said on the subject of *wedding rings*. Aulus Gellius, then, tell us that the Greeks and Romans wore their ring "in digito sinistræ manus qui minimo est proximus,"—on that finger of the left hand which is next to the least, and assigns as a cause, from the authority of Appian, that a small nerve runs from this finger to the heart: Macrobius gives the same reason:—and, therefore, it is fair to conclude that if their nerve existed (which is tacitly allowed by all married people), there is no good objection to be started against mine.

By the way, Mr. Editor, it has surprised me much, that there has been no book yet published, containing all the *infallible* cures that our good old ladies in England are acquainted with; consider only how vast would be the saving in that vile article, "'poticary stuff;"—for example, instead of buying the expensive medicine, Peruvian bark, how cheap are the following among a thousand similar cures of the ague.

First.—"Take a spider, shut him up in a small paper case, and wear it in the breast; as your spider languishes, so will languish the disease,—and when he dies, your illness will be over."

The only reason I can devise for this, is, that the spider having nothing else to eat, subsists himself on the ague, and when it has eaten it all up, it necessarily is starved to death, which is really very natural. As a proof, too, that such effect is not merely imaginary, or to be lightly esteemed, let me cite the following passage from the diary of honest old Elias Ashmole: "March, 1681.—I hung three spiders about my neck, and they drove my ague away, Deo gratias!"

Second.—"Every ass has the figure of a cross on its back; take some of the hair which grows on the point of intersection, and wear it in your bosom: the disease will very soon fly away."

To understand the rationale of this process, it must be observed, that this mark of a cross is supposed to have been impressed on the ass on account of our Saviour having used this animal in his triumphal entry into Jerusalem, and hence its miraculous power.

Third.—Write on a piece of paper the following charm:—

A. B. R. A. C. A. D. A. B. R. A.<br>
A. B. R. A. C. A. D. A. B. R.<br>
A. B. R. A. C. A. D. A. B.<br>
A. B. R. A. C. A. D. A.<br>
A. B. R. A. C. A. D.<br>
A. B. R. A. C. A.<br>
A. B. R. A. C.<br>
A. B. R. A.<br>
A. B. R.<br>
A. B.<br>
A.

And wear it in the breast,—the ague will speedily be cured. For this I cannot pretend to account, "Ni Deus intersit"—but by calling in the aid of the Dom-Daniel professors of "the art that none may name." I must observe, however, it is one of the oldest talismans we possess; and I might, if I chose to sport my learning, quote to you sundry crabbed hexameters of Serenus Simonicus's, giving directions how to form it properly. It has sadly plagued the brains of the learned to discover some good reason:—the most ingenious is perhaps Father Hardouin's, who, by assigning its due power to each of the Hebrew characters which would form the word, has discovered that it is an invocation to the Trinity, saving mankind by the cross; but as it is a very old Egyptian amulet, this cannot be its origin.

Fourth.—"Drink sage tea, and you will be cured"—for this simple reason—sage tea cures every disease in the *known* world, or, *poetice*, it overcomes the whole febrile cohort which that awkward young lady, Pandora, let slip out of the *reticule*. The panaceatic virtues of sage have been celebrated in the following verse:—

"Cur moriatur homo cui Salvia crescit in horto."

"Why will a man die who has got sage growing in his garden?" Why indeed! "Yet," as Goldsmith says, "notwithstanding all this, there are many who now and then think proper to be sick:—only sick did I say? there are some who even think proper to die! Yes, by the head of Confusius, they die; though they had the health-restoring specific growing in every corner of their gardens!"

I could give fifty others all equally *infallible*, but the above are sufficient to explain the plan of the book I wish for, and which is a real desideratum in literature. For the title of this work, perhaps "The Family Recipe Book," or the "Old Lady's Assistant," might serve;—but as it is the fashion now to entitle treatises of all kinds thus—"Every Man his own Gardener," "Every Man his own Cook," "Every Man his own Chimney Sweeper," &c. &c., I see no reason why our work should not receive a similar kind of denomination, and the following would do excellently—"Every Man his own Old Woman." Whether this book would not very soon supersede "Buchan's Domestic Medicine," I will not take on me to say, nor will I state my opinion of the comparative merits of the two; for, as Dogberry says—"Comparisons are odious;" but hoping that these hints will receive due attention, and that I shall be thought to deserve well of my country for them,

I remain, &c.

BENEVOLUS.

## CURIOUS ERRORS OF MISS HAMILTON, MISS OWENSON, AND MRS. RADCLIFFE.

Sir,—In your last I ventured to offer a few critical remarks on a passage in Dr. Ash; and I now propose to be so rude as to attack one or two of the fair sex: yet let them not be afraid—their character is perfectly safe in my hands. The ladies of whom I am about to speak, stand so deservedly high in the opinion of the public, that to say how much I admire the elegance of their writings, and the justness of their sentiments, would be rather to pay a compliment to my own taste than to their talents. To mention only the name of Miss Hamilton is to have said every thing. Let not any of my readers be offended if I attempt to prove that this polished writer has been *once* in error;—then too the mistake was but trivial, and fully compensated by a thousand beauties; yet am I right in pointing it out, for to detect any error, however trifling, or wherever it may be met with, is laudable. The fair fame of Miss Hamilton cannot be sullied by one petty inaccuracy, nor, in commenting on it, shall I be thought, I trust, to entertain the most remote wish of detracting from her well-earned reputation:

> "Verum, ubi plura nitent....non ego paucis
> Offendar maculis."

Every candid reader will, I hope, do justice to my motives. But to the matter at once. Miss Hamilton, in her "Letters on the Elementary Principles of Education," (vol. ii. p. 186) gives it as her opinion that poetry should not form part of children's studies, because they have not acquired a sufficient stock of ideas to understand it. She justly observes that where the mind is incapable of keeping pace with the rapid associations of the poet; where the finest allusions are lost for want of conception to apprehend their meaning; where the finest imagery presents no object to the mind; the emotions that are excited have surely no affinity to the sublime or beautiful. To defend her proposition, she thus gives an instance:—"Let us suppose a little girl, whose acquaintance with natural objects extends to the grass-plat which ornaments the centre of some neighbouring square. In order to cultivate a taste for descriptive poetry, she is enjoined the task of getting by heart Gray's celebrated Elegy, which abounds in imagery at once natural and affecting. Let us follow her in the conceptions she forms from it. Two lines will be a sufficient example.

> 'The curfew tolls the knell of parting day,
> The lowing herd winds slowly o'er the lea.'"

Having gone through her observations on the first line, and convinced us that the mind of a child is not adopted to form correspondent ideas of it, she thus proceeds in her remarks:—"What does she make, what *can* she make, of the succeeding line?

A *herd* she has probably heard of, as one who takes care of sheep, goats, or other animals; but why the herd should *low*, is certainly beyond her comprehension. How, or in what manner, he *winds*, is equally so."

Can it be believed that Miss Hamilton, the well-informed, correct, elegant Miss Hamilton could have made so egregious a mistake as to take *herd* for *herdsman?* And yet that it is so, is too evident; the context, unfortunately, will admit of no palliation.

And how, supposing the word to signify "one who takes care of sheep, &c." does Miss Hamilton understand the line? For it should be observed, that she does not criticise the words themselves, but merely observes that they are above a child's comprehension. In this case, I must confess myself a "mewling infant;" for were the line to stand thus—

"The lowing *Swain* winds slowly o'er the lea,"

I must candidly own I should not understand it. It is very strange how such a blunder could have been committed, and equally so how it could have proceeded to the public eye,—for the compositors for the press, nay the printer's devils, one would have thought, must have corrected it.

As to venial errors like the following, one may easily excuse them, for a lady is not obliged to understand Latin. Miss Owenson, in her excellent

Novel "The Wild Irish Girl,"—in speaking of an *old woman* and her *two cows,* very learnedly calls them a *triumvirate.* And yet, perhaps, if any body ought to be brought to an account for displaying this kind of ignorance, it should be Miss Owenson, as she is not slightly partial to talking "rotundo ore" on deeply learned subjects; and in her "Ida of Athens," impresses on us in every page a thorough conviction that she is deeply imbued with classical knowledge.

The mighty "Enchantress of Udolpho" has also committed a blunder very much resembling the above—speaking of one of the magnificent Venetian halls, her glowing fancy has created, she says, "it was brilliantly illuminated by vast *tripods* suspended from the vaulted roof."—Either etymology or Mrs. Radcliffe must blunder here most terribly, for I need not observe that it is generally considered as a *sine quâ non* with *tripods,* that they should stand on three feet. But enough of this cavilling at words.

Yours, &c.

PERCONTATOR.

## ON THE EYES OF PORTRAITS.

---

PLINY remarks of a certain Painter, that he was the first, who, in a portrait, drew the eyes with so peculiar a skill, that they seemed to follow the spectator as he changed his place, and still to look at him. A writer in the Gentleman's Magazine for August 1766,—observes on this passage, that Pliny discovers great ignorance in making the remark, and further adds that the effect is constant, and impossible to be otherwise. He says—"the most ignorant Painter does the same thing without intention, and the most skilful can never represent the eyes looking at the spectator, standing in any one place, but they will also have the same direction to him standing in any other. The cause of this effect, it is plain that Pliny did not know:—it is, that the direction of the eyes towards the spectator, remains the same in whatever place he stands, for that direction, or turn, of the pupil, bears still the same relation to the position of each feature, and to all parts of the face, which being on a plane, suffer no apparent changes; and it is on this relation that the whole depends; whereas, in a living face, or statue, that relation is continually changing with every change of place of the spectator."

With all due deference to the above elegant writer, I must observe, that in my opinion, he has censured Pliny without sufficient reason. I allow that no painter can represent the eyes look ing at the spectator, standing in one place, but they will also have the same direction to him standing in any other,—and the cause of this, he has, I think, justly assigned to proceed from the nature of a plane. Yet it is certain, that there are some portraits which do, and others which do not, seem to look at us,—and as the painter regulates this by a little artifice, I conceive Pliny's encomium to be on the man who first discovered it. I speak now only of what are technically termed *three quarter faces ;* (for in completely full ones I do not recollect the effect ;) —in these, then, if the nose and eyes have a similar direction, as is most natural, they will in no place appear to look at the spectator,—but if they are turned in opposite directions, then, whereever they may be viewed from, they will appear to return our regards. This is so ingenious an optical delusion, that I cannot but agree with Pliny, in praising highly the painter who first discovered it. Nor is it merely on the score of science, that he claims our thanks. Let those who have hung delighted over the portrait of a deceased or absent friend, lover, or parent :—who have fancied, in the fond returning gaze they met, that the canvass had started into life,—let these appreciate,—for they only can,—the value of such a discovery; and such sensations, I confess I have myself felt, nor do I envy him who has not;—yet I own that at these times, I never checked my pleasure by enquiring to what cause, or to whom, my gratitude was due; for of these exquisite joys, I agree perfectly with the almost too-sweet Anacreon of the present day:—

> "No, Science! to you
> I have long bid a last and a careless adieu:
> Still flying from Nature to study her laws,
> And dulling delight by exploring its cause,—
> You forget how superior, for mortals below,
> Is the fiction they dream, to the truth that they know.
> Would ask how we feel it, or why it is sweet;
> How rays are confused, or how particles fly
> Through the medium refined of a glance or a sigh!—
> Is there one, who but once would not rather have known it,
> Than have written, with Harvey, whole volumes upon it?"

That one,—if one there be,—certainly am not I!—yet, did I know the name of him to whom I am thus indebted, he should receive my warmest gratitude, and hold in my estimation a far higher place than Apelles, Zeuxis, or any other master of the graphic art.

An Amateur.

## BIRTH-RIGHT TO STEPNEY PARISH.

---

Sir,—Being naturally interested by being myself a native, I have lately enquired rather particularly into the origin and truth of a very generally received opinion, that all persons born in this country (Bengal) of British parents, belong to the parish of Stepney. This is continually asserted with confidence; and not only in our behalf, but that the benefit extends to all British children born at, or beyond, sea. I have vainly, however, sought for any authority in support of this. Stow, Maitland, and Pennant, in their several accounts of the place, are silent on the subject, which silence is, of itself, conclusive against the fact.

But there are still stronger grounds for classing it among vulgar errors: Mr. Barrington, in his "Observations on the more Ancient Statutes," affirms the opinion, though a very prevailing one, to be erroneous,—and on such a subject, the assertion of so learned a judge must be considered as decisive. The belief in it may have originated thus;—Stepney was formerly an extremely large parish, and included within its limits Wapping, Limehouse, Poplar, and several other places on the

Thames, which, from having been always the almost exclusive residence of seafaring men, may have given rise to the popular opinion, that all born at sea belong to that parish.

A NATIVE.

## LETTER ON THE IRISH REBELLION.

MR. EDITOR,—You will at once perceive the nature of the following jeu d'esprit,—it is certainly at present somewhat out of date, but, as it has never appeared in print, and may prove amusing to your readers, you may, perhaps, choose to give it admission.

Yours, &c.

A GATHERER.

"MY DEAR SIR,—Having now a little peace and quietness, I set down to inform you of the dreadful bustle and confusion we are in, from these blood-thirsty rebels, most of whom, are, however, thank God, killed and dispersed. We are in a pretty mess,—can get nothing to eat, nor any wine to drink, except whiskey; and when we sit down to dinner, we are obliged to keep both hands armed; whilst I write this letter, I hold a sword in one hand, and a pistol in the other. I concluded, from the beginning, that this would be the end of it, and I see I was quite right, for it is not half over yet; at present there are such goings on, that every thing is at a stand. I should have answered your letter a fortnight agó, but I only received it this morning. Indeed, hardly a mail arrives safe without being robbed. No longer ago than yesterday, the coach, with the mails from Dublin, was robbed near this town; the bags had been judiciously left behind, for fear of accidents, and, by good luck, there was nobody in the coach but two outside passengers, who had nothing for the thieves to take.

Last Thursday, notice was given that a gang of rebels were advancing hither under the French standard, but they had no colours, nor any drums, except bagpipes. Immediately every man in the place, including women and boys, ran out to meet them: death was in every face, but to it we went, and by the time half of our little party was killed, we began to be all alive. Fortunately the rebels had no guns, but pistols, cutlasses, and pikes,—and as we had plenty of muskets, and other ammunition, we put them all to the sword: not a soul of them escaping, except some that were drowned in an adjoining bog; and, in a very short time, nothing was to be heard but silence. Their uniforms were all of different colours, but mostly green. After the action, we went to rummage a sort of camp they had left behind them: all we found, were a few pikes without heads, a parcel of empty bottles full of water, and a bundle of blank French commissions, filled up with Irishmen's names. I have only leisure to add, that I am in great haste.

Yours, &c.

P.S.—If you do not receive this in course, it must have miscarried, therefore, I beg you will immediately write to let me know; but to prevent you doing this, I am advised to send a duplicate. I therefore inclose one in this, and refer you to that for farther intelligence.

## ON BIGNOR PARK IN SUSSEX.

---

By hills encircled, in a lofty grove,
Bignor, fond seat of many a parent's love:
From thy wild glens my earliest breath I drew,
And memory still—to every prospect true—
Can trace each shrub, the lawn, the daisied green,
For 'tis with eyes of infancy you're seen;
When the young bud of life was in its glow,
And youth in embryo scarce began to blow.
Oft in wild vision's fancied joy I'm led
Through scenes, still conscious of the bliss that's fled;
Where fond affection's sad prophetic tear,
Maternal love, and agonizing fear,
Conscious of ills that human life await,
Hung weeping o'er her children's infant state.
Why still should I those long-lost days deplore,
Which, if possess'd again, could charm no more:
For many a year its lingering course has made—
Since I was torn from thy paternal shade:
Life's vernal days of transient bliss are o'er,
And hope's gay wings are closed to rise no more.
 Thy mountains, Bignor, fringed with beechen shades,
Thy verdant meadows—thy empurpled glades,
Brown hamlets shelter'd by the pendant wood,
And antique oaks that crown the wat'ry flood;—
Scenes which my mother's artless strains inspired,
And the ill-fated muse of Otway* fired.

---

* A native of Sussex, said to have been starved to death.

Nor sacred less is Herting's* cottaged vale,
Where Collins breath'd his ever-pensive tale;
Rous'd Echo from her sylvan bed of sleep,
And bade your groves and mountain shepherds weep.
Oft has my sainted mother wept and sigh'd
On the wild banks of Arun's† restless tide;
Whose silver stream still saddening, loves to tell
The vocal numbers which she sang so well;
Bears her sad history into distant deeps,
And with her willowed banks responsive weeps.
No more your sacred haunts, in Spring's attire,
Shall sounds of sweetest harmony inspire.
Or the chaste empress of the starry night,
The muse's meditating steps invite
To the wild pathless copse, or flow'ry dell,
Or where the sheep-fold's melancholy bell
Awakes the solemn silent ear of night,
Or shepherd's boy from vernal dreams' delight.
  What time the hoary owl incessant wheels,
Winnowing, with labouring wings, the misty fields,
And clamorous rooks in black battalions meet,
Slow wearing homeward to their dark retreat,
Oft have I paused upon thy utmost brow,
When evening beams enrich'd the vale below,
And summer suns declining, sank away
In short-lived splendour with the parting day.
Tinkling adown thy turf-clad steeps were led
The folds, reluctant, to their nightly shed:
While jocund labour whistling lagg'd behind,
And village murmurs swell'd the whispering wind.

---

* An obscure village in Sussex, where Collins, who was also a native of this county, wrote his beautiful elegy on the death of Colonel Ross.

† A river in Sussex, which gives its name to Arundel

Slow flew the swallow o'er the glassy lake,
And dulcet warblings fill'd the distant brake;
The nut-fenced hedge, where woodbine flaunts among,
Rang with the blackbird's full impassion'd song:
The skylark, wearied with aerial flight,
Sank tremulous on her verdant bed of night,
Resign'd the music of the live-long day,
To Philomela's soft, but sorrowing lay.
High rose the moon, the traveller's gay resource,
And ranges peerless up her starry course;
Her blossom'd heaths, dark pines and tinted wheat,
In one wide prospect elegantly meet;
There Neptune's wide blue restless waters rise,
And distant ships seem blended with the skies:
High stately groves embrace the flow'ry fields,
And to the sea a woodland contrast yields.
 Where Beechy's* wild immeasurable steep
With pallid horror frowns above the deep,
Oft from the giddy height the shepherd sees
The shapeless vessel in the distant seas—
Struggling with adverse winds to gain the coast,
High in the waste of ruthless billows tost.
Far sounds the tide with never-ceasing roar,
And whitening surges mark the distant shore:
That shore,† where Cæsar's bloody eagle stood,
Hovering in doubtful battle o'er the flood:
That flood which ran in streams so pure before,
Which British valour stained with Roman gore:

---

* Beechy-head. This spot is now classic ground, for it has been consecrated in the verse of the most elegant of the modern muses, a muse, whom, though "melancholy marked her for her own," yet Venus "quintâ parte sui nectaris imbuit,"—but to what reader is this eulogy necessary:—

"Tu quo litoribus nostris,
Æternum scribens famam, Caroletta, dedisti."

† Cæsar, in his second expedition, landed on this coast.

And nobly backward to be Roman slaves,
Turn'd her green azure* into purple waves:
  Drawn from thy woods by promis'd scenes of wealth,
I've lost my friends, my happiness, my health;—
Youth 's wearied out in unavailing toil,
Since pride rejects that wealth obtain'd by spoil:
Virtue unfriended meets with foul disgrace,
And rank corruption revels in her place:—
How far more bless'd, beneath thy mountain's side,
Where Flora triumphs in her vernal pride,
Does many a rustic independent live,
Too proud to ask—too honest to deceive,—
Too low for envy—for a bribe too free,
And crown'd with bliss by fate denied to me.

---

## TRANSLATION OF A SANSCRIT COUPLET.

মাসুজনদর্শনং মেযদি দর্শন মস্তু মাপুন বেহঃ।
স্নেহো যদি মাবিব হো যদি বিব হো মাস্তুজীব
ভা বোমঃ॥

MAY I ne'er know a man of virtuous heart,
Or knowing such, his friendship ne'er obtain,—
But if my friend—O! may we never part,
Or parted, quickly close a life of pain.

---

* The most bloody battles ever fought in England, were those of Hastings, and those on Cæsar's landing in Sussex and Kent. There still prevails, among the lower class, a superstitious belief, that the sea changed colour.

## ODE TO HOPE.

---

Come, sweet Enchantress, come!
  Dress'd in soft visions gay,—
With gentle look and seraph smile,
Thou canst severest grief beguile,
  And charm e'en doubt away:
    My mind serene,
    Shall bless the scene,
Nor own its joys are raised by Fancy's Fairy Queen.

Come, cheerful Hope, again—
  Oh! bless thy votary's prayer!
O'er dark futurity thy mantle throw,
Make ev'ry scene with brighter colours glow,
  And fling behind each care;—
    With Hope my guest,
    How truly blest,
And rich in flatt'ring visions feels my breast!

I e'en will love thee still—
  Though oft the glowing veil delusive proves,
So finely wrought by thy soft magic wand,
Which steals, or seems to steal, from sorrow's hand,
  And from our view each dreaded ill removes.
    Oh! to me yield,
    Thy wond'rous shield,—
Sweet Hope! thine armour ever may I wield!

And will this pass away?—
  Is hope then merely Fancy's child!
Ah no! for her soft angel smile
Can charm Despair, can Woe beguile,
  And soothe the raging Passions wild!
      Her form benign
      Shall be my shrine,
Yes, lovely Hope! my ev'ry vow is thine!

Ah! what has Life to give!—
  Misfortune's hand oft breaks the thread
That binds us to its transient joys,
Its power our short-lived bliss destroys,
  And sorrows deep the mind o'erspread;—
      Still Hope would fain
      The heart regain,
And sure the effort is not made in vain.

Though oft the tearful eye
  Shews Disappointment cradled in the breast,
The humble look, with resignation fill'd,
Displays a heart with grateful fervour thrill'd,
  Where Hope's sweet balm has sorrow sooth'd to rest;
      Hope, which nor clime
      Can bind, nor time,
Till soaring high it rests in heav'nly joys sublime!

## FROM THE PERSIAN OF NIZAMI.

THOUGH grief and rudest pain assail,
  Still hope, through dark misfortune's hour;
From yon black clouds that low'ring sail,
  May fall the lucid crystal shower.

## TO THE BRITISH SHIPWRIGHTS.

### A MASONIC SONG.

THE Briton's best dock is the ocean at large,
His music the sweetest, that sounds to the charge;
His guns and his balls are the tools of his trade,
Which no courage can baffle, no art can evade;—
Britannia's the word,—sure magic is in it,—
Till he comes to close quarters, he chides the slow minute.
Blow briskly ye gales,
And swell her proud sails;
Now windward she wears,
Crowds her sails and makes way;—
Now downward she bears—
See her lightning—hark! her thunder—
While old Neptune beholds, with delight and with wonder,
His Britons build ships in a day.

In proof that the sea is our dock, I'll advance
The names of some shipwrights who've humbled proud France,
Hawke, Rodney, and Vincent, brave Bridport and Hood,
Howe, Duncan, and Warren, and bold Collingwood.
"Britons strike home,"—their word—sure magic is in it,
Till they come to close quarters, they chide the slow minute.
Blow briskly ye gales,
And swell their proud sails;—
Now windward they wear,
Crowd their sails and make way;—
Now downward they bear—
See their lightning—hark! their thunder—
While old Neptune beholds, with delight and with wonder,
His heroes build ships in a day.

As expert as these shipwrights, I will maintain,
That many such craftsmen now sail on the main ;
Who like Nelson would build—like Nelson would die—
Like Nelson, advancing, would exultingly cry—
" Our country's the word,"—sure magic is in it,
Until laid alongside, they chide the slow minute.
Blow briskly ye gales,
And swell their proud sails ;
Now windward they wear,
Crowd their sails and make way;—
Now downward they bear—
See their lightning—hark ! their thunder—
While old Neptune beholds, with delight and with wonder,
His Nelson build fleets in a day.

## FROM THE ITALIAN OF BENEDETTO MENZINI.

Let other bards the Rose's charms proclaim,
And praise the splendor of her beauty gay ;
While I assert the Violet's fairer claim,
To bear from ev'ry flower the palm away.

When to the gale she languidly displays
Her pallid leaves along the verdant ground ;
That pallid hue a languid heart betrays,
Made faint and feeble by love's ling'ring wound !

With rosy wreath let youth his temples bind,
While gay, he quaffs in pleasure's jocund bower ;
But to the tender lover's pensive mind
Shalt thou, fair Violet, be the dearest flower.

## SONNET.

[WRITTEN ON THE RIVER GANGES, ON TAKING LEAVE OF A FRIEND.]

As yon high bourn recedes from painful view,
Where seems to linger still the last Adieu:
Sad sounds the pond'rous splash from ev'ry oar,
That pulls us sorrowing from the distant shore;
Where warm unalter'd friendship ever smil'd,
And many a casual misery beguiled.
Down the unruffled sacred stream we glide,
And pass th'unconscious objects on its side,—
Which serve both joy and sorrow to betray,
As pains or pleasures past have fled away,—
Wrings from fond memory's wounds the fruitless sigh,
And points to long-lost happiness gone by.
So hopeless mem'ry starts with wild dismay,
To find all objects but itself decay.

## TO A SCEPTIC.

You've proved, great Sir, with skill profound,
That nothing certain's to be found;—
To thee respect I always pay,
So doubt the truth of what you say.

## ANECDOTE.

"OBSERVE what an intelligent khidmutgar is mine,"—said a gentleman at breakfast,—"I did but nod to him, and he has brought me the salt, which was precisely what I wanted." "I see nothing very extraordinary in it," observed another, "for, by the way in which you nodded, what you wanted was as plain as *noon-day*." It hardly need be observed, that "*noon dé*" is Hindostanee, and means,—"give me the salt."

"Critics sharp, with brow severe,
Our small volume come not near;—
Authors grave, and learn'd, and wise,
Never this way turn your eyes."

MRS. J. HUNTER.

"Ut pictura, poësis; erit quæ, si propius stes,
Te capiet magis; et quædam, si longius abstes:
*Hæc* amat obscurum."

Hor. *De Arte Poet.* *v.* 361-363.

## PLAGIARISM OF MR. DALLAS'S.

Mr. Editor,—Allow me to offer what you must think a very great literary curiosity,—a writer of hitherto most respectable character, and of deservedly high fame, committing, not merely a venial plagiarism of an expression, or even a line or two,—but shamelessly—for I must call it so—stealing a whole volume!!

Who but must laugh, if such a man there be,—
Who but must weep, when Dallas can be he!

Yet so it is!—Mr. Dallas, by his "History of the Maroons," by his novels of "Percival," "Aubrey," "The Knight's Tales," and lastly, "The Morlands," has acquired a high reputation as an elegant and original writer; and it is with regret I enter on the task of plucking from him what I will prove a borrowed plume.

"The Morlands," (as my readers most probably know) are two tales, which, starting from the same point, arrive at the same end, but by very different means,—the one being a natural and probable train of events,—the other, possible, but highly marvellous. Both of these Mr. Dallas lays claim to; he gives them to the world unequivocally as his own, and great has been the praise bestowed on him by the various reviewers. Yet the marvellous Morland is positively an almost literal translation of the French tale, entitled "Le Lord impromptu," of Cazotte; and the only praise Mr. Dallas can justly claim, is the having given a spirited and elegant version of it!!!

As to accidental resemblance, this is quite out of the question here, for no chance could inspire two writers with precisely similar circumstances and expressions, throughout a volume. Mr. Dallas's second Morland is even a close translation of Cazotte's tale; they differ but in the names of the *dramatis personæ*, and in having altered these, Mr. Dallas has clearly evinced that his plagiarism was wilful, and that he used every precaution to avoid detection.

Some may, perhaps, doubt his wish to impose it on us as his own production, and may think that he intended it simply as a translation, and gave it to contrast with his own: but, as a full contradiction to this, he has said in his title-page,—"The Morlands, by R. C. Dallas, Esq." Why did he, too, so sedulously change every name in the work? And why, lastly, did he engraft on his own, the first Morland, the introductory chapter of "Le Lord impromptu," which he has done? In short, the plagiarism does not admit of a doubt,—his guilt is certain; and, for an offence so heinous, severe is the punishment he merits at the hands of the critic. I will, not, however, assume the office of a Rhadamanthus, but, merely pointing out his crime, leave it to others to chastise him duly for it. "The Morlands" were published by Mr. Dallas in 1805; "Le Lord impromptu" first appeared in 1783; and this is, I believe, the only translation of it. As a specimen of the manner, I will give a page from the beginning of each,—the following is part of a very well-drawn character:—

"Sir George Netting, Baronet, l'un des plus riches de cet ordre en Angleterre, âgé de quarante-cinq ans, n'avait ni vices ni vertus. Comme il donnait volontiers, on démêlait aisément qu'il eût été généreux, s'il ne fût pas né trop riche: mais les flatteurs, les escrocs, l'avaient entouré dans sa jeunesse, et d'après des expériences faites sur ce circle, il s'était persuadé que les hommes ne valaient pas la peine qu'on leur fît du bien par principes: aussi laissait-il aller son argent plutôt qu'il ne le répandait. Il avait trop peu de fonds, trop de besoin des autres, pour être misanthrope, et se jetait dans la société sans s'y livrer. Avec les gentilshommes de son voisinage il tenait table sans boire, et chassait par air jusqu'à se fatiguer."

"Sir Robert Wallingford, of Cray-hill, was one of the richest baronets in England, about five and forty years old, and equally free from vice and virtue. He gave his money so willingly, that it was easy to see he would have been a generous man, if he had not been born a rich one; but having been surrounded, in his youth, by flatterers and sharpers, his knowledge of mankind being gained only from them, he was convinced that men did not deserve beneficence on principle, and he might, therefore, be said rather to part with his money, than to bestow it. He had too little resource in himself, and was too dependant upon others, to be a misanthrope; and he mixed in society without enjoying it: with the gentlemen in his neighbourhood he exchanged dinners, but he never pushed the bottle; and he bore the fatigue of hunting because they did."

The change of names is here seen; Mr. Dallas has also taken many other liberties, to adapt it to the English reader, and to make it pass as his own. The skilful way in which he does this, may be judged of by the following extract, or account of a farmer's dinner:—"Plus d'abondance que de goût: du bon cœur sans démonstration, des attentions sans ménagemens, de la franchise sans ouverture, de la bonne humeur sans gaîté, des mets succulens sans être assaisonnés, de la bierre du temps du roi Jean, et six sortes de poudins."

"More abundant than delicate, good cheer without ostentation, attention without ceremony, frankness without freedom, good-humour without wit, garden-stuff without seasoning, clear old ale, and two large plumb puddings."

To Anglicise it completely, he renders the original very freely, thus, he calls, "des æillades amoureuses,"—"casting sheep's eyes;" "un cabaret chargé de liqueurs," he converts into, "a glass of cherry-bounce;" and "les bergeries de Couperin," he translates, "a number of songs." An expression is also frequently omitted, if it has too Gallic a turn; thus, in the original, the hero is once made to faint away, but such effeminacy would have ill-suited the palate of an Englishman, and it is, therefore, judiciously struck out in the translation. In return for this, a sentence or two of the translator's own writing is here and there introduced:—thus he says of a citizen's wife—"She had deserted the soil of her late husband's harvests, abandoned the chilly East for the balmy West; let her house in Bishopsgate-street, and purchased a villa near Kensington." This is not to be found in the original; nor is M. Cazotte answerable for the following witty passage:—"The Vicar was there before Morland, and no wonder, for the former rode, and the latter walked!"

There is also a long paragraph about Bishop Berkeley and the system of *universal immaterialism*, which is, for aught I know to the contrary, entirely Mr. Dallas's own,—at all events it is not Mr. Cazotte's. In the original there are a few attempts at Anglicism,—thus "Mademoiselle" is never used; it is always—"une jolie Miss,"—"une jeune Miss,"—"de punch,"—"du spleen," &c. In return for this, Mr. Dallas's translation is equally parsemée with French expressions; and this he manages with very slight trouble; it is only to leave the sentence half translated,—"Allons!

Richard, vous plaisez à Miladi; tout le monde ne lui convient pas; voilà vos affaires en bon train."—"Allons! Edward, my lady likes you, and it is not every body that pleases her, I assure you: voilà vos affaires en bon train; you may look upon yourself as a lucky fellow." This manner of introducing French words, as being customary in our novels, would by no means have raised suspicion; indeed they give the work—though it is rather an Hibernicism to say so—a more English appearance; but in spite of all his skill and care, he has betrayed himself in letting a few Gallicisms escape him: thus, in page 145, vol. iv., he says, "Whom they welcomed with the most affectionate embraces:"—this is not an English custom, and it should be observed, that the parties who were thus loving had never seen each other before. Again, "When the women thought themselves alone, they gave a greater latitude to their words and caresses:" and again, "the ladies all praised and embraced her, and the Captain pressed her to his breast with more than common tenderness;" all this is entirely French. In general the idioms are very happily rendered—"assaisonneé d'une exclamation tant soit peu marine," is equally good as "seasoned with a salt-water epithet;" but in one instance, where "tas d'originaux" is translated "a set of originals," he has, I think, failed. This does not give in English a correspondent idea with the French term. When we wish to abuse any one we do not, as in France, call him *an original*. But I have spun out these remarks to a greater length than I intended. I will, therefore, now conclude with giving a brief account of M. Cazotte, the real author of the first chapter of the first Morland, and of the whole of the fourth volume, or the second Morland.

M. Jaques Cazotte, author of the poem "D'Olivier," the tales of "Le Diable Amoureux," "Le Lord impromptu," and of several other small pieces, was, prior to the Revolution, long celebrated in the Parisian circles as a witty and pleasing member of society. M. de la Harpe, in speaking of him, says—"he had an original turn of mind, and an infatuation with the reveries of the Illuminati;" of this his "Diable Amoureux" is a strong proof; but the most singular circumstance recorded of him, is a very remarkable prophecy that he is said to have uttered, in which he foretold not only the deaths of several of the great atheistical philosophers, his friends, but likewise his own; and, strange to say, every part of his predictions was verified! (For an account of this—vide "Œuvres choisis et posthumes de M. de la Harpe," or "Literary Panorama" No. 1., or "Calcutta Magazine" No. 5, in each of these it is detailed.)

When the Revolution broke out in 1792, he was arrested and thrown into prison;—all the horrors of which, an amiable daughter of only seventeen years of age, insisted on sharing, and most dutifully attended him through his imprisonment, never quitting his side for a single moment.

In the horrible massacres of September he was led out to execution; but at the instant when the fatal engine was about to fall on his neck, his daughter threw herself over his body, exclaiming —before you spill one drop of my father's blood, you must first take mine!" So affecting a scene touched even the callous hearts of Parisian executioners; and subdued by the sight of a lovely girl offering to immolate herself to save her venerable parent, they, with one impulse, resolved to spare his life, and demanded to know his enemies, that they might revenge him on them; but Cazotte magnanimously replied—"I cannot have any, for I never did harm to any one." The impression made on these savage cut-throats was, however, but transitory. He was reconducted with his heroic daughter to prison, and before the month was elapsed, again led to the scaffold, and, in spite of her prayers and piercing shrieks, was inhumanly murdered before her eyes!

It is remarkably singular that M. de Sombreuil, who was of the same age, seventy-four, was saved on the same day, at the same prison, in a precisely similar manner by his daughter; and horrible to relate,he afterwards underwent the same cruel fate! L'Abbé de Lille, in his poem of "Le Malheur et la Pitié," thus beautifully alludes to Cazotte and Sombreuil :—

"Cependant au milieu de tant de barbarie,
Lorsque, parmi les maux de ma triste patrie,
La timide Pitié n'osait lever la voix,
Des rayons de vertus ont brillé quelquefois :
On a vu des enfans s'immoler à leurs pères,
Des frères disputer le trépas à leurs frères.—
Que dis-je ? Quand Septembre, aux Français si fatal,
Du massacre partout donnait l'affreux signal,
On a vu les bourreaux, fatigués de carnage,
Aux cris de la Pitié laisser fléchir leur rage,
Rendre à la fille en pleurs un père malheureux,
Et, tout couverts de sang, s'attendrir avec eux."

## CATCHING SPARROWS IN THE VALLEY OF CAZAROON.

SIR,—Looking over my papers the other day, I found, among some manuscripts written by the late Capt. J. R——, (who died on his passage to Bencoolen, when proceeding to take the command of the forces of that place, by order of the Supreme Government,) the accompanying rough copy of a letter to Sir William Jones. Should the concise account it contains of the Valley of Cazaroon, between Abusheer and Shiraz, and the curious mode detailed in it of destroying the flocks of sparrows which infest the fields of corn in that part of the country, appear of sufficient moment or interest to communicate to your readers, it is at your service. PERSICUS.

TO SIR WILLIAM JONES.

SIR,—As I have never seen a description of the very curious method of catching sparrows in the Valley of Cazaroon, I have extracted from the observations made during my stay there the following account, which, being very short, the perusal of it may not perhaps take up too much of your time.

The valley of Cazaroon, in the middle of which, the capital of the district of the same name is situated, lies half way between Abusheer and Shiraz;—it is from five to seven miles broad, and about fifty-six long. Two ranges of hills of immense height run along the south-west and north-east sides of it; and springs from the latter, which is by much the highest, supply great plenty of water for all the purposes of cultivation; and the climate being temperate, fine crops of wheat and barley are produced in the highest, and rice in the lowest, parts of the valley.

In the middle of June I arrived there, and was the next morning carried by Hajy Khuleel, an eminent merchant of Abusheer, to see what he thought the most extraordinary thing he had met with, the catching of sparrows; which he said were so numerous in the district, that were it not for a poor family, who had the art of catching many hundreds of them daily, not one grain of their wheat and barley would be left for the support of the inhabitants.

The catching of sparrows appearing to me a puerile entertainment, I smiled at the idea, but as he persisted in assuring me that there was something uncommon and curious in the mode of doing it, I was prevailed on to accompany him.

At the distance of a mile and a quarter from Cazaroon, I saw a poor creature sitting down with a rope in his hand, who, I was told, was the bird-catcher. On looking round, I found that he had stuck up poles about ten feet high with bits of old rag at the top of each, round a piece of ground of four or five acres;—these poles were distant forty or fifty feet from each other, and were so placed as to form a long square, at one end of which sat the bird-catcher. The rope in his hand was about —— yards long. He had hold of one end, and the other was fastened to the corner of a net of twenty feet long, and two feet nine inches broad; the lower corners were fixed to pegs in the ground, and one of the upper ones to a rope held by the bird-catcher, as I have before mentioned, the other to a rope of fifteen feet long fixed to a peg. This last rope was slack enough to admit of the net being laid flat on the ground. On either side a small and light pole was fixed, and laid horizontally along the top of the net, in order to enable the fowler to throw it from one side to the other with greater ease; and the ground on which the net was placed was level and clean. The bird-catcher having laid the net flat on the ground, with its highest corner out of the long square before described, that is, with the outside of the net next to the ground, and being in every respect prepared, he desired us to send away our horses, and to sit down, that we might not frighten the birds; and then ordered his son, a boy of twelve years of age, to raise the sparrows. The boy instantly ran about the enclosure, and by shouting and hallooing, put up immense flocks, not one of which attempted to fly out of the enclosed ground, but at the end where the net was placed. The sparrows raised themselves to fifty or sixty feet, flew several times round the enclosure, but the noise made by the boy prevented their alighting; they at length directed their flight towards the end where the fowler was seated, which, having sufficiently neared, the fowler, by putting two fingers upon his tongue, and giving a shrill whistle, magically as it were, caused the sparrows to descend and fly close along the ground, and immediately above the net, which, by a small exertion, was at the same instant, thrown over, and covered the flock or greater part of it.

I saw this method repeated twenty times the same day, and very frequently after during my residence at Cazaroon, and always with success.

I had frequent conversations with the Governor and principal inhabitants of Cazaroon on the subject, and they all assured me that no other man but the person I saw, and a few of his family, could catch sparrows in this manner; nor could the same man catch them in any other place but the Valley of Cazaroon, for he had been carried to two or three places, by order of the Prince of Shiraz, and had not been able to catch one bird.

It is unnecessary for me to intrude on you with any conjectures of my own. You can much better account for the seeming infatuation of the sparrows than I can, but as you may perhaps wish to make some particular enquiries, I send this letter by the servant who accompanied me into Persia; and who having seen the birds caught, and speaking Persian, may be able to give you some satisfaction on this subject.

## CRITICISM ON A PASSAGE IN THE ESSAY ON THE ELOQUENCE OF SILENCE.

SIR,—I take the liberty of communicating the following remarks which occurred to me from the perusal of the Essay in your miscellany on the "Eloquence of Silence," and should you approve, you are welcome to insert them.

It is not my intention to consider the whole of the essay, the subject of which, in my humble opinion, is well chosen and treated, but to confine myself to one or two particular passages, which most attracted my notice. In the first place I shall observe, that, by some readers, the numerous quotations that appear in this paper were objected to. But in this censure I cannot agree, since they appear absolutely necessary not only to elucidate the subject, but to substantiate the argument by the authority of the best writers. Indeed, I should have been very sorry had they been left out, and more particularly that beautiful passage from the Æneid, containing the interview between Dido and Æneas, the translation of which by the author of the essay I conceive to be a very happy one.

The author of the essay, however, in commenting on this passage, and comparing it to that of the Odyssey, which relates to the interview between Ajax and Ulysses in the regions below, gives a decided preference to the latter. This may be very fair as a matter of opinion only, but, in assigning his reasons for forming this judgment, I cannot help thinking the writer passes too hasty a censure on the Mantuan Bard, and too indiscriminate a reflection (if such it may be called) on the lovely heroine, as well as the fair sex in general. Your correspondent, in his essay, observes—"To me the conduct of Ajax is most admirable, and perfectly in unison with his general character; but it is not equally natural in Dido, to vent her anger by silence;—an *enraged* woman adopts a far different mode." That this sentiment, Mr. Editor, may have been universally adopted and even applauded by the followers of Xantippe, I can readily believe, but I most sincerely hope, that by those who have not the honour to be enlisted under her dread banners, it will never be assented to or acknowledged. The contempt and hatred of Ajax for Ulysses was not so well grounded as that of Dido for Æneas; and when we consider the rank and character of the Tyrian queen, and the aggravating injuries she had sustained from the Trojan prince, nothing could be more appropriate than the conduct ascribed to her by Virgil. An *enraged* woman may express her anger and contempt by abusive epithets and other unbecoming actions, and so may an *enraged* and *passionate* man, but the behaviour of either will usually be regulated by their situation and rank in life, by their education and general habits, rather than be governed by a difference of sex. According to Fielding, who quotes from Aristotle, and understood human nature to the full as well,—"The modesty and fortitude of men differ from those virtues in women,—for the fortitude which becomes a woman, would be cowardice in a man; and the modesty which becomes a man would be pertness in a woman." But, in the resentment of an injury, to suppose that in every station of life, the man alone should maintain a dignified reserve and silence, and that complaint and clamour would be more characteristic of the woman, is paying the former a compliment entirely at the expense of the latter. Indeed it reminds me of Isabella's excellent reply to Angelo, in Shakspeare's comedy of "Measure for Measure," when the Lord Deputy, the crafty Angelo, in his attempt to seduce the innocence and virtue of Isabella, remarks—"Nay women are frail too,"—the latter replies—

> "Ay, as the glasses where they view themselves,
> Which are as easy broke as they make forms.
> Women! help heaven! men their creation mar,
> In profiting by them: nay, call us ten times frail;
> For we're as soft as our complexions are,
> And credulous to false prints."

To conclude, I am willing to believe the "tetigit et non ornavit" cannot with justice be applied to Virgil, in the admirable passage of his Æneid above alluded to, and, on consideration, the writer of the essay will, I dare say, acknowledge as much.

Yours, &c.

LYSANDER.

## REPLY TO THE FOREGOING CRITICISM.

MR. EDITOR,—I am much obliged to you for having favoured me with a perusal of Lysander's strictures, previous to their insertion in your miscellany; and if you will indulge me by letting my reply accompany them, a matter of so little moment, will not detain longer than it ought the attention of your readers.

To Lysander, for his very handsome and well-turned compliments, I have many thanks to give,—my vanity has been pleased in spite of my judgment, and I am almost as much gratified as had I merited them. But with respect to the point in agitation, viz. the comparative merit of Homer and Virgil, in the scene in the shades below, I am sorry to say, I retain my former opinion;—sorry, because Virgil is my favourite poet, and I like not in any instance to withhold from him the palm, nor can I, but with regret, differ from one who has so well treated me as Lysander.

Before, however, I attempt to support the opinion I have advanced, I must strive to conciliate the good graces of any of the fair sex with whom Lysander's arguments may have done me injury. To admire or not a passage in a musty old Greek or Latin poet, is of little consequence,—but to be supposed not duly to admire "Woman! lovely woman!" would weigh heavily on me indeed: under such a stigma I hope I shall never *justly* lie;—for my very essence and nature must be altered, before I can cease to be one of the warmest, nay, almost idolatrous admirers these Houries, in a mortal shape, possess. Dryden, when he says—

> " Imagine something between young men and angels,
> Fatally beauteous, and have killing eyes,
> Their voices charm beyond the nightingale's ;
> They're all enchantment ; those who once behold 'em,
> Are made their slaves for ever"—

is, in my opinion, but feeble in his expressions ; and Otway, in observing that angels are only " painted fair to look like them," is far nearer the truth :—but enough of rhapsody, which, on such a subject, might last for ever. I confess I did insinuate, that angry ladies are apt to be loud in their grief, and this opinion I still hold, though I by no means allow that it is a reflection on the sex,—nor, had it been one, would the gentle Euripides, I think, have allowed Andromache to express a similar opinion, in observing, that—

> " Women are by nature formed
> To feel some consolation, when their tongue
> Gives utterance to th' afflictions they endure."

I merely meant to say, that there is an essential difference in the general nature of men and women ; and, as Lysander has kindly quoted for me, that the modesty and fortitude of the one, differ widely from these virtues in the other,—the fortitude becoming a woman being cowardice in man. This being granted, I cannot think it just or natural that no discrimination should be made between the venting the anger of a woman of so particularly warm a temperament as Dido, and of the rude, stern, inflexible Ajax. I must agree with Dr. Johnson,—whose opinion on this subject is, that "Virgil's judgment was overborne by his avarice of the Homeric treasure, and for fear of suffering a sparkling ornament to be lost, he has inserted it where it cannot shine with its original splendor." This dignified silence of Dido, though most beautiful as an insulated scene, yet, as it relates to the character she sustains in the poem, is, I think, particularly unhappy, for it is at direct variance with every other part of her conduct. Thus, when she first becomes enamoured of the Trojan prince, she by no means lets "concealment feed on her damask cheek," but immediately, in an eloquent speech, "tells her love" to her sister Anna;—again, when she suspects Æneas of wishing to leave her—

> "Sævit inops animi, totamque incensa per urbem
> Bacchatur,"—

or, in other words, she runs distracted about the city, more furious and noisy than a bacchanalian; attacks Æneas roundly for his treacherous behaviour, and bestows on him every term of abuse politeness would allow. She calls him perfidious, and says that a goddess was not his mother, nor a Trojan his father; but that he was born in the horrible caves of Caucasus, and received suck from Hyrcanian tigers; she wishes he may be shipwrecked in his passage, and threatens to kill herself, that she may have the pleasure of hunting him, and witnessing his sufferings. She owns—"furiis incensa feror"—that she is burning with fury; and at last works herself into such paroxysms of anger, that her strength is exhausted, and she faints away. When she recovers, she next assails him, though in vain, with prayers and tears, then sends her sister to supplicate his pity, and, when every effort has failed, and the base Æneas has cruelly deserted her, she at last lays violent hands on herself.

To all this I have not the slightest objection,—it is strongly drawn, but beautifully natural, and in character. But, in afterwards representing her in the shades below, as acting so entirely different a part, Virgil has, I think, offended against the Horatian precept,—

> "Servetur ad imum
> Qualis ab incepto processerit, et sibi constet."

He is not consistent; and can only have been thus misled by his ardent admiration of, and wish to emulate, the beautiful passage in the Odyssey. This striking deviation of character, has been noticed, and endeavoured to be palliated, by several writers; one, in number eight of a series of essays, entitled, "The Old Maid," imputes this change of conduct, and profound silence of Dido, to "the consciousness of her guilt, and her consequent shame, on finding herself in the presence of the most virtuous of all women,—the Cumæan Sybil." This is refining with a vengeance!! Nor has a writer in the "Gentleman's Magazine" for May, 1772, succeeded better, I think, in loosing the Gordian knot;—he sets off, allowing that Virgil is inferior, in this passage, to Homer in the corresponding one, and then, in accounting for Dido's silence, so very unlike her former conduct, gives the following highly natural and philosophical reasons for it:—"I have sometimes been inclined to fancy, that the poet, in this passage, might possibly design to hint to us, in his delicate manner, the difference between the states of the *living* and the *dead;* to intimate, that, though the *latter* may retain all the passions and resentments to which they were enslaved upon earth, yet, in this state of separate beings, those passions can only prey upon the spirits that entertain them, and so much the more keenly, as they are now deprived of the power of gratifying, or giving vent to them. The duration of the vicious appetites beyond the grave, and their attendance on the soul in the next life, is a favourite doctrine of Plato. As Virgil was a great admirer of this author, and has evidently adopted his principles of philosophy, his shadowing out this favourite tenet of his master, in the conduct of Dido, may, perhaps, be thought no improbable conjecture." Perhaps, also, this solution may, by some, be considered as strained and far-fetched; for my own part, I think that the bow of Ulysses waits a far stronger hand.

I grant, with pleasure, that situation, rank,

education, and general habits, have the strongest influence on the conduct of either sex; and had Dido been represented throughout as the dignified queen, in whom every ebullition of womanly feeling was kept in a due state of subjection, and constantly repressed when verging on the bounds of regal decorum,— such a character,—though, perhaps, not so interesting as the one Virgil has given her, as coming less home "to our bosoms and business,"—yet, would have been perfectly unobjectionable;—but, as this is certainly not the Queen of Tyre's general character, the partial assumption of it, offends, I think, against that consistency, which ought to mark every part of the Epic.

Homer has avoided a transgression of this nature with the greatest care,—his characters are always preserved with the strictest and most beautiful integrity; and the speech of any one of his heroes, would scarcely, in any case, be adapted for the mouth of another. Nestor is always Nestor,—and Ajax never other than himself; but Dido of the myrtle grove, differs widely, I think, from Dido raging in the streets of Carthage. I, therefore, strongly protest against Lysander's opinion, that her conduct is appropriate, as considering her *character*;—this I deny.

When he says of the beauteous Eliza's wrongs, that her contempt for Æneas was well founded, I entirely agree with him, for the conduct of the

Trojan was as base and despicable as it was possible to be; nor, after such unmanly, ungenerous treatment, did he merit a single syllable from Dido. Yet I will not allow that this could have any influence on her character in the poem; for Virgil, had he allowed her to entertain aught *more* than anger, would have failed in one of the most essential requisites of the Epic,—which is, that the hero preserve throughout the *esteem* of the reader. If he has failed in this, it has not been from want of exertion;—he was obliged to adhere to truth, and relate Æneas's cruel desertion; but he endeavours to palliate it as much as he can, and would represent it as an action in which his hero was deprived of free-agency, being compelled, with regret, to succumb to the mandates of a deity. The Mantuan Bard has not, I believe, generally succeeded in winning over the reader by his arguments; but with the personages of his poem, who are all creatures of his own management, to have granted that they were unconvinced by his reasoning, and looked on that conduct with contempt, which he himself extols, would have been to have condemned *himself*, and to have allowed that his hero was unworthy his praises, which is so much at war with all epic propriety, that the idea cannot be entertained. Dido, therefore, ought not to be considered as *despising*, however angry she may be with Æneas; and for anger alone, silence was not equally natural with complaint and invective, all the other circumstances of the case being considered.

Thus much in defence of the opinion I have formed on the passage in question, but as it is so entirely a matter of taste, I am by no means either surprised or displeased that Lysander should differ from me; nor do I expect to make him alter his sentiments by any arguments I may advance; for in points of this nature it is generally the first feeling that leaves an indelible impression on our thoughts,—so much so, that it has been decided —"nil disputandum,"—there must be no disputing; which will, I hope, plead my excuse for being invulnerable to even Lysander's ingenious arguments,—could any have done so, they must oblige me to relinquish an opinion dependent unfortunately on this stubborn perception. Lysander is not the only one from whom I here dissent, for as I have before observed, l'Abbé Hénault also gives a decided preference to Virgil. *Authority* I do not look upon as *argument*, yet I think it but fair to oppose the opinions of one great man with those of another;—in reply therefore to the French critic, I give the following quotation from our brightest English one. Dr. Johnson thus expresses himself in the "Rambler," No. 121 :—

"When Ulysses visited the infernal regions, he found, among the heroes that perished at Troy, his competitor Ajax, who, when the arms of Achilles were adjudged to Ulysses, died by his own hand, in the madness of disappointment. He still appeared to resent, as on earth, his loss and disgrace. Ulysses endeavoured to pacify him with praises and submission; but Ajax walked away without reply. This passage has always been considered as eminently beautiful, because Ajax, the haughty chief, the unlettered soldier, of unshaken courage, of immovable constancy, but without the power of recommending his own virtues by eloquence, or enforcing his assertions by any other argument than the sword, had no way of making his anger known, but by gloomy sullenness, and dumb ferocity. His hatred of a man whom he conceived to have defeated him only by volubility of tongue, was therefore naturally shewn by silence, more contemptuous and piercing that any words so rude an orator could have found, and by which he gave his enemy no opportunity of exerting the only power in which he was superior. When Æneas is sent by Virgil to the shades, he meets Dido, the Queen of Carthage, whom his perfidy has hurried to the grave;—he accosts her with tenderness and excuses, but the lady turns away like Ajax in mute disdain. She turns away like Ajax, but she resembles him in none of those qualities which gave either dignity or propriety to silence; she might, without any departure from the tenour of her conduct, have burst out like other injured women into clamour, reproach, and denunciation;—but Virgil had his imagination full of Ajax, and therefore could not prevail on himself to teach Dido any other mode of resentment."

With many apologies for having taken up so much of your paper and time,

I remain, yours, &c.

PHILO-TACITUS.

## ON THE SPANISH REVOLUTION.

SIR,—The accompanying paper was, as you will perceive, written at the commencement of the glorious contest which Spain has now so long and so heroically held against the usurpations of France. The late intelligence from Europe gives a new interest to the subject; and if you deem my paper likely to add interest or amusement to your miscellany, you can insert it.

THE information lately received in this part of the world, of the gallant and generous exertions of the Spaniards in the cause of liberty, cannot fail of re-animating the most despondent from that depression, to which the preceding victories of the oppressor of Europe had given birth.

"If plagues or earthquakes break not heaven's design,
Why then a Borgia or a Cataline?
Who knows, but He, whose hand the light'ning forms,
Who heaves old Ocean, and who wings the storms,
Pours fierce ambition in a Cæsar's mind,
And turns young Ammon loose to scourge mankind?"

The political bears a considerable analogy to the natural state of the world; and in the above-cited lines, the poet, with great energy, deduces the foresight and omniscience of the Deity, by a comparison of the physical and political evils, which apparently result from his government.

In making this remark, I am deviating from the subject I commenced upon;—my intention being merely to hazard an opinion on the present struggle, in which the Spaniards are engaged for their liberty, independence, and religion: to this I shall endeavour to confine myself; and by comparing the state of France at the commencement of the revolution, to that of Spain at the present moment, I hope to point out the probable result of the operations and efforts of the Spanish arms, as exerted in the field against a foreign enemy. France, at a period when the people assumed the reins of government, was distracted in her councils, and torn to pieces by the dissention and animosity of various parties, which, having destroyed the Monarchy, were contending for power against each other, with the greatest hatred and fury imaginable. In the midst of these commotions, she found herself engaged in immediate and active warfare with almost every established government in Europe. The forces of the most powerful states were put in motion to invade the country. In the cause of honourable independence, the spirit of the nation was roused, its enthusiasm knew no bounds; and when liberty was the watchword and order of the day, a nation of citizens was converted into an army of soldiers, and their country assumed the martial appearance of a camp, which not only defied, but continued impervious to the hostile attacks of the most regular and best disciplined troops of the age.

In a neighbouring country, a similar revolution has, to the admiration and astonishment of the world, disclosed itself to our view. Spain, with a better cause, has assumed the same attitude of defiance. She breathes the manly spirit which animated her sons of old. Attacked by the insiduous policy and gigantic force of Napoleon, she nobly spurns at her oppressor, and crushes, with a single effort, the mercenary armies which were sent to despoil the country of its riches, and the nation of its honour, rank, and independence. From the Pyrenees to the Straits of Gibraltar, from Valencia and Saragossa, to Corunna and Oporto, the sacred flame of liberty is kindled; from the noble's palace to the peasant's cottage, its enlivening influence is known and felt: it invigorates the arm with more than mortal power; elevates the mind to sentiments of honour, love, and patriotism, and gives an energy, unknown before, to all the noblest passions and affections which sway the human soul. Such appears to be the present state of Spain; how far the mass of force, directed by the Gallic Emperor, may be able to operate on a country thus situated, cannot with certainty be decided upon.

By reference to history, which, with great propriety, is said to be "Experience teaching by example," one may form a reasonable conjecture, that, eventually, the cause of liberty and freedom must predominate; and that the issue of the present contest will prove favourable, not only to the interests of the Spanish patriots, but of Europe in general. History informs us, that the spirit of a nation, once roused, and well directed, will never succumb to an armed foreign force; witness the annals of Greece, of Rome, and America. "Divide and rule" is the maxim of every despot; and, where the clashing interest of different parties allow of this principle being acted upon, it has, in many instances, succeeded; witness Italy, Switzerland, Germany and Holland. England is almost a solitary instance to the contrary. After the defeat and death of Harold, the British nation offered little or no resistance in the field to the Norman conqueror. The English historian, in elucidating the character of William, observes—

that "his attempt against England was the last great enterprize of the kind which, during the course of seven hundred years, has fully succeeded in Europe; and the force of his genius broke through those limits, which, first the feudal institutions, then, the refined policy of princes, have fixed to the several states of Christendom." But it is elsewhere remarked, in the same history, that —"Although the loss, which they (the English) had sustained, was considerable, it might have been repaired in a great nation, where the people are generally armed, and where there resided so many powerful noblemen in every province, who could have assembled their retainers, and have obliged the Duke of Normandy to divide his army, and probably to waste it, in a variety of actions and encounters. But there were several vices in the Anglo-Saxon constitution, which rendered it difficult for the English to defend their liberties, in so critical an emergency. The people had, in a great measure, lost all national pride and spirit, by their recent and long subjection to the Danes; and, as Canute had, in the course of his administration, much abated the rigours of conquest, and had governed them equitably by their own laws, they regarded with the less terror the ignominy of a foreign yoke, and deemed the inconveniences of submission less formidable, than those of bloodshed, war, and resistance."

This, however, as above noticed, is almost a solitary instance, and the circumstances which led to it, are satisfactorily explained by the philosophic historian. Spain, undoubtedly, is not in a similar situation, at the present moment. The Spaniards have ever been noticed as a valiant, proud, and jealous people; tremblingly alive to honour; noble, generous, and disinterested; impatient of a superior, and possessing an inveterate dislike to foreigners. Such are the outlines of their character, as sketched in former times, and which they appear in the present day to merit; their zeal, enthusiasm, patriotism, and bravery, cannot be exceeded; for where shall we find a people who have ever exerted themselves with more bravery, or evinced more disinterested loyalty and attachment to their country and religion? or who, among their leaders, have produced greater characters, either in the field or cabinet? It is the mark, or rather, the principle, of a generous mind, to forego, as long as possible, its resentments, and to stifle petty animosities. That the forbearance and apparent apathy of the Spaniards, did not originate in any want of spirit, has been satisfactorily demonstrated by their subsequent conduct. Their valour in the field, their vigour and wisdom in council; their proclamations, inspired with a commanding and manly eloquence, pourtray the indignant feelings, the ardent passion, the genuine freedom, of a much injured nation! their sense of shame, their contempt of danger,—all bespeak a noble and high-minded people, who are at once worthy of independence; and who will command it.

---

TO THE EDITOR OF THE MOOFUSSUL MISCELLANY.

---

SIR,—Having received, from my correspondent in Europe, the enclosed letter, covering the detailed account of an action fought on the same ground where the Count's predecessors have often been victorious, I now send it for your perusal, and beg you will make what use of it you please.

PEREGRINE QUIDNUNC.

---

COPY OF A LETTER FROM T. FABRICATE, ESQ. CHARGÉ D'AFFAIRES, TO C. RANGALL, ESQ., PRIVATE SECRETARY TO THE PRESIDENT OF THE STATES UNITED FOR THE SUBVERSION OF ALL GOOD.

SIR,—I have the honour of forwarding the enclosed despatch, relative to an action which is said to have taken place near Braggadocia. As I cannot find any such place laid down in the maps of either Spain or Portugal, I am apt to think the termination in the orthography cannot be correct, though I have reason to think that the French arms have been often successful in that quarter. This victory appears to have been one of the most complete and extraordinary ever recorded in the annals of the French; for when you take into consideration the gallantry of the attack, the intrepidity evinced, the judgment displayed, and the trifling loss sustained; when you reflect on the determined spirit with which it was continued, and the complete success with which it was crowned, I am confident you must allow it to have been seldom equalled—never surpassed!

I am, with the highest consideration,

&c. &c.

(Signed) TIM. FABRICATE.

---

*Braggadocia,—Brumaire 13th.*

SIR,—I have the honour to acquaint you, that this morning, at a quarter before eleven o'clock, I was on the alert, and, by a masterly movement, reached the garrison before the drum had beaten to breakfast. After driving in the advanced posts, storming the steps, and forcing the outward verandah, I commenced a well-directed attack on the inner works, where the breakfast forage was deposited. After a spirited defence by Major-General Fowler,—who had been commissioned to act during the absence of the Commandant,—I carried the place knife in hand. With incredible satisfaction, I have to inform you, that in a few minutes I was in possession of two plates of muffins, a considerable quantity of buns, and cakes of all sorts, biscuits of various sizes, three stands of dry toast, six manchets, (three of them rasped) two hot buttered rolls of large dimensions, two loaves of smaller size,—one white and the other brown,—several canisters of sugar, (as per margin) with various other stores.

I then secured the military (tea) chest, spiked nine eggs, after first unloading them, seized the coffee redoubt, and made a considerable impression upon Fort Chocolate. All this was effected without the loss of a single tooth,—and I feel much pleasure in being able to add, that my bowels and stomach are in excellent order, not having lately suffered by the marauding attacks of that free-booter General Bile, who, on a former occasion, considerably annoyed me, and of whose attacks I was in some alarm, during the time I was carrying on my operations.

I am under infinite obligation to Brigadier Leg, and Colonel Foot, whose exertions on this and other occasions, demand my warmest gratitude.

They were particularly serviceable to me during my rapid march. I also beg leave to recommend to your notice, two very deserving officers, Lieut.-Col. Foretooth, and Major Grinder; but for whose penetration, and unremitting exertions, in the laborious post which they occupied, I should have been ill able to have accomplished this undertaking. Nor ought I to pass over in silence the activity and intrepidity of my staff in general, particularly of Adjt.-General Thumb, and Assistant Quarter-Master-General Middle Finger, to whose lot it fell to be more individually engaged, and who were extremely active on the occasion; and I endulge a sanguine hope, that they will meet with that distinction to which their long-tried and faithful services entitle them.

Health and Fraternity.

COUNT BOBADIL.

## PERSIAN ANECDOTE OF CHESS.

A KING and a Fakeer were once playing at this game, when fortune, or rather skill, invariably favouring the latter, he won from his Majesty his palaces, jewels, treasure—in short every thing he possessed! Maddened with ill-success, the King offered his beauteous Queen, Dil-aram, as a last desperate stake against his losses. The challenge was accepted, and again the Fakeer triumphed, for in a very short time the game was brought to such a point, that check-mate seemed inevitably to await the hopeless King. At the next move, in a rage of vexation, he threw it up, and sent for Dil-aram to yield her to the victor; but when she was sorrowfully led in, she glanced her eye on the board; immediately her countenance brightened, and she joyfully exclaimed—

اي شاه دو روخ بده مده دلارام را
پيل پياده پيش كن اسپ شهٔ مات كن

"King,—yield me not, but both thy rooks resign,
And Dil-aram shall still continue thine.
Move on thy pawn, then let the knight advance,
And o'er thy fallen foe, his beauteous steed shall prance."

The event justified her opinion; for the King having moved his pieces according to the direction, won the game, kept his Queen, and retrieved his losses.

This situation, according to the Persians, occurred in a game of "*shutrunj*," and involves unfortunately a move which is inadmissible by our rules;—the Orientals, though this is not generally known, have two modes of playing at chess; one is termed شطرنج "shutrunj;" the other, دابا "dâba." The first differs very widely from our manner, inasmuch as, among other distinctions, the bishops have their range of action confined to the second square from that on which they stand, and that it is allowable for them to move *over* any piece that may be on the intermediate square;—an example of this occurs in the present instance. The other game, "dâba," very nearly resembles ours;—the first move of the pawns, however, is limited to one square; and that very beautiful movement "castling" is unknown to them.

The following is the situation of the game above alluded to:—

Black-King at his Queen's square; K. R. at its Q. Kt.'s square; Q. R. at its square; Q. B. at its Q. R.'s 3d.; Kt. at its Q. Kt.'s 4th; Pawns at the adversary's; Q. B.'s and Q. Kt.'s 3d.

White-King at his Q. R.'s square; K. R. at it's adversary's K. R.'s 2d; Q. R. at its K. Kt.'s square; K. B. at its adversary's K. B.'s 4th.

The solution it were hardly necessary to give, but that the first move was one not customary with us. The Black Q. Bishop moves to the adversary's Q. B.'s 4th, *passing over* the Knight, and opening check. The two Rooks are then successively lost; the Q.'s Kt.'s pawn advances in checking; and, lastly, the *coup mortel* is given by the Knight at the Q. R.'s 3d.

There is a somewhat similar anecdote to this in the "Sporting Magazine" for May 1800; but the situation there pointed out could never have occurred in the Persian game, as it is asserted to have done, for the Bishop is made to act from a distance of four squares off, to which, its Oriental powers, as I have before observed, are inadequate.

---

## TO THE EDITOR OF THE MOOFUSSUL MISCELLANY.

SIR,—The *embonpoint* of the French Empress Louisa-Maria has at length produced, what I am sure none of us expected, an heir to the great Napoleon. On such an occasion I could not refrain from mounting my Pegasus, however much it may be "invitâ Minervâ." The poets of the Seine have very probably anticipated me in their birth-day compliments; yet, though conscious of my inferiority, I could not resist the temptation of entering the list, and immortalizing one lay by attaching it to the future fame of the rising King of the Romans. O! that there may soon be occasion to blazon forth his or his father's deeds in dirge, elegy, or epitaph! This last, sad, pious office to their manes, I would perform with the most heart-felt joy; and in my invocation, exclaim with Virgil—

> "Extremum hunc, Arethusa, mihi concede laborem.
> Pauca meo *Gallo,*"—

## APOLLYON.

Ye Imps of Corsica! begin the song:
To themes like this demoniac strains belong.
The mossy fountains, and the peaceful shades,
Great George's virtues and the British maids,
Delight no more.—O thou, my voice inspire,
Who shall requite Napoleon's deeds with fire!

Rapt into dreaded times, the bard began!
Maria shall conceive, Maria bear a son!
From root obscure behold a branch arise,
Whose baleful flower with stenches fills the skies;
A hellish spirit o'er its leaves shall spread,
And on its top descend the raven dread.

Ye heavens! from high the forked lightnings pour,
Let thunders crash, and clouds in anger low'r!
Nor sick nor weak the pois'nous plant shall aid,
From storms no shelter, and from heat no shade.
All crimes shall rage, and every fraud prevail,
Despairing justice drop her loaded scale;
War o'er the world her bloody hand extend,
And red-robed guilt from gaping hell ascend.
Slow roll the years, avaunt the dreaded morn!
In darkness rest, nor, hated babe, be born!
See, Nature dreads her wonted wreaths to bring,
Nor breathes her incense now the drooping Spring:
See lofty Alp his angry head recoil,
See shudd'ring forests sink into the soil:
See noisome clouds from bleeding Jaffa rise,
And Europe's blasted plains invoke the skies!

Hark ! a dread voice the deserts hear with fright;
" Avoid his way ! a demon blasts the light !
A demon comes !"—the trembling hills resound,
Th' approaching curse the rocks proclaim around.
Lo, earth receives him from wide-yawning hell;
Hills sink with fright, with rage the valleys swell;
Ye cedars droop, the sad event deplore;
Be rough ye rocks: ye rapid floods, loud roar !
Th' avenger comes ! by ancient bards foretold:
Who hears, is deaf;—he's blind who shall behold !
In thickest films he shall immerge the sight,
And on the eye-ball pour eternal night:
'Tis he that shall obstruct the paths of sound,
And with dire noise the deafen'd ear astound:
The dumb shall yell, the lame his crutch forego,
And fly in terrors like the stricken roe.
But sighs and murmurs the sad world shall hear,
And every face shall feel the frequent tear.
In chains no more shall cruel death be bound,
And hell's grim tyrant roam the world around.
As the stern butcher tends his fleecy prey,
Coops up in pens, or lets them harmless play;
Alone on slaughter turned his savage mind,
By day his flocks are watch'd, by night confined;
The tender lambkin from its mother torn
He slays, nor knows its hapless fate to mourn;
Thus shall mankind his tyrant care engage,
The promis'd butcher of a future age.
See how the nations against nations rise,
And ardent warriors meet with hateful eyes,
The fields with blood-smear'd steel be cover'd o'er,
And brazen trumpets, kindling anger, roar:
The useless scythes shall into spears be made,
And rusty plough-shares yield the falchion's blade.

Then too shall prisons rise—the cursed Son
Shall finish what his too-old Sire begun.
No vines a shadow to their race shall yield,
Nor the same hand shall sow, and reap the field.
The swain to barren deserts with surprize,
Sees meadows turn, and blasted verdure dies:
And starts, amid the gushing rocks to hear
Old falls of water check their 'mid career;
Where green reeds tremble, and the bulrush nods,
Hard mounts are form'd,—the dragon's dire abodes.
Where spiry fir and shapely box adorn,
Are now waste valleys, thick perplex'd with thorn:
To flow'ry palms the leafless shrub succeeds,
And to the od'rous myrtle noisome weeds.
With gore of lambs the wolves shall stain the mead,
On sprightly boys the rav'nous tigers feed;
Not then unharmed shall steers the lion meet,
Nor venom'd serpents spare the pilgrim's feet.
The crested basilisk, and speckled snake,
In murd'rous coils shall tender infants take;
In many' a slimy fold their young limbs crush,
And with their forky tongue their shrieks of anguish hush.

Sink, stained with blood, imperial Paris, sink!
Bow down thy head, and from thy prospects shrink!
See not the miscreants that thy courts disgrace;
See not thy future sons and daughters base,
Who rise in crowds, and clam'rous prey demand,
Impatient for the meed from Satan's hand!
See not the groaning nations who attend,—
Thy sway they curse, but in submission bend;
Nor view thy altars, throng'd with abject kings,
And heap'd with spoils, thy bandit army brings.

For thee Avernus' death-fraught breezes blow,
And seas of fire in realms Tartarian glow.
See Heaven enraged, its red right arm displays,
And breaks upon thee in a lightning-blaze!

No more the sun shall gild thy towers laid low,
Nor trembling Cynthia fill for thee her bow;
But lost, o'erwhelm'd by fate's avenging doom,
One rush of night, one all-prevailing gloom,
Shall seize thy courts; the Light its sway resign,
And Satan's everlasting night be thine!
The seas shall waste, the skies in smoke decay,
Rocks fall to dust, and mountains melt away;
But fixed shall God's avenging power remain;
Thy punishment shall last, nor cease Napoleon's pain!

## TO THE MEMORY OF ——.

The angels bend from heaven to chide thy stay,
Oh friend beloved! thy happy flight delay:—
Anxious we kneel, submiss to Fate's behest,
Though keen corrosive sorrow load our breast.
E'en here, while kindred worth, in manhood's bloom,
Sinks prematurely in the silent tomb;
Oh teach our wayward hearts to kiss the rod!
And bear the fiat of a gracious God.

Alas! could warm affection's ardent prayer,
Prefer'd in vain! thy valued Being spare;—
Could aged virtue move the pitying skies—
Heard were the mother's vows, the sister's cries;—

Still had thy liberal and exalted mind,
A firm example granted to mankind;
Proved faultless friendship not an empty name,
And taught the selfish heart a generous aim.

Resign'd the parent weeps! her guardian son
Torn from her arms!—exclaims, "Thy will be done!
Father Supreme! to whose omniscient power,
I bend in dark affliction's heaviest hour.
The great Redeemer lives! who soon shall call
My trembling steps from this terrestrial ball
To mansions bright; where lull'd on Jesus' breast,
By seraphs welcom'd to immortal rest;
Unfading happiness his virtue crowns,
For human frailties, Christian faith atones."

Each mournful sister, wild with piercing woe,
Vainly attempts to check the heart's o'erflow;
Oh! snatch'd from earthly view and kin beloved!
By us adored, by virtue's self approved;
O'er thee, with just affection, still we hung,
And caught the pious dictates of thy tongue:
Convulsive pain in ev'ry feature spoke,
Yet Christian fortitude sustained the stroke.

Tho' regions vast a brother's life divide,
Sad pilgrim he, near Ganges' ample tide;
Nor time, nor space, the raging grief controul,
Uncheck'd by time or space, it rends his soul;
Till sympathetic sorrows gently flow.
Oh, guardian of my child! by death laid low!
Shelter'd in mercy!—While we weep thy doom,
With deep regret we contemplate the tomb.

A few short years to faith's clear eye disclose
Seraphic union! free from mortal woes.
From ills to come the righteous oft is borne,
To countless joys, while we presumptuous mourn!

Oh! spirit pure! celestial palms be thine—
With fervent prayers approach the throne divine.
For us, forlorn, implore Almighty God,
That rays benign may cheer our darksome road;
From selfish cares our erring souls redeem;—
Thy manly worth, our darling, endless theme;—
May kindred virtues emulation move,
Till pleased we follow to the realms of love.

فريدون فرّخ فرشته نبود
ز مشك و زعنبر سرشته نبود
بداد و دهش يافت ان نيكوي
تو داد و دهش كن فريدون توي

## TRANSLATION.

Feridoun the Great—no etherial was he—
But formed like the rest of mankind;
He justice displayed in every decree;
To mercy was ever inclined.

By justice and mercy his acts stood confessed,
Thus Feridoun immortal became;
For the worthy, the guilty, the rich, the oppressed,
In their prayers repeated his name.

If a king, or a judge,—take him for your guide;
Be merciful, mild, just, as he;
O'er faction thou shalt then triumphantly ride,
And, like him, thou immortal shalt be!

---

## ANOTHER TRANSLATION.

---

FERIDOUN the Just was a great man of yore,
Whose fame as a justice was great;—
But why?—He was sure not compounded of more
Than is common to this mortal state.

By his bounty and justice he gained this good name,
Impartial to every degree;—
Be as just, and as good, and in all just the same,
You'll be just such a justice as he.

---

MR. EDITOR,—Two gentlemen have sent you what they call translations of a Persian quatrain,—but in doing this they have displayed consummate ignorance of the language they wished to render;—nothing can be more remote from the truth than their versions. I speak decisively, for I am, without flattery, an excellent Orientalist. But they will perhaps say—"si quid novisti rectius istis candidus imperti;" well then—take the following—on its fidelity you may rely. I have observed in it the Horatian maxim of giving *verbum verbo;* but though it is strictly faithful, it may not, perhaps, be perfectly intelligible. This is not my affair, nor will I attempt to elucidate its obscurities. Sir William Jones praises it—his reasons for so doing I care not about;—they might have been the same which influenced the University of Aberdeen, when they so highly extolled the *quodlibetical* questions of Duns Scotus;—viz. because they did not understand them!! You will remember too, that—"omne ignotum est pro magnifico"—

In error headstrong, and of morals base,
No claims had he to Missionary grace;
And, strange to say,—his form was kneaded in
Nor leathern bottle, nor a fish's skin.
By alms he got, he here was well to do,
But was as unrelenting as a Jew:
Do thou like him, and thou shalt quickly be
Just such another stubborn rogue as he.

Some of the words certainly possess a double meaning, as may be seen by a reference to Richardson's Dictionary. I give them both under, but it is past a doubt that they are wrong, and I right.

| | | |
|---|---|---|
| فريدون .... | a name .... | obstinate in error |
| فرخ .... | happy .... | base, vile |
| فرشته .... | angel .... | missionary |
| مشك .... | musk .... | leathern bottle |
| عنبر .... | ambergris .... | fish's skin |
| سرشته .... | form'd .... | kneaded |
| داد .... | justice .... | revenge |
| دهش .... | liberality .... | alms |
| نيكوئي .... | reputation .... | *(well-to-do-ness)* |

## EPIGRAM FROM THE FRENCH.

THIS rhymer says he can't write prose,
However much he tries;—
Now read his verse—it plainly shows
How much the fellow lies.

## THE BATTLE OF BARROSSA.

HAIL Graham! who hast nobly won
Thy country's battles with firm arm,
And made thy star of war so bright;—
The last brave deed which thou hast done,
Shall strike the foe with dread alarm,
And crown with glory wild Barrossa's height:
Whilst future ages with applause shall pay,
The hardy laurels thou has snatch'd this day.

Though fierce Napoleon strive to dim,
And mar the lustre of the day
So full to thee of fair renown,
Ah! never shall it rest with him,
To turn bright Glory's steps away,
Who e'er will love to claim thee for her own;—
Dauntless in war,—'mid rudest perils great,
Thy country hails thee—pillar of her state!

Though stern when War attention calls,
And bids thee arm thy heart in steel,
And drown each selfish sigh in fight;

Though vers'd in scenes that life appals,
Thy soul can truest friendship feel,
And in each softer tie delight;
Thee, Friendship, Love, their willing vot'ry find,
Yet most thy Country sways thine ardent mind.

Thy bright career still bold pursue,
And make Britannia's foes bend low,
Wild seized with just alarm;
False Gallia's wretched sons shall rue,
The dreadful strength of Graham's blow,
The conquering might of Graham's arm.
Glory's bright beams shall sparkling bind thy brow,
And thy proud deeds exulting nations know!

## ANECDOTES.

THE following is a ridiculous Grub Street mistake I once met with. Lord Bacon mentions as a proof that the Turks are barbarians, "their want of *stirpes*, or hereditary rank." A learned writer, who did not quite understand the term, said—"he thought it very hard that a whole nation should be stigmatized as barbarians, merely because they *did not ride with stirrups!*"

---

I HAVE heard the following anecdote related of Mr. Boyd, the author of the "Indian Observer," and by some supposed to have been Junius. In a party, after dinner, where the "pouting vine" was made to "weep" rather too copiously, an Hibernian gentleman, taking umbrage at something or other, threw (though fortunately without effect) a bottle at Mr. Boyd's head;—this placed the latter in an unpleasant dilemma;—the Hibernian was his particular friend, and he saw that his intoxication alone had caused the act: he could not then justly resent it, yet custom forbade his passing it over unnoticed, and a duel seemed inevitable. A happy stroke, however, concluded the affair amicably. Turning to the company, he said—"I believe, gentlemen, we must overlook this on the score of my friend's general excellences;—indeed, he has but one fault—that of passing the bottle a little too quickly." Such admirable presence of mind and good-nature restored order instantly. All were delighted; and the Hibernian himself, so completely sobered by it, as to make an immediate and ample apology.

---

"Voulez-vous du public mériter les amours?
Sans cesse en écrivant variez vos discours."

BOILEAU.

" Ipsâ varietate tentamus efficere ut alia aliis,
Quædam fortasse omnibus placeant."—

PLIN. EPIST.

## ON AMPHIBOLOGY.

> " Next an uncertain and ambiguous train,
> Now forward march, then counter-march again;
> The van, now first in order, duly leads,
> And now the rear the changeful squadron heads;
> Thus onward Amphisbæna springs to meet
> Her foe—nor turns her in the quick retreat."—
>
> CAMBRIDGE'S SCRIBBLERIAD.

SIR,—Having already troubled you with dissertations on Anagrams and Chronograms, I come now to those " difficiles nugæ," which range under the the generic name of Amphibology,—and the subject, as it is curious, will, I trust, plead my excuse for indulging rather largely in quotation.

Of simple equivocation, or merely the doubtful signification of one word, I do not so much intend to treat, as of that artificial construction, by which the sense of a sentence or more, is thrown into ambiguity, and made to admit of a double interpretation. That the ancients excelled in this art, we cannot doubt, when we recollect that there were numerous schools instituted among them, where this was the chief, and almost the only, science studied.

I allude to the temples at Delphi, &c. For an idea of the proficiency to which they attained, it is only necessary to read a few of their infallible oracular responses,—infallible they were necessarily, for, being ever constructed in ambidexter form, they were ready to coincide with any event that might happen. Thus, as an instance, the dreadful prediction pronounced to Æneas by Celæno. She informs him, that he and his companions should never possess a city in Italy, until they had been compelled, by hunger, to eat up their own tables!!

> "Non antè datam cingetis mænibus urbem,
> Quàm vos dira fames, nostræque injuria cædis,
> Ambesas subigat malis absumere mensas."

Had they been devoured by the Cyclops, lost in the storm, or had they perished in any other way, the oracle had been pronounced divine and true; but, as it was also possible for them, as the event proved, to arrive safe in Italy, and build there a city;—observe what an excellent *coup de réserve* in this case was prepared by the oracle, to justify its response,—"to keep it to the ear, but break it to the sense." It was very natural, on a long perilous voyage, that some of the sailors should, in a fit of hunger, attack "orbem fatalis crusti, patulis nec parcere quadris,"—eat up the biscuits which they used as *trenchers* for their meat, and these, by a very allowable poetic license, were easily termed *tables.*—

> "Heus! etiam mensas consumimus, inquit Julus;"—

and thus the gods always come off victoriously.

Of more artful construction was the answer given by the Pythia to Phyrrhus, when he consulted her respecting his future success in war; she replied,—"Aio te, Œacide, Romanos vincere posse,"—"I say that you, Phyrrhus, shall the Romans conquer,"—thus leaving the pronoun so happily dubious, that it might serve either as agent or object:—also the oracle to Crœsus—

Χρόισος 'Αλυν διαβας, μεγαλην ἀρχην διαλυσει.

"Crœsus having crossed the Halys, shall destroy a great empire."

But, exclusively of the oracles, where, indeed, it was a "sine quâ non," the ancients frequently indulged in Amphibology in their compositions; the following is an example from Terence:—"Ego me amare hanc fateor,"—where the sense may either be, "I confess that I love her,"—or, "I confess that she loves." A precisely similar one frequently occurs in Persian, from the similarity of the inflection in the two nouns:—

اي خواجه ضيا شود زروي تو ظلم
با طلعت تو سور نمايد ما تم

is either,—"your countenance converts darkness into light; at your presence, mourning is turned into joy;"—or, "light is turned into darkness by your countenance; at your presence, joy becomes sorrow." The confusion in the vowel-point, also, often gives rise to ambiguities like these; thus—

روز وشب خواهم همين از كردگار تا سرت باشد هميشه تا جدار

may mean either,—" day and night I am incessantly imploring God, that your head may ever be crowned,"—or, "I am praying that your head may be upon the wall—that you may be beheaded."

Indeed, the orientals, in all matters of this kind, ever keep pace with us—" haud inequali passu." And the following anecdote from their records, is not inferior to anything of the kind that can elsewhere be shewn.

" Akul being displeased with his brother, the celebrated Ali, went over to Moaweyeh, who, as a proof of the sincerity of his intentions, desired him to curse Ali. As he would admit of no refusal, Akul thus addressed the congregation:—' O people! you know that Ali, the son of Aboo-taleb, is my brother; now Moaweyeh has ordered me to curse him, therefore, may the curse of God be upon him!' So that the curse would apply either to Ali or Moaweyeh."

That England herself has not remained quite free from this kind of evasion, the well-known sentence, "Noli regem occidere timere bonum est" testifies: —this was the order sent by an Archbishop to the barons, who were then in arms against their sovereign, and who had applied to him for advice respecting their conduct to his majesty. It served as a salvo to his conscience, and, at the same time, left the barons at liberty to do what they pleased; for they might read it (according to Fuller's very happy translation) either as,—" to kill the king fear, not to do it is good,"—or, "to kill the king fear not, to do it is good." On a similar plan, viz. the ambiguity of the comma, are constructed those riddles, one of which commences, "I've seen a comet drop down hail," &c.; and by a similar misplacing of the comma, occurred the facetious mistake recorded by the modern Josephus, where, when the parson should have read—"A man going to sea, his wife desires the prayers of the congregation," read it—"A man going to see his wife, desires the prayers of the congregation!"

But the most difficult, and at the same time amusing examples of Amphibology, are those which commonly go by the name of Jesuitical verses,—verses which receive directly opposite meanings, if read in different order. Thus the following lines, if read as they stand, must be admired for their staunch loyalty, but let them be perused according to the order of the figures prefixed to them, and nothing can more strongly savour of rank Jacobinism.

1 I love my country—but the king—3 Above all men his praise I sing,
2 Destruction to his odious reign—4 That plague of princes Thomas Paine;
5 The royal banners are display'd—7 And may success the standard aid,
6 Defeat and ruin seize the cause—8 Of France, her liberty, and laws.

The above, I am sorry to say, was not sported off as a mere jeu-d'esprit, but was actually composed to lend its artful aid to the cause of anarchy. I have it from a friend, who himself picked it up with many other similar productions, as they were circulated, previous to the rebellion in 1798, amongst the United Irishmen! I do not doubt but the following translation of another such poem into monkish Latin, was applied to the very same laudable purpose!

1 Pro fide teneo sana— 3 Quæ docet Angelicana—
2 Affirmat Quæ Romana— 4 Videntur mihi vana—
5 Supremus quando rex est— 7 Tum plebs est fortunata—
6 Seductus ille grex est— 8 Cui Papa imperator
9 Altare cum ornatur—11 Communio fit inanis—
10 Populus tum beatur—12 Cum mensa, vinum, panis—
13 Asini nomen meruit—15 Hunc morem qui non capit
14 Messam qui deseruit—16 Catholicus est et sapit.

I have here ventured to supply myself a couplet that was wanting, but I will not so far affront my reader's penetration as to point out to him which couplet that is. In prose also there have been similar compositions, but of these the most ingenious and entertaining, is a letter of recommendation written by the celebrated Cardinal Richelieu. Monsieur Campy, a Savoyard friar, solicited the Cardinal for a letter of credence in his behalf to the French Ambassador at Rome, to which court he was proceeding, and this Richelieu readily granted; but as an exercise of his ingenuity, he amused himself by composing it in this very singular form, that if it be read as consisting of single lines only, it is couched in the most flattering terms, and gives the most favourable view of Monsieur C.; but if it be considered as divided into two columns, and the first only read, then, alas! the poor friar comes woefully off indeed!

I have heard this letter adduced as a specimen of the Cardinal's general epistolary style, and the whole transaction brought forward as a proof of his duplicity, artifice, and cunning. In the same place it is asserted that Monsieur Campy, in consequence, long lived in fruitless hopes, and at last died through disappointment and vexation. But as this is a mere gratis dictum, unsubstantiated by any proof, I consider it as a malevolent, uncharitable insinuation, and have followed the more probable and favourable interpretation of his conduct. The letter, then, was simply an admirable jeu-d'esprit, and Monsieur Campy without doubt received an ample reward, for giving Richelieu so excellent an occasion for displaying his ingenuity. I am sorry I cannot give it in the original French, for this I have in vain searched.

Sir,—Mons. Campy, a Savoyard,
is to be the bearer unto you
of this letter. He is one of the most
vicious persons that I ever
knew. He has earnestly desired me
to give him a letter unto you of
recommendation, which I granted to
his importunity; for believe me, Sir,
I would be very sorry you should be
mistaken in not knowing him,
as many others have lately been
who are of my excellent friends;
I earnestly desire to advertise you
to take especial notice of him,
and say nothing in his presence
in any sort,——for I may
assure you there cannot be a more

Friar, of the Order of St. Bernard,
of news from me by means
discreet, wise, and indeed, the least
(amongst all I have conversed with)
to write to you in his favour, and
credence in his behalf, with my
his merit, I assure you, rather than to
he deserves infinitely your esteem.—
wanting to oblige him by being
I would be afflicted if you were so,
on that account who now esteem him, &c.
hence, and from no other motive
that you are obliged more than any
and to afford him all imaginable respect
that may offend or displease him
truly say I love him as myself, and
convincing proof or argument of an

unworthy person in the world. I know that as soon as you shall be acquainted with him, you will thank me for this advice:—civility, doth hinder me to say more on this subject. I am To the Ambassador of France at Rome.

than to be capable of doing him ill. cease to be a stranger to his virtue and will love him as well as myself, and the assurance which I have of your write further of him to you, or to Your most obdt. servt., Richelieu.

Paris, 29th Nov. 1658.

It will here very probably suggest itself to many of my readers, as it did to me, that this mode of writing letters would form a very ingenious cypher for the correspondence of lovers, &c. It would certainly, it must be owned, be rather difficult, but this difficulty would only enhance the ultimate pleasure, and the grateful vanity attending success would fully compensate the labour of attaining it. This idea I find has not escaped others, and the following is a specimen, of which the key is the same as to the Cardinal's letter.

"I cannot be satisfied my dearest friend! unless I pour into your friendly bosom, the various sensations which swell my almost bursting heart; I tell you my dear I have now been married seven weeks, and repent the day that joined us. My husband is ugly, cross, old, disagreeable, and jealous a wife,—it is his maxim to treat as a plaything, or menial slave, the woman he says, should always obey implicitly; An ancient maiden aunt, near seventy, lives in the house with us. She is the —vil to all the neighbourhood round, I am convinced my husband likes nothing more than the glass:—and really his intoxication often makes me blush for the unworthiness of the man whose name I bear. To crown the whole, my former lover is returned, and I might have had him! may you be as blest, as I am unhappy! is the fervent wish of yours, &c.

blest as I am in the matrimonial state which has ever beat in unison with mine, with the liveliest emotions of pleasure husband is the most ámiable of men.—have never found the least reason to both in person and manners, far from like monsters, who think, by confining, to secure bosom friend, and not at all as a whom he has chosen — neither party, but each yield to the other by turns. a cheerful, venerable, and pleasant old lady, delight of both young and old. She is ci- generous and charitable to the poor. than he does me, he flatters me much more (for so I must call the excess of his love) of its object, and I wish I could be deserving say all in one word then, and to is now my indulgent husband, my love a prince without the felicity I find in able to wish that I could be more

The following very elaborate trifle may also be considered, from its Amphibological construction, as belonging to the above species; though from its being able to be read either backwards or forwards, it has also a right to the name of "*devil's verse*." It was the work most probably of some monk, who pored over it in his solitary cell for weeks or months; and though this time may justly be deemed as misapplied, yet it would certainly cost any one as much more to produce a match to it,—not that I mean to defend such useless labours. I readily acknowledge "turpe est difficiles habere nugas," yet I cannot but admire the curious felicity here attained. The verse is applied to the sacrifices of Abel and Cain;—in one way it is very well adapted to the first,—

"Sacrum pingue dabo, non macrum sacrificabo,"

or,—"I will give a fat sacrifice, not offer up a lean one;" but read backwards, and altering the punctuation, it will produce a speech equally applicable to the sentiments of Cain; thus—

"Sacrificabo macrum, non dabo pingue sacrum,"

or,—"I will offer up a lean sacrifice, not give a fat one." In the first way, the line is an hexameter, in the second, a pentameter; and what renders it still more extraordinary, both verses are Leonines,—that is, the middle and ending of each, rhyme to one another, so that this, from the numerous difficulties to be overcome, may fairly be considered as the very *ne plus ultra* of the art. By the way, as I have mentioned "*devil's verses*," I might as well here explain the meaning of the term, and this simply is, verses that read backwards and forwards the same: the difficulty of composing which has procured them the above appellation.

I only at this moment recollect two examples; —one in Greek—Νίψον ἀνόμημα, μὴ μόναν ὄψιν,— which is frequently inscribed on baptismal fonts in England,* and signifies, "wash the sins, not the face only;" and this in Persian, ارام داد مارا which means "he gave me rest." Apropos of which, it is fully time for me to give this to my readers. I will therefore conclude.

NUGARUM AMATOR.

## ON MARRIAGE CONSIDERED AS A RELIGIOUS CONTRACT.

SIR,—Having heard various opinions sported in company respecting the Institution of Marriage, considered by some as a civil, by others as a religious, contract, I beg leave to offer some observations on the subject, through the medium of the "Moofussul Miscellany;" and though not any

* This inscription is on the font in St. Mary's, Nottingham, and may also be found on the font in Sandbach Church, Cheshire, and on that at Harlow in Essex.

thing in them may be new or striking, yet, when thrown together, and duly considered, they will, I think, tend to prove that Marriage is of divine institution ; and that, consequently, it is more a religious than a civil contract. Prior having claimed a collateral descent equally long as that of Bourbon or Nassau, as the son of *Adam and of Eve*, so I, being almost as nearly related to that couple as Mat himself, feel myself authorized to take the liberty of first adverting to their marriage. We are taught to believe, by the highest authority, that when the great Author of our being brought these good folks together, "He blessed them,"—(Gen. chap. 1, v. 28) this, without twisting the meaning of the word to my own purpose, was, that he pronounced a blessing upon them, and thus *consecrated by prayer their union.* (vide Johnson.)

The Jewish marriage was solemnized by the Rabbi, who used to pronounce the following benediction :—"Blessed be thou, O Lord, who hast created man and woman, and ordained marriage," &c. When we advert to the marriage of Christians, we find that our Saviour blessed and sanctified it by his presence. We are also told that it was at a marriage-feast where he wrought his first miracle. In our ceremony, we begin with, "We are gathered together here in the sight of God," &c. We call it "holy matrimony,"—and why? Because it was *instituted of God*, or, according to the Jewish benediction, *ordained.* Let us now seriously reflect on the following expression:—"Those whom *God hath joined* together, let no man put asunder." If we consider that we are correct in saying, "those whom *God hath joined* together," we cannot but consider the institution a religious one, for if it be a civil ceremony, we ought to say,—"those who have *joined themselves* together,"—or, "those whom I" (the officiating layman or priest) "join together." I feel convinced, in my own mind, that any person who reads, without prejudice, *but with attention*, the marriage service of our Church, must allow that it is a religious, and an awfully religious, ceremony.

I well know it will be advanced, that the form of the marriage service is of human invention;—granted. And is not our form of public worship equally so? But is our attending that public worship of less moment—less expected of us,—or more lightly esteemed, as, what Johnson terms it, "*a religious act of reverence?*" At the same time that I allow the *form* of matrimony to be of human invention, I aver that the *institution* of it is founded on Divine Authority. In proof of this assertion, I must beg leave to note some passages in addition to those to which I have already adverted. Is not the giving the woman to the man, founded on the *Almighty bringing the woman to the man?* Does not Adam then say, (Gen. chap. ii. v. 28) "This is now bone of my bone, and flesh of my flesh." And does not the man, in our service, make a declaration to the same effect, though not in the same words? Does he not conclude by marrying the woman in the name of the Father, and of the Son, and of the Holy Spirit? Can any compact be more solemnly or more religiously ratified? I may be asked, from whence came the form of marrying with the ring:—is it not a civil ceremony? I grant it may be; and it is of so ancient a date, that the primitive Jews used it in their marriage ceremony, with the following words:—"By this ring thou art my spouse, according to the custom of Moses, and the children of Israel." But to proceed. The man and woman are afterwards blessed in the name of the "Eternal God," &c.: they are then declared to be man and wife, *in the name of the Father*, &c.; and, lastly, receive a blessing in as awful a form as our Church admits; and in as solemn language as any Church service can give it.

To close what I have adduced in favour of marriage being a religious ceremony, and of divine institution, I will subjoin the three following verses from the 19th chapter of St. Matthew:—"Have ye not heard that he, which made them in the beginning, made them male and female; and said, for this cause shall a man leave father and mother, and shall cleave to his wife; and they twain shall be one flesh,—wherefore they are no more twain, but one flesh: what, therefore, God hath joined together, let no man put asunder."

If we refer to the heathen nations, we shall find

that they ever held marriage so religious a ceremony, as never to have it performed without their priests solemnizing the same by sacrifices, and by calling on their deities to witness the sacred contract, and by invoking them to bless the marriage covenant. Thus, then, by considering the marriage ceremony simply a civil contract, we, in this, outdo the heathens themselves. I am convinced in my own mind, that if the marriage ceremony was performed in a more awful and solemn manner than even the canons of our Church direct; and if the divine institution of it was more thoroughly impressed on the minds of those who are married, we should not see so many couples *putting themselves* asunder, as we now do, in this Frenchified age of fashionable inconstancy, vicious politeness, and licentious gallantry. If it was my province to give advice, I should recommend to parents and guardians, to impress on the minds of their children and wards, that marriage is of *divine institution;* that they should seriously reflect on the state of their own hearts, and cautiously observe the conduct and disposition of each other, before they enter into a religious engagement;—and that, having been pronounced man and wife in the name of God, no sophistry of the present age should induce them for a moment to consider that engagement a mere civil contract; for when once the marriage ceremony is lightly esteemed, the bonds of union are easily snapped by the artful casuistry of the designing libertine, or by the more dazzling acquirements of the unprincipled man of fashion. These are my undisguised sentiments: and had I a sister, a daughter, or a son, I should use every endeavour to convince them, that though the *form* might be considered *in part* as civil, yet the actual marriage was of divine institution, and therefore ought to be most *religiously observed* by both parties, if they have any regard for their happiness hereafter, or their respectability here.

As I consider religion without morality to be a farce, so do I mean, by the words "religiously observed," true fidelity, which is a strictly conscientious observance of that virtuous and faithful love, which the contracting parties so honourably promise, so openly avow, and so *sacredly pledge* to each other till "*death do them part.*"

To the pen of Gisborne, both married and un married are under the greatest obligation. His "Considerations antecedent to Marriage," cannot be too carefully read,—his duties of matrimonial life cannot be too strictly practised. By an attentive perusal of his pages, the most beautiful and accomplished woman may make her charms still more attractive; and the most gay and elegant man may obtain that knowledge of the human heart, as to ensure to himself, by a kind and affectionate attention to the woman of his choice, that blissfulness, which domestic felicity, arising from a mutually honourable and virtuous conduct, can alone give.

Frequently do we bachelors smile at the expression—"for better, for worse;" and unblushingly allege, that the dread of the latter deters us from becoming Benedicts. How far are we surpassed in this respect by the Athenians, the burthen of whose song, at their marriage feast, was—"'Εφυγον κακὸν, εὗρον ἄμεινον,"—"I quitted the bad, I found the better." From this we read, they never dreamed of such a thing as finding a lady *worse:* and I am persuaded that it is, nine times out of ten, the fault of a bad husband, when the wife becomes *worse.* The Greeks had also another custom, viz.—that of writing over the door of the bridegroom's house, "Μηδὲν εἴτο χαχόν,"—"Let no evil enter here." This induced Diogenes once to observe, that the master had no right to go in:—and if the same custom was still in vogue, I am afraid the same sarcasm might very justly be applied to some bridegrooms, who, when they do enter, carry with them as much evil as the man to whom the Cynic alluded.

As a bachelor, I shall, for the future, lay aside the idea of a lady becoming worse; and I hope other bachelors will follow so excellent an example. The only fault that can possibly be laid to the charge of the ladies, and for which they often smart most grievously through the rest of their lives, is, parting with their hearts without consulting their judgment. Of the danger arising from fixing the affections, without first giving reason the command of the vessel, at the commencement of the voyage through life, Fielding thus expresses his conviction:—

> " Safe o'er the main of life the vessel rides,
> When Passion furls her sails, and Reason guides;
> Whilst she, who has that surest rudder lost,
> 'Mid rocks and quicksands by the waves is tost;
> No certain road she keeps, nor port can find,
> Toss'd up and down by every wanton wind."

In having left the vessel to be tossed about at random,—and as there are shoals of jealousy and ill-temper—quicksands of treachery and seduction —whirlpools of ruin and infamy—besides innumerable rocks of destruction, scattered over the ocean of life,—it is natural to suppose that the vessel must at last strike or go down: I therefore venture to give you the following lines on the same idea.

When o'er the gently-flowing tides,
    While soft the gale,
    Which swells the sail,
The weak, frail bark of woman rides,
The mind undisturb'd, and passion asleep,
Reason will pilot her over the deep.
    But when clouded the skies,
    Dread tempests arise,
And that tempest of love, dreaded most;
    The pilot is blinded,
    The helm is not minded,
And this way and that the vessel is tost;
    She rocks and she reels,—
    She settles,—she heels,—
She founders at last,—and is lost!

Having trespassed so long on your patience, and that of your readers, I now take my leave, with a sincere wish, if you are a bachelor as well as myself, that we may meet with women whose attractions are heightened by virtue, good sense, and good humour.

Thus solaced by the assiduous endearments of a tender and affectionate wife, we may scoff at the unthinking dissipation of some—smile at the ambitious folly of others—and, like Gil Blas, write over our doors—

> "Inveni portum—opes et fortuna valete,
> Sat me ludisti—ludite nunc alios."

MILESOLIM.

## ON THE CANARA CAVES IN SALSETTE.

ON the north of Bombay, and opposite to Mahim, lies the Island of Salsette, of which Tanna is the capital, on the eastern side; and, this being the frontier coast towards the Mahratta country, is defended by a small fort, which is garrisoned by two companies of Sepoys.

Salsette has long been celebrated for its subterranean temples, of which those of Canara, situated near the centre of the island, are the principal.

On the morning of the 16th November, 1800, I

set out early from Poullec to visit them, and crossing the ford at Sion, proceeded on, through a romantically beautiful tract of hilly country, which is but little cultivated. After a journey of fifteen or sixteen miles, and at the hour of eleven o'clock, I reached the foot of this majestic mount. Here I was obliged to leave my palanquin, as the surrounding thickets covered the small path, which leads to its ascent, and rendered it extremely difficult, without some guide to point out the way. At this place, the mountain appears to be of vast circumference, and is clothed on every side with the thickest foliage, but terminating, near to the summit, in a barren rock, which appears greatly elevated above the adjacent hills. After ascending by a circituous route, the distance of one mile, I reached the entrance to the caves, where the first object that strikes the eye, is a flight of rude steps, leading into a large cave or temple, through a lofty and extensive portico, which is hewn out of the solid rock, and ornamented in the front with a colonnade of plain pillars, formed to support the immense surface of the roof. Those pillars bear some resemblance to the Tuscan order. On the right and left hand of the portico, there are two colossal statues, chiselled from the stone wall in bas-relief, and rising to the height of about twenty-five feet. These figures are of an uncouth form, and are decorated with various fantastic ornaments, such as ear-rings, &c. And by being placed in so conspicuous a position, at the entrance of the caves, one would suppose were intended to represent the guardian deities of this hallowed recess.

Besides those, there are also a number of smaller images, and groups of figures, embossed on the walls of that apartment, and in several chambers lying contiguous to it,—which but little exceed the natural size of man, and are, in general, well executed. Many of the figures are mutilated, and, in some, the work of the sculptor is totally effaced by the destructive hand of time.

Further on is a plain but spacious apartment, formed also out of the solid rock, in the shape of an oblong, and rising to a considerable height, with an arched roof. The walls of this inner apartment, or temple, as it appears to have been originally, are rough and unadorned; but, at the extremity, is a curious kind of altar, eight or ten feet high, which, in all probability, was intended to answer some holy purpose, in the ceremonies of that religion (whatever it might be) which, no doubt, existed here at the period of its fabrication, although the knowledge of it is now hid in obscurity. The exterior of this astonishing excavation is a little damaged, and some part of the stone work also, that was originally placed for its defence and support, has been broken down, or has given way on that side, which is most exposed to the action of the elements.

From the place here described, a broken road

winds towards the left, higher up the mountain, and leads to a variety of smaller caves, which are situated at different heights; many of them include extensive suites of rooms, which are connected by narrow passages; and others are entirely detached from the rest. But these excavations are so numerous, and are so widely separated from each other, that it was not in my power to view them all; I was, therefore, obliged to content myself with visiting those amongst them, which were pointed out to me, as being the most remarkable, in the vicinity of the spot from which I began my tour of observation. A great similarity of appearance is observable in all the different caves, which consist, for the most part, of long ranges of single apartments on either side, running parallel to each other, with an open portico in front. They are, however, of different dimensions, and many of them extend so far into the rock, as to be obscured in total darkness throughout the year.

In some of the most celebrated pagodas of the Hindoos, that I have had an opportunity of seeing, their images are rude and misshapen, and not at all similar to these, in the caves of Canara, which are executed in a more masterly manner, and, to an ardent imagination, would seem to approach nearer to the simplicity of the Attic style. I do not, however, intend a comparison. The nations of this quarter of the globe, seem, by the indolence of their habits, and the languor of their mental exertions, to be precluded the hope even of approaching the perfection of the Greek artists. Various aqueducts, leading to the different caves, are cut in the rock, and communicate with reservoirs, at the top of the mountain, which are abundantly supplied with water during the periodical rains.

On different parts of the rock, a number of ancient characters had been inscribed, which are still discernible, but, whether it be now possible to decypher them, must be left to the judgment and knowledge of those who are skilled in the Sanscrit, and other ancient languages of the country. On the whole, I was not surprised to hear the natives who accompanied me, attributing the cause of this assemblage of artificial wonders, to a supernatural agency; but, if a reasonable conjecture may be hazarded on the subject, they are the performance of several ages, and not the work of any particular individual. The caves of Canara might originally have been the residence of a religious society, who, after forming their first settlement, increased in number, and extended their cells in proportion, until successive revolutions drove them from their haunts, and desolated those mansions of their Gods.

The similarity which exists between the site of these caves, and that of the celebrated temple of Delphi, may be adduced in support of an idea, that the form of worship observed in the one, was something similar to the mysterious rites which, we are led to believe, were practised in the other, since the situation of the former could not have been better adapted to inspire the minds of the devotees with reverential awe, than these gloomy shades, which are now sacred only to silence and to solitude.

If, as it is generally admitted, human nature is alike at all times, and in all countries, it is allowable to suppose, that the same means had been employed in the east, and in the west, to fetter the human mind, by alarming the imagination, and filling it with terrific images and superstitious notions. Whence, it is possible, that a similar kind of worship might, originally, have been celebrated at Delphi, and at Canara; although no historic proof can be brought forward in support of this inference. For want of time, my own observations were rather more confined than I could have wished, although I could hope to add but little to the description that is here given, of objects, which had attracted the notice of antiquarians, philosophers, and architects, but, which have hitherto, and perhaps ever will elude, the researches of accurate investigation. For, what curiosity could here expect to withdraw the veil of fiction,—or what labour hope to illumine these subterranean abodes, by that faint glimmering, which strives to penetrate the thick shades of fable and romance?

X. X. X.

## A CURIOUS INSTANCE OF NATURAL ANTIPATHY.

---

MR. EDITOR,—You have favoured your readers with a few essays on various subjects—*Silent Eloquence*, Chronograms, and one or two others;—I should like much to see some ideas thrown together on the subject of Natural Antipathies,—and, by way of text, ground-work, or, as a professional man (an engineer for instance) would say, as a foundation to build upon, I will relate you a circumstance in that way, which I was actually a witness to. I was acquainted with a gentleman, who could not bear the smell of a shoulder of mutton, (he had no dislike to any other part) and happened to spend a day in his company, at a friend's garden-house, near Calcutta.

To pass away the forenoon, cards, backgammon, and other amusements, were resorted to. I was engaged at the same card-table with Mr. M——, and we did not break up till some little time after dinner was announced on table. I mention this as a proof that he could not have had an opportunity of knowing what was for dinner; (as may naturally be supposed by some) add to which, he was one of those of the party least acquainted in the house.

On approaching the door of the dining-room, he stopped short, and was observed to turn quite pale; being asked what was the matter, he instantly said—"Oh! there is a shoulder of mutton on table!" Examination was made, but nothing of the kind appeared: he was told so, and made another attempt to enter the room, but he could not—declaring, he was certain there must be a shoulder of mutton, however disguised, on table. On a second, and more minute investigation, a shoulder of mutton was found in a pye at the farther end of the table; which being removed, all uneasiness ceased,—and Mr. M—— eat his dinner as comfortably as any other person!!!

I never heard whether this gentleman ever made any serious effort to overcome his antipathy; but I knew a lady, whose dislike to cheese was equally strong, (so much so, that she would faint at the mere sight of it) very prudently and resolutely determined to overcome her dislike to it,—and completely succeeded in doing so. For which victory, obtained by her perseverance and good-nature, I have seen her repay herself by eating cheese like other people.

## LETTER OF ADVICE TO YOUNG LADIES.

---

My dear Girls,—As you are now entering into "*Life*," you no doubt sometimes study the "*Way to get married*;" and having years and experience to authorize me, I venture, though an "*Old Maid*," to point out "*Ways and Means*," which may put you on the "*High Road to Marriage*." First let me entreat you to beware how you act the "*Romp*," or play the "*Inconstant*;" a slight indiscretion may cost you "*Many sighs*;" and the "*Way to win him*" that may be worthy of you, will be, never to indulge the "*Caprices of a spoilt child*," or imitate the manners of "*Maids as they are*." Keep clear of the "*School for Scandal*," and place little confidence in "*Fashionable Lovers*." In your "*Election of a Husband*," let me advise you to shun the "*Miser*," who will neglect you for his "*Iron Chest*," and a "*Gamester*," who will certainly run the "*Road to Ruin*." There is a sort of "*Love à la Mode*," whose only object is the "*Purse*,"—whose only attention is an "*Heiress*;" but there is also a "*Trial*," which will in time unmask the "*Votary of Wealth*," and bring him to disgrace. Do not let any "*Gay Deceivers*" ensnare your affections,—such "*Lovers' Vows*" are lighter than air, and seldom last "*Three Weeks after Marriage*." Show your contempt for

"*Fashionable Follies*;"—do not be dazzled by "*Accomplished Fools*," who make a transient figure in the "*World*," till the "*Wheel of Fortune*" turns, and they repent the "*Follies of a Day*."

When at length your good fortune presents you with a "*Man of Ten Thousand*," rising superior to all his "*Rivals*," do not let "*False Delicacy*" occasion "*Delays and Blunders*," but prevent all "*Mistakes*" by accepting the "*Prize*," with a candour that should prevail amongst "*Conscious Lovers*." If you meet with a "*Good-natured Man*," think yourself peculiarly favoured;—a "*Choleric Man*" will assert his ways in the "*Honey Moon*," and early show an inclination to "*Rule a Wife*." May you escape equally a "*Careless Husband*," and a "*Suspicious Husband*," and defy the evil offices of the "*Busy Body*," and the "*Double Dealer*." May discord ever be a "*Stranger*" in your mansion, or if "*Family Quarrels*" should happen, never make "*Much ado about Nothing*." You will, by yielding gracefully, appease a "*Provoked Husband*," and make him own himself "*All in the Wrong*." 'Tis a "*Secret worth knowing*," before you enter into "*Matrimony*," that, "*Every one has his faults*." May you and your "*Tender Husband*" present to the world, that "*Wonder*" in the present days—a "*Constant Couple!*" Still emulate "*Wives as they were*," and you will find it the true "*Way to keep him*," who, I hope, will reward you with "*Love for Love*." May you look on your "*Wedding Day*" as the happiest of your "*Life*," and find in "*Mutual Affection*" an infallible "*Cure for the Heart-ache*, and the genuine "*Secret*" of happiness!!

LUCRETIA SINGLEDAME.

## CHENGEZ KHAN.

SIR,—I have the pleasure to send you another paper of my late friend Captain J. R. It is a short memoir of Chengez Khan, the greatest and most destructive conqueror that ever existed. It was, I imagine, written during the author's residence in Persia. Much of the information it contains may be met with in other books, but as there appear to be a few particulars relative to this extraordinary personage, which may not be found elsewhere, I am induced to transmit it for insertion.

PERSICUS.

This celebrated conqueror, who was born at an encampment in Tartary, called *Dekun-buldok*, in January A.D. 1155, was eldest son of Pisuky Behadoor, a royal prince who had become famous among the Tartar tribes for warlike exploits. At Pisuky's death, great part of his subjects revolted, presuming on the youth of Chengez Khan, who was then only thirteen years of age. This drew him into wars with those ferocious tribes, and with the neighbouring Khans, in which he continued to be engaged from that time to his fortieth year, with various success,—sometimes carrying off the herds and horses of his competitors, and sometimes defeated, and taken captive in his turn.

From his fortieth to his forty-ninth year, was the first great æra of his successes, in the course of which he added greatly to the number of his troops, and subdued various tribes that were hostile to him.

At length, in 1202, having overcome a powerful prince named Uny Khan—the most considerable with whom he had hitherto waged war—he was that year proclaimed *Great Khan* by the class that had submitted to him. And thus supported and established, he proceeded next to subjugate the *Naiman* and *Mickit* tribes, bordering on China, as well as others to the west; and seeing himself then in a condition to attack greater powers, and his way open on that side, he invaded China repeatedly.

On his return from one of these invasions in 1212, he ordered all the young children whom his troops had taken, in ravaging the northern provinces of that empire, to be inhumanly butchered in his camp!

After these expeditions, he finished the conquest of the rest of Tartary, and had soon completed the extirpation of *Khuslup Khan*, (who reigned in Cashghur, and who was the last of his competitors in those parts,) when the slaughter of his ambassadors, by Sultan Mohammed of Khorasan, who possessed all the countries from the western boundaries of India to the Caspian Sea, afforded him a fair pretext for invading the Southern Asia. That region was then crowded with populous cities, abounding in riches, and sunk in luxury and effeminacy; and he came down upon it with a prodigious number of Moguls and Tartars, all inured from infancy to hardship, danger, and fatigue; equally strangers to the comforts and refined feelings of civilized life, and habitually exercised in war and bloodshed.

He passed Turkistan in his way to the Khorasan Mountains, in 1218, when he was sixty-three years old; and, after effecting their entire reduction, he returned to Tartary, in 1223, where he died soon after.

Jagy Khan was the eldest son of Chengez Khan. The present Khan of the Crimea is a descendant of Jagy Khan. Uzbek Khan was the seventh in succession from Jagy Khan. Hulaker Khan was the fifth son of Tutûg Khan, the fourth son of Chengez Khan. His elder brother Mungo Khan succeeded to the throne of his ancestors Korakorum in the Hedjira year 648, or A.D. 1250; and in consequence of complaints made to him of the state of Persia, and the adjacent countries, which his grandfather had subdued thirty years before, he sent his brother Hulaker, in 1253, with a chosen army of Moguls into these parts. His principle achievements on coming thither, were, the extirpation of the *Mulahidu*, called also *Ismaelions*, and Fedays, who had established themselves in Persia Irak; and the taking of Bagdad, which city he entered on the 9th of Safer A.H. 656, or A.D. 14th February 1258. He was the patron of the famous astronomer *Nasir Ud-deen Toosy*, for whom he built an observatory at Meraga, near Tauris, in *Azirbajan*, at which place the prince died in A.H. 663.

## CHRONOGRAM ON THE CONQUEST OF JAVA.

I HAVE the pleasure to send you a Persian chronogram, which, from the nature of its subject, you may perhaps deem worthy of a place. The present tribute, humble indeed for so glorious an occasion, is the composition of a learned Native of Moorshedabad; and an Asiatic muse celebrating in her song a British triumph, is a circumstance, I think, not slightly deserving of praise and publicity.

شد چواز حسن تردد فتح جادا شکار
پر ز شور تهنیت گردید ملک وکوه ودشت
سال این است فتح مسرت بجش گفت از من خرد
ازسر جرات بگو شاغل کر جاوه فتح گشت

"When the braVe onset open'D ConqVest's roVte,
O'er pLaIns, o'er hILLs, far rang th' eXVLtIng shoVt,
A year of VICtory, Late foretoLD the wIse,
Lo! JaVa faLLs to gLory, VaLoVr's prIze."

To understand this fully it must be explained that سرجرات not only lends its aid to form the above sense, but must also be taken in another more literal one, or for "the head or beginning of the word جرات" of course the letter ج the numerical power of which, according to the rules of the ابجد being added to those of the letters which compose these words جادهفتح کشف will give the date required; — thus ج3 + ج3 + ا 1 + و6 + ه 5 + ف80 + ت 400 + ح80 + ک20 + ش 300 + ت 400 = 1220, year of the Hedjira, which corresponds with A.D. 1811. "Shaghul" in the last line is the تخلص or poetical appellation of the composer. This in my translation I have omitted, for which, and for the very paraphrastick, incorrect version, I have above given, the only excuse I can offer. is, that I was obliged to sacrifice much for another object which I had in view, namely, to transfuse into my lines not only the sense but the date of my original. The

Roman numerical letters which they contain being added together, will give agreeably to chronogrammatic rules, the year 1811.

## TOMB OF SELIM KISHTEE.

Sir,—Perhaps the following description of the tomb of Selim Kishtee, &c. may be acceptable to some of your readers, if you think it worthy of insertion in your Miscellany.

On the 10th February, 1807, we visited Futteh-poor-Sicri, distant from Agra about twelve coss (or twenty-four miles.) At this place is the tomb of Selim Kishtee, the saint through whose prayers and intercessions Ackbar first obtained his wishes of an heir to his throne, his former children having died in early infancy. His eldest son, born at this place, was named after the holy man; in further gratitude to whom Ackbar erected the tomb above mentioned, about 241 years ago. The gateway was built nearly thirty years after. It stands on a stony eminence, and the ascent is by a steep flight of red granite steps. With the simplicity and unity of the design of this grand and noble structure we were highly pleased. It is formed of red granite, having borders and ornaments carved in stone of a pale ochre colour; there is also some inlaid work of white marble, but the subserviency of parts is so well preserved, that the effect produced by the whole is chaste and simple in a degree seldom witnessed in Indian architecture. From its summit, to which the ascent is by a flight of 117 steps, the eye commands an extensive prospect over a barren and sandy plain, but from whence some interesting spots are noticed: on one side, at the distance of eighteen coss are seen the hills of the Brima Pass: at a nearer extent of five coss, rise the walls and bastions of Bhurtpoor, rendered famous by its obstinate and successful resistance against five attempts to carry it by storm, by the British army, under Lord Lake, in the beginning of the year 1805. In an opposite direction, the white dome of the Taj Mah'l is descried above the horizon.

Through this beautiful gateway, under a bold, and astonishingly elevated arch, the passage leads to a square and spacious area, paved with stone, round which, on the four sides, are arched cloisters of red granite, supported by pillars, richly carved, of the same stone, having small cells ranged within the walls. In the centre of the western side stands the Musjid. This building is in the same style and of the same materials as the gateway, but less elevated, and has a greater variety of beautiful borders, carved in stone. The corresponding building on the western side of the area, is a gateway; and a third, which stands on the same side as that in which are deposited the ashes of Selim, is nearly filled with stone and marble tombstones, which cover the remains of the descendants of the saint.

The tomb of Selim Kishtee is a square building, covered by a dome, formed entirely of white marble. The pillars which support the square porch, by which the building is entered, are richly carved, and are hollow in their centers, to admit of water being conducted through them, for the egress of which is a marble rose near the base of each pillar. Beyond the porch is a verandah, which surrounds the interior apartment on the four sides, enclosed by a marble network, the most beautiful we had seen. The effect produced by the richness and variety of the designs, together with the lightness of their execution, was such as we had never witnessed at any other building in this country.

Within this verandah is a room ornamented by paintings and designs, in coloured chunam or stucco. The floor, inlaid in coloured marbles, has a handsome effect. In the centre stands the canopy, regarded by the natives with superstitious reverence. It is composed of a dome, supported by four pillars; the frame is of wood, but entirely covered with mother-o'-pearl, which was procured from Surat, cut into small pieces of various shapes, and fastened to the wood by brass pins, in regular designs. A low marble railing runs round the canopy, over which is stretched a piece of red flowered silk, covering a plain white tombstone, which occupies the centre of the canopy; on its top are two vessels for rose-water, encrusted also with mother-o'-pearl; and over the whole is thrown a silk net, substituted for one which is said to have been originally of silver.

During the period that the place was in the possession of the Mahrattahs, Scindia allowed the descendants of the saint 10,000 rupees (£1,000) per annum, towards the repairs of the tomb. It is now kept up by the revenue yielded from four villages, that have ever been attached to it, and which produce from 5 to 7,000 rupees a year.

Adjoining to the tomb of Selim Kishtee are the ruins of Ackbar's palace. This was a favourite residence, where he spent much of his time. What remains of it are only sufficient to convince that it could never have boasted either elegance or splendour. A contiguous residence, which belonged to Rajah Beer Bull, the Vizier of Ackbar, affords more interesting speculation, and displays in its ruins the vestiges of its original ornaments. The architecture is Hindoo, and consequently irregular, but the carved designs on the red stone pillars and cornices are extremely rich, and exhibit great boldness and freedom of design.

The town of Futtehpoor is a mere mass of ruined and falling buildings, and offers nothing worthy of observation.

## ADDRESS TO LOVE.

---

O THOU ! or Fiend or Angel, —by what name
Shall I address thee,—how express thy power ?
Strange compound of extremes of heat and cold,
Of hope and fear, of pleasure and of pain ;—
Most credulous Infidel !—now trusting none,
Now anchoring on a feather ; craving all,
With nothing satisfied,—perplexed with doubt,
Yet dreading to be sure ; surcharged with thought ;
Of speech incapable ; in absence curst—
Yet eager still to rush on certain pain !

They call thee blind,—yet have I known thee, Love,
More keen and watchful than the sleepless eye
Of that dread serpent, whose terrific glare,
Hung like a comet o'er the Hesperian boughs ;
Nor ken of griping miser, nor of lynx,
Nor his, whom poets feign'd with hundred eyes,
Argus,—nor that majestic bird, which looks
Undazzled on the sun, is half so sharp,
So vigilant as thine. All-seeing love !
No look, nor motion, gesture, deed, or word,
No,—nor the secret councils of the heart,—
Can 'scape thy scrutiny. How wretched thou,
If aught thou see'st, which thwarts thine ardent wish :
And oh ! how ravish'd, if thou mark'st one glance;
Which tells the latent longings of the soul.

In that high fever, the delirious brain,
Coins gaudy phantoms of celestial bliss;
Of bliss that never comes,—for now, e'en now,
Now, while Love sleeps, and eyes the rainbow hues
With child-like rapture,—e'en now comes jealous Fear,
With trembling hand, and thunders at the door;
At this rude noise, alarm'd the dreamer starts,
Looks round appall'd, and finds the vision fled!

Where now th' angelic tongue, the dimpled cheek,
The moisten'd eye-ball, and the hidden blush,
Of love's delicious smile?—All, all are fled!
From airy joys he wakes to solid pain.
Quick to his sight upsprings, in long array,
A tribe of hellish ills,—the cold reply,
The unanswer'd question, and the careless look
Of blank indifference,—the chilling frown
That freezes to the heart, the stony eye
Of fix'd disdain,—or more tormenting gaze
Bent on another. These, with all the train
Of fears and jealousies that wait on Love,
Are no imagin'd griefs,—no fancied ills
Are these—or fancied, worse than real, woes.

Such art thou, Love! and who, that once has known
Thy countless rocks and sands that lurk beneath,
Would ever tempt thy smiling surface more?

Long toss'd on stormy seas of hopes and fears,
How willingly at last my wearied soul
Would seek a shelter in forgetfulness.
Oh! kind Forgetfulness! Love's sweetest balm,
Come, rouse thee from thy bed, if still thou sleep'st

On Lethe's shore,—come, take this willing breast,
And fold it in thine arms;—through all my veins,
Thy dead'ning power infuse,—close up each gate,
And avenue to Love,—clear off the lime
That clogs the spirit, which fain would wing its flight,
To sense, to reason, liberty and peace.

## RESIGNATION.

Why droops the head, why languishes the eye,
What means the flowing tear, and frequent sigh?
Where are the lenient med'cines, to impart
Their balmy virtues to a bleeding heart?
Fruitless are all attempts for kind relief,
To mix her cordial, and allay my grief;
So strong my anguish, so severe my pain,
Weak is philosophy, and reason vain!
Such rules, like fuel, make my passion glow,
Quicken each pang, and point the sting of woe.
Imagination labours but in vain,
And dark'ning clouds intoxicate the brain.
Fancy no sweet ideas can suggest,
To lull the raging tumult in my breast;
In vain or mirth invites, or friendship calls,
Wit dies a jest,—and conversation palls—
Nature and art supply fresh springs of care,
And each obtruding thought creates despair;
No scenes amuse me that amused before,
And what delighted once, delights no more:
Though all creation beautiful appears,
And Nature's aspect a rich verdure wears,

Yet still her bloom with sick'ning eyes I see,
And all her luxury is lost on me.
The budding plants of variegated hue,
The blossoms opening with the morning dew,
The vernal breeze that gently fans the bow'rs,
The laughing meadows, and enliv'ning show'rs—
Th' enamel'd garden, where the works of art
Give strength to nature, and fresh charms impart;
Where gaudy pinks and blushing roses bloom,
Rich in array, and pregnant with perfume;
Where Flora smiling sees her offspring vie,
To spread their beauties, and regale the eye;
All,—all in vain with charms united glow,
To deck the scene, or gild the face of woe.

So when the morning lark ascending sings,
While joy attunes his voice, and mounts his wings,
Though to the cheerful notes the hills reply,
And warbling music gladdens all the sky,—
Still in his strains no pleasing charms I find,
No sweet enchantments to compose the mind.
In vain the sun his gaudy pride displays,
No genial warmth attends his brightest rays;—
And when his absent light the moon supplies,
Or planets glitter to enrich the skies;
No gleam of comfort from their lustre glows,
No harbinger of peace, or calm repose:—
But gloomy vapours o'er the night prevail,
And pestilence is spread in ev'ry gale.

Thus weaken'd by a gradual decay,
Life's bitter cup I drink without allay,
Nor taste the blessings of one cheerful day!

Come then, kind Death! thy sharpest steel prepare,—
Here point the dart—and snatch me from despair!
But stop, O! man—Thy plaintive notes suppress,
With Christian patience learn to acquiesce—
Th' instructive voice of reason calmly hear,
And let religion check the flowing tear.
Whate'er the will of Providence assigns,
'Tis infidelity alone repines.
But they, who trust in God, disdain to grieve,
And what our Father sends, resign'd, receive;
Whose sharp corrections testify his love,
And certain blessings in the end will prove.
Who sees how man would err without controul—
Afflicts the body to improve the soul,
And by chastising part, preserves the whole.
Hence the dark low'ring skies, and angry gales,
Conspire to raise the storm, and rend the sails.
Yet if calm reason at the helm preside,
My little bark will stem both wind and tide;
And adverse currents shall at last convey
The shattered vessel to the realms of day.

Thus taught by Faith how rash it is and vain
For man—mere dust and ashes—to complain!—
My soul, with sad disquietude opprest,
Directs her flight to Heav'n in search of rest,
And refuge takes (which peace at last will bring)
Beneath the shadow of th' Almighty's wing.
On him I fix my mind, and place my trust,
A being infinitely wise and just.
And should his providence new beams create,
To brighten the complexion of my fate,
A cheerful tribute to his throne I'll raise,
And stamp my song with gratitude and praise;

But should indulgence suit not his designs,
Who evil into happiness refines,
Let due submission make my burden light,
And may I think "Whatever is, is right."
Then be not thou disquieted my soul;
Have lively faith—and faith shall make thee whole.

When Heav'n inflicts, with calmness bear the stroke,
Since to repine, is only to provoke—
Learn to adore the justice of thy God,
And kiss the sacred hand that holds the rod,—
That sacred hand, which first the heart explores,
Probes ev'ry wound, and searches all the sores;
Then the right med'cine properly applies,
To cleanse the part where all th' infection lies;—
Hear this, thou coward man,—nor dread the smart,
Which, though it stings, will purify the heart;
For Resignation will promote the cure,
And though the means are sharp, the end is sure.

Since, then, afflictions are in mercy sent,
To be of good the happy instrument;
Since for the noblest ends they are design'd,
To form the judgment, to improve the mind;
To curb our passions, to direct our love,
To awe mankind, to speak a God above!
O! may I view them with religious eye,
Nor lose the guard of virtue till I die!
Thence shall I taste the sweets that evils bring,
And suck the honey, while I feel the sting:
Hence shall I learn the bitter cup to bless,
And drink it as a draught of happiness!—
A wholesome potion—which, tho' mix'd with gall,
May still preserve my life, my soul, my all!

Thus fix'd my heart, tho' fruit should fail the vine,
The fig-tree sicken, and its bloom decline;
The culture of the olive be in vain,
And flocks, infected, perish on the plain;
Though corn, and oil, and wine, at once decrease,
The field grow barren, and the harvest cease;
Though baffl'd hinds their fruitless toils deplore,
And vales uncheerful laugh and sing no more,—
Yet still with gladness would I serve the Lord,
Adore His wisdom, and obey His word.
Hear, then, O God! regard a suppliant's pray'r,
Soothe all my pangs,—and save me from despair!
Illuminate my soul with gladsome rays,
And tune my voice to Thy eternal praise;
Dispel the clouds of darkness from my eyes,
And make me know, that to be good—is wise:
Let christian precepts all my soul employ,
And be not more my duty, than my joy.
Let Conscience, void of art, and free from guile,
Still in my bosom innocently smile;
Her cheerful beams will gild the gloom of fate,
And make me happy in whatever state:
Hence shall I learn my talent to improve,
If poor, by patience, and if rich, by love.
If fortune smiles, let me be virtue's friend,
And where I go, let charity attend;
Within my bosom let compassion dwell,
To soften all the woes which others feel;
T'assuage by kind relief affliction's sighs,
And wipe the falling tear from widow's eyes.
To feed the hungry, the distress'd to cheer,
The needy succour, and the feeble rear;—
Hence shall I scorn temptation's gilded bait,

Look with disdain on all the pomp of state,
And, by humility, be truly great.

But should it be Thy blessed will to spread,
Clouds of thick darkness low'ring o'er my head,
Let me have grace to know they are design'd
To check my follies, and correct my mind:
Let me have grace to know, in my distress,
I still to Thee may have a free access,—
And be an heir, (tho' all the world should frown)
Of heavenly glory, and a future crown.
From these reflections true contentment flows,
Contentment—such as grandeur seldom knows.
Hence, in the lowly cot a relish springs,
Above the taste of courts, and pride of kings:—
Thus, on the flood of wealth, be thou my guide,
And steer my course 'twixt avarice and pride,
Or, in the ebb of fortune, teach my mind
To know its duty, and to be resigned,
Prepare me to receive or good or ill,
As the result of Thy almighty will—
Thy will—whose chief design and general plan,
Tends to promote the happiness of man.
Be ev'ry sensual appetite suppress'd,
Nor the least taint lie lurking in my breast.
Let steady reason my affections guide,
And calm content sit smiling by my side.
Teach me with scorn to view the things below,
As gaudy phantoms, and an empty show.
But guide my wishes to the things above,
As the sole object of a Christian's love;
Make me reflect on my eternal home,
A dying Saviour—and a life to come.

Direct me virtue's happy course to run,
And let me, as instructed by Thy Son,
In ev'ry station say—" Thy will be done."

## ON FANCY.

Can it be Fancy all?—ah, no!
The beating heart, the cheeks' high glow,
Declare, alas! too plain,
That no ideal pain
Throbs in my pulse, and from my breast
Steals its content, its wonted rest.

Say, does imagination guide,
And over all my thoughts preside?
Does fancy prompt the sigh?
Does she instruct the eye—
Ardent to gaze when thou art near,—
Absent—to drop the tender tear?

Though frequent borne upon her wing,
Of groves and sylvan shades I sing;
I own not now her sway;—
Alas! to Love a prey,
My soul acknowledges his chain,
Of real torments I complain.

She o'er my dreams indeed is queen,
And as she pleases paints the scene;
She not affects the heart—
She points no love-barb'd dart;

The morning drives her from her throne,
And reason must her spells disown.

Yet let me not disclaim her power,
Her potent smile may soothe the hour,
When far from you and love,
In other climes I rove,
Her airy wand may ease impart,
And soothe my agonizing heart.

## HOPE.

We're taught by Young, or our immortal Pope,
That our chief happiness consists in *Hope*,—
"Man never *is*—but always *to be*, blest:"
Come, then, fair Hope, and cheat my soul to rest.
Fortune, suspended, bids me free to use
Thy genial influence to 'wake the muse.
Indulge me, then, with thy inspiring lay.
To soothe the present, in the future day.

Since we, thus distant from our friends and home,
Have sought the plains of Hindostan to roam;
Where Britain's standard has been long erect,
Her legal rights of commerce to protect;
Let me the path of glory still pursue,
Our country's claim must still be honour's due;
And when bright Fame the patriot bosom warms,
The noblest science is the law of arms.

But if Ambition drives th' impetuous war,
'Tis then a rage the good and wise abhor.

May conquest crown us then, as we display
Our scorn of tyranny, the base betray.
Yet, as hostilities will sometimes cease,
And seasons claim a temporary peace,
In these cessations would I ask of heaven,
What would compensate the volition given?

When war relaxes, or subsides, O Jove!
Give me to taste the softer sweets of love,
The bliss supreme of purest love to share,
With genuine friendship to divide my care.
And if a sacrifice of all that's dear,
Be no mean title to th' imperial ear,
From England be the mistress of my heart,
Her charms will thence more solid joys impart;
Kind, meek, and gentle,—and, if passing fair,
I ask not beauty exquisitely rare.

Care-soothing sweetness, with an ample mind,
Ever to please, and to be pleased inclined:
With cheerful ease and elegance, I'd seek,
The smiles still playing on her lovely cheek;
Wit, sense, and song, harmoniously should move,
In sweet succession to the tune of love.

Ye powers divine! ye virtues which controul
And move the softer passions of the soul!
Had I the confidence of such a maid,
With all these captivating charms array'd,
Such glowing extacies would then inspire
My grateful heart, that not a new desire
Should find admission to my anxious breast,
Yet anxious still—for nothing could divest

My eager soul of the unceasing care,
How best, how surest, to delight my fair.

But, Love, thy rights, thus claiming highest praise,
Must now secede for Friendship's humbler lays;
For thy soft transports, exquisite, require
Some intervals, to renovate their fire;
The calmer sentiments of Friendship then
Haply recruits the generous flame again.
Zeal, thus receding, serves but to increase
And harmonize the higher joys to peace.

Give me a friend, in whose good-will and sense,
I may repose unbounded confidence,
One, who'll be free to give advice, but who
Will let that counsel be rejected too—
When on deliberation we incline,
Still to prefer what we ourselves opine:
For ever generous, enlarged and free,
Let him have latitude, and give it me.
Good-nature, candour, must inspire the youth,
But, above all, the beauteous goddess, Truth.

Hail, sacred deity! whose province lies,
To root out error in whate'er disguise.
Thy essence 'tis, philosophers explore,
And which, unfound, enthusiasts adore.
Oh, be thy laws as sacred with my friend,
As if their breach did his existence end:
That, led by Thee, his ev'ry act and word
Should fail in no one instance to accord;
Thus, honour, mistress of his steady mind,
More firm than oaths, would all his compacts bind.

With friends like these, of either sex, to share
My joys, my hopes, my interests, my care;
To gain a competence in this sojourn
Then, but remains;—that so we might return
To our dear friends at home, while yet our powers
Were equal to enjoy the gliding hours:—
Thus, greatly happy, at some rural seat,
In blest society our friends we'd meet,—
And there delight them, by recounting times,
Past unregretted in these adverse climes.
Transporting thought! O, what a close were this,
How far transcending ev'ry other bliss!
Enjoy then, Fancy, thy unbounded scope,
And still sustain us with inspiring Hope!

## THE DYING SOLDIER.

[OCCASIONED BY A SIGHT OF THE MILITARY HOSPITAL.]

Lo! where pale sickness rears her mournful dome,
  The sad receptacle of human pain;
Where the poor soldier, distant far from home,
  Writhes his rack'd limbs on mis'ry's couch in vain.

No more to him shall Hope's gay visions rise,
  Nor Fancy waft him to his native soil;
Unknown, unnoticed, here he lingers—dies;
  Nor feels the blessing of one cheering smile!

No friend appears to soothe the hour of death;
  Nor can conviction of his country's good,
By his decease, arrest his fleeting breath,
  Or cool the burning fever of his blood.

Yet, hopeless Soldier! o'er thy lowly grave
A tear I'll shed—the tribute to the brave.

## TO AN ÆOLIAN HARP.

Sweet Harp! whose magic power,
In sorrow's lonely hour,
    Gives to th' afflicted ear,
Thy friendly aid to feel;
And woes it cannot heal,
    Doth teach the heart to bear.

Gladly I hail thy lay,
Which sheds a cheering ray,
    To calm my aching breast;
Those heart-felt notes alone,
With trembling plaintive tone,
    Can bid my passions rest.

    Ah! then again
    Repeat that strain,
Whose dying cadence, soft and low,
    Steals o'er my soul
    With sweet controul,
And lulls the sense of woe.

Sure, sounds like those were given,
To raise the soul to heav'n,
To make men wise and good;
Hark! how they pour along,
Now in full tide of song,
Now pity's tend'rest mood.

Oh Music! maid divine!
Before thy heav'nly shrine;
Whether in solar ray,
Or where the polar star,
Gleams faintly from afar,
To light the pilgrim's way;—

A suppliant low,
I votive bow,
And claim from thy benignant pow'r
A sweet relief,
The balm of grief,
In sorrow's lonely hour.

## VERSES ON A LADY.

I own I'm wholly at a stand,
How to obey my friend's command—
That the poetic lyre be strung,
To sing a lady fair and young.
How shall description mark out one,
By attributes unclaim'd by none?

Should I an angel face pourtray,
With eyes that emulate the day;
Or radiant with a milder beam,
With love and langour softly gleam;
With skin as white as mountain snows,
With cheeks as crimson as the rose;
Made up in short of sweets and graces,
And all that's usual in such cases;—
There's not a woman with an eye
Dull as baked gooseberries in a pie,
Eyes that, unless a friendly nose
Did amicably interpose,
Each, as if jealous of its brother,
Would cross-examine one another;
With teeth alternate black and yellow,
With cheeks most biliously sallow;
With hair grey, carroty, or black,
With skin as coarse as rind of *Jack*,*
Like nine-pins squat, or maypole tall,
With figure of no shape at all;
Whom surgeons could, from bones projecting,
Anatomise without dissecting,—
But would, if called upon, aver
The picture might be meant for her.
Exclusive then, of form and face,
Unless you name some other grace;
And with corporeal charms combined,
Disclose some beauties of the mind;
The muse in vain her voice shall raise,
To fix on *one*, divided praise;—
Yet know I one of lovely mien,
Of roseate hue and sweet sixteen;

---

* A very rough-coated fruit.

Whose youthful beauty, tho' it warms,
Yet constitutes but half her charms.
Her Hebe-face, although 'tis true,
Is heighten'd by the rose's hue;
Her eyes with liquid lustre shine,
Her flowing tresses intertwine;
Her ruby lips perchance awhile
Distended sweetly with a smile,—
But oft'ner laughing, give to sight,
Teeth even rang'd of iv'ry white;
Her form majestically bold,
With limbs conform'd of nicest mould;
Softness with life and vigour join'd,
Firmness with symmetry combined;
Though she displays in form and face
A model of the female race;
Yet those alone would fail to move
My praise, my wonder, or my love.

But when with these I see combined,
The nobler beauties of the mind—
See goodness, temper, sense, and ease,
Give both the power and will to please;
See her the several duties blend,
Of daughter, relative, and friend;
Trace in a conduct void of art,
The best emotions of the heart;—
Not touched by selfish woes alone,
But grieved for sorrows not her own.
See her those studied arts disdain,
That stigmatize the weak and vain;—
See each accomplishment unite
To win the heart and charm the sight;

Without a thought to covet praise,
Yet merit it a thousand ways:
With mirth, the chasten'd child of sense,
And laughter-loving innocence,
Joyous the passing hours beguile,
Extort from dullness' self a smile;
But with the gaiety of youth,
Blend solid sense and spotless truth,—
These added charms I own e'en move
My praise, my wonder, and my love.
You smile, my friend—why then I ween,
This is the very girl I mean!

## ON A STATUE OF NIOBE—FROM THE GREEK.

The Gods, in anger, chang'd my form to stone,
And from my breast the spark celestial tore;
But see!—Praxiteles hath their work undone,
And warm'd to life what marble was before.

## ANECDOTE.

Belinda was celebrated in this country both for her wit and beauty, and if a patriotic Hibernicism now and then escaped her, it only added to the piquancy of her character, and gave a zest to the originality and brilliancy of her remarks. That she did sometimes, however, betray by implication which was her native country, the following anecdote will serve to evince. At the time of which I speak, the church in Calcutta was not built, but divine service was regularly performed to a numerous congregation in a room appropriated to this purpose. At Chinsurah there then stood as now the church, built long ago by the Dutch, but which, at that time, used to be very thinly attended. Belinda and a large party—amongst whom was Warren Hastings—in an excursion on the river, happened to pass by Chinsurah; and, at the sight of this religious place of worship, and being told to how little use it was applied, the lady could not help exclaiming—"Is it not very strange now, Mr. Hastings, here is a fine church, and nobody at all goes to it,—and, in Calcutta, where there is no church, why every body goes to it?"

"Haply the little simple page,
Which votive thus I've traced for thee,
May now and then a look engage,
And steal a moment's thought for me."

T. Moore.

"Extremum hunc, Arethusa, mihi concede laborem."

VIRGILIUS.

## ON CENTOS.

"From different nations next the Centos crowd,
With borrow'd, patcht, and motley ensigns proud;—
Not for the fame of warlike deeds they toil,
But their sole end, the plunder and the spoil."

CAMBRIDGE'S SCRIBLERIAD.

SIR,—As many of your readers, I doubt not, feel emulous to shine in your poetic department, yet are restrained from making the attempt by foolish qualms of diffidence, conscious inability, &c. &c., things totally exploded from the new school, I shall consider myself as rendering you an important service, in discovering to these a *mechanical* way of making verses, by which they may ascend Parnassus with as little trouble or genius, as may serve a person to cast up half a dozen figures on Neper's bones.*

The following is my recipe;—let the lover of the Muses first purchase any one of the fashionable poets' *vade mecums*,—"Enfield's Speaker," "Beauties of the Poets," or "Elegant Extracts," for

* Neper's Bones,—an instrument, by which multiplication and division of large numbers are much facilitated and expedited—so called from its inventor, J. Neper, or Napier, Baron of Merchiston, in Scotland, born in the year 1550; died 1617.

Neper's name was chiefly immortalized by his fortunate discovery of logarithms, and their application to all trigonometrical calculations, by which, improvements in the sciences of astronomy, navigation, &c. have been wonderfully facilitated.

instance;—let him then choose his subject, (the larger and more common the better,) and some easy measure. The index will guide him to those poems that relate to his subject, and running with his finger and eye down the rhymes of these, he must examine those in different poets that happen to co-jingle; and when he has gotten together a sufficient number, let him interweave them *secundum artem,* and his poem will be finished.

It is of course necessary that his lines should have some slight relation in subject to each other, but this may be as faint as he pleases. With respect to much sense it is not required—sound is quite enough; should it indeed be possible to preserve good sense without much trouble, it may be as well not to forego it; but it must always be remembered that this is a work of supererogation, for in the most finished poems of the present day, it will be seen that wit is not now included, as formerly, in the Muses' sacrifice.

The true definition of a poem is a "metrical composition,"—Dr. Johnson says nothing about thoughts, nor are they by any means indispensable; indeed I would have really good ones avoided as much as possible, for they are often very troublesome in the management. Yet as from the custom of antiquated writers, the remembrance of whom the new school has not yet quite effaced, many people are in the habit of expecting a thought to close the verse with, to prevent disappointment it will be as well, if not attended with too much labour, to gratify this old-fashioned taste with something that at least resembles thinking; thus in concluding a poem on Sunset, the following couplet may be mistaken for a sentiment:

> "Alas! bright Phœbus sets—the Sun is gone,
> Thus ever when the day is closed—the Night comes on!"

Now that I am on the subject of modern versification, it may be as well to observe, that, most of the writers of the present age will be of vast assistance in forming the taste for sweetly-elegant and original sonnets, canzonets, fragments, impromptus, extempores, &c. Some there are, it is true, that must be interdicted,—of these I need scarcely mention Cowper, Rogers, or Crabbe, for a moment's glance will convince the reader that though they have lived in our times, yet their writings are quite of the antediluvial order, their style is quite antique and out of date, and they might as well have lived in Queen Anne's time for the little good they have derived from existing in a polished age. But the most dangerous are those, who, while they are stout ancients at heart, disguise themselves in a modern costume; these must be particularly avoided; the most prominent are Charlotte Smith and Kirke White,—

> "If thou readest thou art lorn,
> Better hadst thou ne'er been born."

A perusal of their works will infallibly ruin all good and modern taste, by inspiring the reader, in spite of himself, with a most improper relish for the vulgarly natural, the horridly simple and pathetic; and, in short, for all that was improperly called *poetic* some hundred years ago. In lieu of these let Tyro revenge himself by taking *ad libitum* of Wordsworth, Cottle, Lewis, and a thousand others.

The way that I have proposed is not only easy, but it is certain of being attended with success and applause. You do not come before your readers trembling to know whether your new-born ideas may be agreeable to their palate, but you boldly offer them what they have already confessed they admire; and to frown therefore on your labours, it becomes necessary for them first to forswear their primary decisions, and to give up all pretensions to established taste. Like Zeuxis you offer a concentration of beauties, and your work, like that of his, cannot but be admired.

Some may term this mode of proceeding plagiarism, but in my opinion it does not quite deserve the name, for, if I understand the term aright, it generally is considered as the crime of taking others' thoughts or words, and serving them up to the reader with a large proportion of *our own;* but here as they are given quite unalloyed, it ought not to be thus termed. I am not, however, very tenacious of this argument; I do not care to allow that it is plagiarism, and what then? Is there any harm in this, or if there be, are we not countenanced on every side? And take it from me as a very convenient and good doctrine, that where there is no *shame* there is no *crime;* let us not then fear to follow the fashion whatever it may be. Besides, does not Shakspeare say, "he that is robbed not knowing what is stolen, is not robbed at all;" and what can these dead people know about the matter? Indeed, even in common plagiarisms I think we may be considered as conferring a favour and compliment on the gentlemen whom we so far honour as to borrow from; for in their original state they are scarcely ever read, being in general too nauseously strong and racy for the exquisite taste of the present day; but when diluted with a proper quantity of our gentle effusions, and introduced to the public in double hot-wove, with meadows of margin, morocco-binding, elegant *illustrations,* and black-letter notes, they become indebted to us both for fame and perusal; it is true they only enjoy this by proxy, but—by the way "discretion is the better part of valour," and I will not argue the point farther, as it might go perhaps farther against me.

To strengthen my precept by example, I offer the following *morceau,* in which I have strictly observed the directions I have laid down. (The names annexed to the several lines are those of their original proprietors.)

'Twas Spring,—'twas Summer,—all was gay, *Johnson*
But now the skies have lost their hue, *T. Moore*
No fragrant blossoms crown the May, *Miss Whately*
But sullen gloom obscures the view. *Collins*

| | |
|---|---|
| And now the Storm begins to lower, | *Gray* |
| And see, the fairy Vallies fade, | *Collins* |
| The feathered songsters love no more, | *Mallet* |
| And Spring now drops her gay parade. | *Miss Carter* |
| | |
| Alas! for man! so frail, so fair, | *C. Smith* |
| The vernal joys thy years have known, | *M. Bruce* |
| Oppressed with grief, oppressed with care, | *Burns* |
| Soon youth's fair heritage is gone. | *E. Moore* |
| | |
| Thus pleasure ever on the wing, | *E. Moore* |
| At Noon decays, at Evening dies, | *Pitt* |
| Its Sun is set, soon gone its Spring, | *Gray* |
| And Evening spreads obscurer skies. | *Parnell* |
| | |
| For Life is short, and wears away, | *Anon.* |
| It sickens on the languid sight, | *H. K. White* |
| Nor then regret those scenes so gay, | *Percy* |
| For soon, too soon, it will be night. | *Anon.* |

I remain, Yours obediently,

NUGARUM AMATOR.

## ON SNORING.

SIR,—In a former Number, mention is made of an infallible cure for nose-bleeding, by tying the middle joint of the little finger very tightly with a piece of packthread. Equally ingenious with this, Mr. Editor, and equally simple, is a mode lately detailed to me by a fair lady, for the prevention of what is commonly called snoring. Possibly there may be some more fashionable name for this kind of music, and, in this case, I must beg of your fashionable readers to attribute the use of so uncouth a word as *snoring*, rather to a lapse of memory than to sheer vulgarity, or even to the affectation of it. But to the point. In married life many are the comforts, (as is well known to those who have tested them,—and to those who have not, it would be useless to recommend sour grapes) and, happy am I to say, few are the inconveniences; but, taking Hotspur's advice to Glendower, and with it, Truth for my motto, inconveniences and troubles there certainly are: such as satiety, a numerous offspring, and slender income, &c. Leaving these things to graver authors, I shall confine my remarks to an inconvenience which many, if not most, married people have laboured under,—and that is, the harsh, uncouth, heart-piercing, sleep-rending sound, which breaks upon the stillness of the night—grates dissonant upon the tremulous ear, and harrows up the troubled soul. I cannot say with Armstrong, "That power is music"—but parodying his words, I may justly say—"That power is snoring," the sleeper's comforter—our loved companion's bane!

"Still it cries to all the house
Duncan sleep no more!"

Surely, Mr Editor, it is an object of some consequence to rid ourselves and others of so very disagreeable an inmate, which may be said to pillow us at night, and haunt us through the day; and to married people, what so simple as the following mode of prevention, which I am told is certain, although I cannot from my own experience vouch for it.

When your companion (male or female) is subject to this infirmity, you have nothing more to do than quietly with your finger and thumb to stop the nostrils of the sleeper, and this repeated for half-a-dozen successive nights, effectually removes the uncouthly custom of snoring. The sleeper may be incommoded in a trifling degree, but who could urge this as an objection, who did not feel a pleasure either in blowing, or listening to, what may emphatically be termed the *French night horn*.

You perceive, Mr. Editor, that, like your correspondent Benevolus, I prefer the civic to any other wreath, and, who knows what dreadful misfortune the knowledge of this circumstance may avert. Nose-bleeding in many cases is healthful to the body, since it appears to be a spontaneous effort of nature to relieve the system; but snoring is an evil counterbalanced by no good, or, at least, none that I ever heard of. It disturbs the happy mansion of quiet and repose, banishing slumber from our couch, and with it all those charming airy dreams of happiness which perhaps exceed our real bliss; or, what should most be dreaded, excites dislike, disgust, antipathy; and where these obtain the smallest footing in a family, "ware pitcher and ware stone"—the unhappy consequences may be too readily foreseen,—bickerings and quarrel, if not separation and divorce!

PHILO-SOMNUS.

## ON THE POETRY OF PHINEAS FLETCHER.

IT may be a remark of general truth, that what is little read, is read as much as it deserves to be; but it is equally true, that there are few general observations which are not liable to exceptions; thus, in the present one, it is on record, that there was a considerable period of time, in which even the beauty and sublimity of Milton were unfelt and disregarded: yet, who shall dare to say that they deserved to be so? Another poet is nearly in the same state at present as our great bard was in at that time,—certainly by no means to be compared to him in merit, yet, still, deserving of more fame and perusal than he now enjoys;—this is Phineas Fletcher. In his day he was termed, and justly so, the "Spenser of the Age;" but had he not now, by good fortune, obtained a place among Anderson's Poets, and received much well-deserved praise from Mr. Headley, in his "Select Beauties of Ancient English Poetry," his name would scarcely have been known, and his works never read. Yet, to the admirers of Spenser, (and what poetical mind can be unfeeling to his beauties?) the "Purple Island" of Fletcher must afford the highest gratification, for it is replete with the truest poetry, clothed in the most melodious versification. To use the words of Anderson, and, in doing so, I perfectly coincide with him in sentiment, the images of Phineas Fletcher "are distinguished by a boldness of outline, a majesty of manner, a brilliancy of colouring, a distinctness and propriety of attribute, and an air of life, that rarely mark our modern productions, and that rival, if not surpass, every thing of the kind even in Spenser, from whom he caught his inspiration." The other works of Fletcher are possessed of considerable merit; but it is to his "Purple Island" alone, that I purpose confining my present remarks.

This is an allegorical poem, in twelve cantos, on man: by an unfortunate error of judgment he has devoted the first five to an anatomical description of him; an attempt, which, as is obvious, however much credit it may reflect on his scientific knowledge, can in no way be made subservient to the display of his poetical powers. His readiness of rhymes, and volubility of syllables, indeed, it amply proves; and it must be allowed, that he has overcome with wonderful success, difficulties beneath which almost any other writer would have sunk. When we look on him struggling through this part of his work, it reminds us of Satan wading through Milton's chaos; we mark his progress with surprise, but with little desire to accompany him. His descriptions here are certainly clear and harmonious, we admire them, but we only admire; the poet should, nevertheless, receive a tribute of praise. When we enter, however, on his succeeding labours, this tribute we pay with eagerness, "here fatigued attention is not merely relieved, but fascinated and enraptured," for he then describes, in a beautifully chaste and highly-coloured allegory, the various virtues and vices which may inhabit the bosom of man. Between these a contest then ensues, and the poem concludes with giving the victory, according to poetic justice, to our better qualities. This whole part of the poem is filled with beauties of the highest order; in the marshalling his bands, his personifications are at once nicely discriminative, warmly animated, and richly poetical; and throughout the battle, in his images, his verse, and his judgment, a master's hand is every where perceptible. But critical remarks, as Dr. Johnson well observes, are not easily understood without examples; and of these, therefore, I will give a few, which will, I trust, fully justify the warm admiration I feel for the poet. What then can be more beautiful, more happy, than his following figures of Death?—

> "A dead man's skull supplied his helmet's place,
> A bone his club, his armour sheets of lead;
> Some more, some less, fear his all-fright'ning face,
> But most, who sleep in downy pleasure's bed."

His Hope, too, is so glowingly poetical, that, though long, I cannot but extract it.

> "Next went Elpinus, clad in sky-like blue,
> And through his arms few stars did seem to peep,
> Which there the workman's hand so finely drew,
> That, rocked in clouds, they softly seemed to sleep:
> His rugged shield was like a rocky mould,
> On which an anchor bit with surest hold,
> 'I hold by being held,' was written round in gold.
>
> Nothing so cheerful was his thoughtful face,
> As was his brother Fido's:—fear seemed to dwell
> Close by his heart: his colour changed apace,
> And went and came, that sure all was not well:
> Therefore a comely maid did oft sustain
> His fainting steps, and fleeting life maintain:
> Pollicita she hight, which ne'er could lie or feign."

The representing his fainting steps as supported by the beautiful maid Promise, is particularly correct and felicitous. It is true this picture cannot vie with the one drawn by Collins, "But thou, O Hope, with eyes so fair," &c.—but Collins' touches are all exquisite, and ever soar far beyond competition; yet, it is no mean praise that Fletcher stands second in a path that all have trod. Spenser's "Hope," though beautiful, is very much inferior; and for Cowley's, which Johnson so much praises, it cannot be read but with disgust after this.

To extract all the beautiful passages which this poem contains, would be to fill a far larger portion of paper than you, Mr. Editor, would be willing to allow me; I shall, therefore, content myself with recommending to the reader's particular attention, the rich aud exquisite delineations of Faith, Fear, Envy, and Mercy; many more there are beautiful, but these, in my opinion, are prominently so. On his nice judgment, in allotting to the various combatants their fit opponents, too great praise cannot be bestowed; thus, as an instance, Fear is made to attack Hope, who, when about to sink, is relieved by Faith: one cxample will suffice; all is equally chaste. Nor does the poem reflect less credit on his heart than head; he imitates Spenser, and he is not ashamed to avow it; he gives him continually the warmest tributes of gratitude, and declares that, but to *lacky* him, "is all his pride's aspiring." How different this from the conduct of the Dean of St. Patrick; Swift, though he owes so much to the author of "Hudibras," never once in his verse even mentions his name! The sentiments and images of Phineas Fletcher, breathe, likewise, the purest strain of fervid piety; his indignation of vice is warm and honest; his praise of virtue, innocence, and peace, such as proclaims him to have known their value, and to have possessed them: this, indeed, is the character handed down of him by his contemporaries; to use a figure of Mrs. Klopstock's, he was in every relation of life, what he is in every relation of poetry; but let him speak for himself,—the passage is too long to quote, but the reader who will turn to Canto I. Stanza xxvi. et seq. will be well repaid for his trouble by the most beautiful sentiments and poetry.

It is no slight praise, also, for Phineas Fletcher, that, living in an age when *conceit* was so prevalent, when the works of Donne, or Quarles, and of Jonson, overflowed with it; and possessed as he was both of sufficient invention and learning, to have shone in the metaphysical school, he was blessed with so pure a taste and excellent judgment, as to turn from these, to relish the simpler beauty and more genuine poetry of Spenser. That a few *conceits* should disfigure his works, was, however, to have been expected; for it was impossible to dwell in the very vortex without being rendered a little giddy; and, consequently, a few—but very few—there are. I recollect but two in his "Purple Island;" the one is, when speaking of the creation, he says, that, at the command of God, "first stept the light," and then, he very unnecessarily adds,—"not that he meant to help his feeble sight to frame the rest:" another, when in speaking of Orpheus playing, he observes that Charon's boat, at the sound of the music, "came *dancing* o'er the moat;" but these are "like rocky islands in a sunny main,—like spots of cloud amid an azure sky;" his beauties had more than compensated a thousand of such faults. Another testimony to the merit of Fletcher's poetry is, that Milton and Pope have both paid him the compliment of borrowing from him; only in insulated expressions 'tis true, but still this is a proof that they read and that they valued him. Milton's "shapeless shapes," "imparadised," "flaggy soils," and many other remarkable turns of expression may be traced to this source; it is also very probable that he took his idea of Sin and Death creeping from the mouth of Error from Phineas Fletcher, Canto 12th. St. xxvii., where he says, "The first that crept from his detested maw was Sin, a foul deformed wight," &c.; and his description of her as half woman, half serpent, is precisely the same. Milton's better to "reign in hell than serve in heaven," is also very like Fletcher's "in heaven they scorned to serve, so now in hell they reign." Pope, in his Eloisa to Abelard, has—

> "See my lips tremble, and my eyeballs roll,
> *Suck my last breath*, and catch my flying soul."

And Phineas Fletcher, in his beautiful Elegy on Eliza,—

> "And by his side, sucking his fleeting breath,
> His weeping spouse Eliza."

What Pope also calls "damning with faint praise,"

may owe its origin to part of Fletcher's description of Envy. He says of him very happily—

> "When needs he must, yet faintly, then he praises,—
> Somewhat the deed, much more the means he raises:
> So marreth what he makes, and praising most, dispraises."

In the following too may be traced a strong similarity to a well-known couplet of Dr. Sewel's—

> "He is as cowardly
> That longer fears to live, as he that fears to die."

But I have already, I fear, extended my remarks to too great a length. I will therefore now conclude with offering a humble tribute to the memory of a poet, from the perusal of whose works I have received very exquisite gratification. It is necessary to inform my readers that I have attempted in the following verses to imitate the style of the bard I address. The allusions which occur in them are to passages in his poem; Colin, it is hardly necessary to observe, is his great prototype—Spenser.

---

## IMITATION OF PHINEAS FLETCHER.

Forgive me, Fletcher! if I dare presume
  In my weak verse thy matchless flights to praise,—
Such praise on thy strong light but throws a gloom,
  And serves to lower more thy fame than raise;—

Yet can I not my teeming muse contain,
For, fill'd with thee, to curb her fire is vain,
And thou so sweet a theme—shalt have her sweetest strain.

Yes, gentle Shepherd! thou who tunest thy reed
To tell how sweetly thy lov'd Colin sung,—
Dost merit well for this an equal meed,
Dost merit wreaths by every poet hung!
Yet ah! I fear—howe'er thy claims divine,—
Their praise of thee will ne'er like Colin's shine,—
For tho' thou equall'st him—their powers not equal thine.

A skilful painter, tho' his nymph be plain,
Will with his art create a beauteous form,—
But *daubers* gaze on Venuses in vain,
Nor can with e'en one grace their canvass warm;—
'Tis not the subject but the powers that glow,
And were it otherwise, full well I know
The song that sings of thee, would far all songs outgo.

Oh! much I love thee when with generous rage
Thou hurl'st thy bolts at deep-wrong'd Colin's foe,—
Much, when indignant at th' ungrateful age
Thou dost upbraid it with thy Colin's woe;—
And oh how warmly in thy prayer I join—
May that rude churl who scorns the Muse divine
Alive, nor dead, e'er know one Muse's gentle line!

But why would'st thou the virgin Queen excuse?—
For Essex' wrongs why feel no virtuous ire?—
Such murder foul deserved an angry Muse—
And should have waked the thunders of thy lyre;—
'Twas wrong to say in thy too-polished song
For deed so base she could repent too long,—
Oh no!—for murder ne'er can grief too great belong.

When proud Eliza rises in her might,
And teaches haughty Spain her power to know,
Dazzled, enraptur'd at the glorious sight,
My breast distends with all a Briton's glow;
But when I see the beauteous Mary slain,—
When bleeding Essex sues—and sues in vain,—
Ah, then fast flow my tears,—and all her glories stain.

But why do I thus rashly dare to chide?
My eye-balls strain'd, one spot minute to spy
On thy bright sun-like disk, where all beside
Is glory beaming strong, and majesty,—
So strong, that when but at that spot I gaze,
Amazed and wilder'd at the neighb'ring blaze,
I feel my censure drown'd in wonder, love, and praise!

With what a master's hand thou know'st to ope
Each passion's cell, and give its form to day;
How stands aghast thy Fear,—how smiling Hope,—
And oh! what glories round thy Mercy play;
E'en Envy jaundice-eyed his portrait views,
And though he can't t' applaud thy skill refuse,
Yet with his praises faint he would dispraise thy muse.

And when thou chant'st the heav'nly King of Kings,—
But hush my lyre, nor dare th' Almighty theme;
To soar so high not e'en thy muse had wings—
To venture, then, would me but ill beseem.
Enough,—'tis time my tedious song to close;
Farewell dear bard,—my heart thy spirit knows,
My verse receive, tho' cold,—for warm my bosom glows.

## ON DIVINATIONS, ANAGRAMS, ETC.

I HAVE read with much pleasure the letters that have been addressed to you under the signature of "Nugarum Amator," and, as the subjects on which he treats have also formed a part of my desultory reading, I will avail myself of the invitation he holds out, of following his steps, and give you a few similar instances on the same topics.

He rightly observes, that the Persians, in their divination, by taking an omen from the opening of a book, chiefly resort to the works of Hafiz. Scott Waring, in his "Tour to Shiraz," mentions the practice as being very common; and states his having in his possession a Diwan—*i.e.* Hafiz, or collection of his odes, in which the ceremony necessary to be previously gone through, is particularly detailed: in general, however, he says, there is little other ceremony used, than propitiating the poet by some couplet, as this,—

حافظ شيرازي　　كاشف هرر ازئي

"O Hafiz of Shiraz! thou art the opener of all secrets!"

But that the custom existed before Hafiz himself, is certain, for the poet frequently mentions it in his poems, and, by his own confession, sometimes resorted to it;—thus, in one place, he brings it forward as an excuse for his manner of living:—

بعزم توبه سحر گفتم استخاره کنم
بهار توبه شکن میرسد چه چاره کنم

"I resolved this morning, with an intention of repenting, to consult an omen;—it proved to be—'The Spring, the breaker of vows, has returned,' What therefore can I do?" By this it will be seen that this divination is not only termed "tufal," as stated by "Nugarum Amator," but also استخاره "istukharee."

In speaking of divination by *lots*, Nugarum cites an instance from the book of Esther, in which it is mentioned that "Pur" was the Hebrew term for this species of oracle. I have to observe, that among the Jews, even of the present time, there is a kind of carnival annually held, which is called "Purim, or the Feast of *Lots*," and which I doubt not has relation to this very instance, the defeat of Haman.

Of anagrams, to enumerate all that have been made would be an endless task; but I cannnot forbear adding a few more, of, I think, equal excellence to those that have been already offered. To match the Greek one on Ptolemy, I present the following from the same author, Lycophron, which pays Arsinoë the pretty compliment of calling her Juno's violet—Ἀρσινοή ἴον Ἥρας. For single words, as the making is easy, there must be some peculiar felicity in the coincidence, to entitle them to our attention,—such as when "Logica" is converted into "*caligo*;" for *logic* will, by very many, be readily allowed to be *darkness*;—or the English one, which hinted to us, that the cry of "*opposition*" was "O poison Pit!" This is generally known, but not the less happy on that account; and I have therefore mentioned it. It may not be amiss, in the same way, to acquaint Sir Francis Burdett, that his name makes "*frantic disturbers*."

The fate of Sir Edmundbury Godfrey must be familiar to all my readers: it is not slightly singular, that the letters of his name compose the following sentence,—"*I fynd murder'd by rogues.*" But the most remarkable instance with which I am acquainted, is on that sentence in St. John (chap. xviii. v. 33.) where Pilate said to Christ,—"What is truth?" This in Latin would be "*quid est veritas?*" and the anagram of it is the most excellent answer that could be given—"*est vir qui adest!*"—"*Behold truth in the man now before you!*" Really this is a most beautiful anagram, and, in my opinion, must take precedence of the celebrated one on Nelson.

I recollect, too, at the time of Bonaparte's assuming the consular dignity, the following anagrams being made on the words "Revolution Francaise;—"*Un Corse la finira!*" The chief beauty of this anagram consisted, very remarkably, in what, at first, appears to be its imperfection, viz.

in its wanting four letters, to coincide strictly with the other; for after having predicted that a Corsican should put an end to the French Revolution, those four letters added to it, a most emphatic, though, alas! a vain "*veto!*"

Nugarum Amator is perfectly correct with respect to the great prevalency of the anagram among the effusions of "the wits of either Charles's day;" not one of them, according to Ben Jonson, but "pumped for those hard trifles;" a little bad spelling never stood in their way;—thus, one of them boldly asserts that *car* and *crashaw* are the same; but, gentle reader, take the proof:—

> "If you do say these anagrams not are,
> Take *crashaw*, and invert it,—*pshaw* 'tis *car!*"

Another of the poets of this age concludes an amatory poem with the following couplet:—

> "My heart thy altar is, my breast thy shrine;—
> Thy name for ever is—my breast's chaste valentine."

More is meant here than meets the ear,—there is a *posy*, Mr. Editor, to this ring, and one which I doubt not its author would have called a *posing posy;* it must certainly have cost him an infinite toil of brain: it would not readily be guessed, perhaps, that in the words, "is my breast's chaste valentine," is contained an anagram of his fair lady's name, or "*Maystress Elisabetha Vincent!!* —"cedite Romani Scriptores, cedite Graii,"—

"Homer and Virgil, hide your diminished heads;" for when did you ever display such exquisite, such refined ingenuity, as this!! The *learned* reader who wishes to know more on the subject, may consult "Gulielma's Blancus," who has written an art of Anagrammatism; or the celebrated Lepsius, who has given a list of such as have excelled in it.

Of Chronograms I could only offer you a few dry pieces of Persian, for which you would scarcely thank me; the traveller, however, may examine the inscription on the bridge at Juanpore: it is chronogrammatic; and you may, if you please, insert this on the death of Nelson,—"Flebilis in certamine decessit!"—"He died lamented in battle!" This, according to the regular rules, expresses the date, or A.D. 1805.

On Amphibology, since Nugarum Amator speaks of the cautious ambiguity ever preserved in the responses of the ancient oracles, I will adduce for him an instance equally to the point as the one he has cited. A Roman general, on his being about to enter on a campaign, consulted the oracle as to its success, and received for answer—"Ibis—redibis—nunquam per bella peribis;" this, of course, he interpreted,—"you shall go,—you shall return,—never by war shall you perish;" and, accordingly, went away fondly calculating on the highest success. But, whether Apollo and the Fates had quarrelled, or to whatever cause it may be imputed, it turned out as though they had determined to bring his prophecies into disgrace, for they unrelentingly allowed the general to be killed, and the whole army to be destroyed. On receipt of this intelligence, the friends of the deceased instantly posted off to the oracle, to reproach it with its fallacy; but the god was not so easily to be put to shame,—he had not been so little chary of his reputation, as to trust it to such slippery dames as the Fates,—but had, very prudently, like a Newmarket jockey, who takes the odds both ways, so framed his answer, that let whatever might be the event, he had predicted it. When, therefore, the general's friends began to taunt him for having deceived them, and related to him what had happened, his priests very calmly replied, that such was the event the oracle had predicted; for, said they, the response was,—"Ibis—redibis nunquam—per bella peribis!" that is,—"You shall go—you shall return never,—by war shall you perish!"—and by war he has perished. On hearing this, the poor general's friends were fain to go away—more than ever impressed with the conviction of the wonderful wisdom of the triumphant Phœbus.

Of devils' verses, or those which can be read backwards and forwards the same, I can add to Nugarum Amator's stock by the following Persian couplet:—

شکر بتر از وي وزارت برکش
شو همره بلبل بلب هر مهوش

of which the following is a paraphrastic translation: —"Sweetness shall find weight in the scales of government—let the nightingale ever dwell on the lips of the lover."

I cannot, Mr. Editor, take my leave of you without making one more attempt on my worthy friend the great Emperor,—and I think if you knew what trouble it has given me ("*stultus labor*,") you would excuse my offering the following anagram on Napoleon Bonaparte. I have the pleasure to address him thus—"*plan on—atone b'a rope*."—And that this hint may be prophetic is the wish of Yours,

PHILO NUGARUM AMATOR.

## CRITICISM ON A PASSAGE IN ST. JOHN.

MR. EDITOR,—It has frequently been suggested that a new translation of the Bible should be made; not only to correct the errors which the present one contains, but to adopt altogether a more modern and elegant phraseology. Against the latter proposition, however, the sense of the nation is almost unanimous; the most competent judges have declared themselves decidedly in favour of the version as it at present stands; and one of the most able of these, Sir W. Jones, in adducing from it several instances of beauty and sublimity, clad as they are in the garb of primitive simplicity, challenges any modern periphrasis, any ornamented rounded periods, to give to the sense a closer expression, or one that produces a more striking effect. The present translation is indeed the most simple, the most pure, and the most perfect model that could have been chosen for the purpose to which it applies, namely, in general, a plain historical narrative, that needs not the meretricious glare of ornament to engage our attention and belief, but receives them from us as voluntary tributes; while, in energetic simplicity, it details a system of morality the most pure, and a chain of truths which but to read is impossible to doubt. But even were its language a little antiquated or defective, which it is not, yet still the *prejudice*, if it may be so called, that is entertained in its favour, should not lightly be outraged; even prejudices, if harmless and sanctioned by good feelings, deserve some respect; and though no sanctity exist in effect, yet if an innocently-entertained veneration be attached to any place or thing, it would be both cruel and indecent unnecessarily to violate it. But with respect to the *errors* that occur in the present version, the case is very different: to correct these is not a mere matter of taste; it is not one in which the voice of prejudice is to be heard even were it raised; it is not even a matter of choice, but of imperious duty and necessity. That there are some few faults is certain; indeed, in a task of such length, this was almost unavoidable; and our chief wonder ought to be, that there are so few: of the propriety of correcting these, however, there cannot be, I think, a doubt;—the more beautiful the edifice, the more requisite that it should be free from faults. Yet still it is an office that demands the utmost delicacy and skill. As for an entire new translation, this is by no means necessary; the end desired may be obtained without this. I would not, however, have any presumptuous hand permitted to exert his critical acumen, at merely his own discretion, on so beautiful a fabric; nor indeed ought so important a charge to be confined to any single individual, even though that one were possessed of all the mighty learning of a Bentley or a Johnson. It would perhaps be best that a committee of the most learned and religious men were instituted, like the one which first performed the task of translating. The duty of these should be to revise carefully the present editions, to compare them attentively with the original, to take into consideration all that has been already written on the subject, to invite the farther discussions of the literary world, to examine whatever might be submitted to them; and, as the result of all this, to make such emendations as the text requires, rendering, however, at the same time, the most full and satisfactory reasons to the public for every correction they proposed to make. In so highly important a duty nothing should be done lightly. Some may say, "the present version is sufficiently correct,—there may be a few faults, but these are of no consequence; our fathers have been contented with this, and why should not we be so? To this, I reply, that had such reasoning always prevailed, we should not at this day have been Christians, or being Christians, we should not have been Protestants. No—nothing is done while any thing remains to do; however trifling the errors, yet as *errors* they call for correction; and indeed in a work of such importance no errors can be trifling;—we should stop at nothing short of perfection, when every letter is connected with, and may involve our highest, our dearest interests.

But that these errors are not quite so venial as may be imagined, the following is a proof. In St. John's Gospel (chap. ii. v. 4.) our Saviour is made to say to his mother,—"Woman, what have I to do with thee?" This speech, to me at least, always sounded most gratingly. I would not, I am sure, have used such expressions to my own parent, and I could in no way reconcile the appearance that it has of undutifulness. All to whom I have ever mentioned the subject, have confessed a similar feeling; it is, therefore, of the greatest consequence that an explanation should be given; for to entertain even a shadow of doubt of the

Messiah's perfect immaculateness, is a sin of the first magnitude. I did, however, entertain none; knowing he could do or say no wrong, I passed the sentence over, as I believe almost every other reader does, under the supposition that it contained some mystical sense, which, though above vulgar comprehension, yet rendered it perfectly innocent. But, still, this was rather a slovenly mode, and, in truth, I regretted to be obliged to appeal solely to my faith in this one instance, when in every other it was seconded by my reason and feelings. I often reflected on the passage, and at each time with increased wonder that it should be ever requisite to resort to mysticism fully to believe in his perfect excellence and purity. It at length occured to me to examine the original; and I there was at once relieved from these unpleasant feelings; and had the pleasure of finding, what I ought never to have doubted, that the Messiah's every word and deed is not only in *reality* the most perfect, but also ever strictly so in appearance. The original stands thus:—Λέγει αὐτῆ, ὁ Ἰησοῦς. Τὶ ἔμοι καί σοι, γύναι; οὔπω ἥκει ἡ ὥρα μου. The translation is perfectly correct in rendering γύναι "woman," but this address has by no means that harshness in Greek which it has in English, and, indeed, "Madam" approaches nearest to the sense in which it is used. But the chief point—τί ἐμοί καί σοι,—which is translated—"what have I to do with thee?" is a most false version of the passage; it means simply and only—"*what is that to thee and me?*" Thus our Saviour merely says, that there being no wine at the feast, is no concern of theirs; and then immediately adds,—"my time is not yet come;" which, that Mary understood as a promise, without any harshness in it, is clear, by her instantly turning to the servants, and bidding them carefully obey his orders. I do think that errors like the above ought to be rectified; and I could point out several lesser,—but not now, for I have already, I fear, taken up too much of your time, Mr. Editor, with a very dry discourse;—and thank you and my other readers, therefore, for the patience exercised.

PHILALETHES.

## ACCOUNT OF AGRA AND DELHI, &c.

SIR,—The following account of Agra and Delhi, extracted from the papers of a friend, will perhaps be acceptable to some of your readers.

"I will now detail a few remarks which may be useful for the information and guidance of those who may be induced to make Agra the object of their research, and may operate as an incitement to those, whose curiosity may not have been sufficiently excited by the general declaration of admiring travellers who have visited the Taj Mah'l, or to such as may have doubtingly withheld due credence from the assertions of public fame in praise of the surpassing charms of this model of perfection, of which no drawing or description can possibly convey an adequate idea to the mind.

I will begin by acquainting the traveller that when I visited Agra, I was previously under the necessity of obtaining a *perwannah* from the Nawaub to pass the Jumna, and a letter from the resident with Scindiah to the Dewan at Agra, intimating the purport of my visit. I pass over several intermediate stages of my journey, and arrive at Omeidpoor, about eighty coss from Cawnpore, and fifty from Futtehpoor.

A mile west of this village, and in the centre of a tank, about 300 yards square, stands a large building, consisting of a single room, with a verandah all round, and a corresponding room above, crowned by a dome. There are some trees round the building. It is a pleasant place to spend a day in, and affords good accommodation for a traveller and his suite. A good bridge leads to the building, and the tank is full of water. From this edifice the splendid domes of the Taj rise in full view, at the distance of twelve miles, appearing like snow-white clouds ascending to the skies.

This place was constructed about 300 years ago by a Patan chief, named Ahmed Khan, whose mausoleum stands on an eminence near the tank. The base of his tomb is a single piece of yellow granite, extremely fine. From this place you should, in the afternoon, send forward your tea equipage to Shah Dera, within a coss of the Taj, with directions to proceed in the morning to Yâtimaud U'Dowla's tomb, and prepare breakfast in a house in the garden directly on the banks of the Jumna. This precaution becomes the more necessary where there is a large party, in order to guard against interruption in your progress next morning; for, as you approach Agra, a bad road leads through a deep and narrow pass, through which there is room only for a single hackery, so that if another should approach in an opposite direction, one of them must turn back, though in most parts an hackery could scarcely turn, and certainly not with its bullocks. It opens about half-way, where a small stream crosses the valley, but narrows again as you advance, and is altogether about a mile long. On arriving at Shah Dera next morning, strike off on the right towards the Rana Bagh. This is an extensive fine garden, whose broad stone walks are highly raised, and amply shaded from the solar ray by rows of full-grown trees; but the solemn gloom and awful silence that reign in the bosom of this dark retreat, check the cheerful current of the spirits, and incline the mind to pensiveness. It must, however, be a delightful refuge from the meridian fervour of an Indian sun, in the oppressive, sultry season of the year.

You thence proceed to the river, where, in the

centre of a delightful garden, surrounded by a high wall, with four handsome central gates, and pavilions at its angles, stands the Mausoleum of Yâtimaud U'Dowla, father of the celebrated Noor Jehan, and grandfather to Momtauz-e-Zemauna, to whose memory her royal consort Shah Jehân erected the splendid building of the Taj. The building is about sixty feet square; and from the angles of a second story, rise four small marble spires, somewhat higher than the edifice, which, on the second story, consists of a single room, about twenty-four feet square; and below, a room of equal extent, surrounded by small apartments; the whole throughout of white marble, elegantly inlaid, inside and out, in beautiful patterns of flowers, vases, cypress trees, and other ornaments, composed of gems, as in the Taj, but of inferior delicacy, yet producing a fine general effect.

The diameter of the spires is too great in proportion to their height—the only apparent defect; but perhaps unavoidable, from the space necessarily required for each ascending stair. The tombs in the lower story are of a yellow cast of porphyry, of a high polish, and extremely beautiful. The cenotaphs in the upper room are of plain white marble; and the walls of open lattice-work throughout, exceedingly delicate, and admitting an agreeable light, that displays the ornaments to the best advantage.

From this building the view of the opposite shore is uncommonly grand and interesting. On one side the Taj, with its rich dome of white marble, rising, as K—— expresses it, "like a most beautiful pearl on an azure ground," and forming with its beautiful spires, its splendid gates, and other buildings, a most delightful picture, softened by the verdant shades of its rich garden.

In front, the extended, high, red freestone walls of the fort, rising with bold abruptness from the river, surrounded by the beautiful marble domes of the Mootee Musjid, and the rich gilt spires of the imperial palace, present a pleasing contrast to the chaste delicacy of the Taj; while farther on, a ray of sadness darkens the happy scene, on contemplating the splendid ruins of numerous palaces scattered in rich profusion along the banks of the river, backed by the magnificent domes of the Jumma Musjid, and a distant view of the town.

As you will here pass the day, you will have time to make the necessary arrangements for crossing the river next morning. Any letters you may have for the person in command at Agra should now be sent, that the necessary orders may be issued to those in charge of the buildings, and a person sent to conduct you to the place.

Having crossed the river, and passed through a large square court some hundred yards in extent, you enter a magnificent gate of red freestone, by a room about forty feet square; whence descending into a delightful garden of great extent, the splendid edifice called the Taj Mah'l bursts upon the view at the extremity of a long avenue of luxuriant lofty trees.

The whole of this rich edifice is of white marble, rising from a noble base of the same material, above a hundred yards square. This base or terrace is elevated more than twenty feet above the level of the garden—a circumstance that gives the building a full and fine relief, and greatly contributes to the grandeur of its appearance. From each angle of this extensive terrace, rises a beautiful white marble minaret of four stories, each having a small balcony, and ending in a neat pavilion, crowned by a dome, whose height from the ground cannot be less than 150 feet; and that of the grand dome of the Taj, I judge to be 200.

In the four great faces of this brilliant edifice a magnificent arch rises to the height of sixty-five feet, above which the wall is raised considerably, to hide the shaft of the dome.

In the four lesser sides, formed by cutting off the angles of the square, a double range of arches rises to the top; but here, instead of raising the wall, whose uniformity would thus destroy its beauty, a small pavilion, crowned by a dome, is raised at each great angle of the building, and rising to the spring of the great dome, fills up the hollow bosom of the shaft, and thus produces the desired effect. The advantage of raising the shaft so high is displayed in the surprising lightness of appearance it gives to the whole building, which is more apparent the further you recede from it, even to the distance of many miles, and the more strikingly so, when contrasted with the distant appearance of the buildings on either side, whose domes not possessing this advantage, seem in close adhesion to the buildings from their very spring,—an opinion you find not warranted on near inspection. These buildings consist of two large edifices of equal dimensions; one a large mosque, the other a *Jamâ,ut Khauna*, or place of assembly before and after prayers.

Each building is supported in front by a grand arcade, of which the central arch is near sixty feet high;—they are open on three sides, the mosque (as usual) being closed on the *Mecca* side, which they always face at prayers. The whole building covers an extent of ground nearly seventy yards in length, and about thirty yards in breadth, and rises to the height of eighty feet—all of red freestone, crowned with three domes of white marble.

These buildings are at the distance of a hundred yards on either side, and erected on a base nearly twenty feet lower than that of the Taj. This seems a judicious measure; for if equally raised with the marble terrace, they must, by being in too full relief, have considerably injured the apparent grandeur of the principal building. Considered as a single piece of architecture, were they duly raised on more elevated bases, their grandeur would be infinitely striking from the great extent of building that fills the eye.

An octagon building of three stories rises at each angle of the garden, affording to visitors excellent accommodation. The garden is in a pleasing style, with broad stone walks, gay parterres, numerous fountains, and a charming white marble reservoir in the centre, which is constantly kept full of water.

The outside of the Taj is highly ornamented with Arabic inscriptions in large black marble letters round the doors and arches, and with flowers composed of various coloured stones, inserted in the white marble ground of the building. The numerous shades of these rich flowers are so elegantly blended, that the strictest eye of scrutiny cannot possibly discover the points of unison in any part. I have head it asserted, that with the aid of a microscope, seventy pieces have clearly been ascertained in one small flower: and I have myself reckoned with the point of my nail even ninety in one flower.

The plan of the Taj appears to be one central octagon room, about sixty feet diameter, having a suite of rooms all round, to the number of eight, which have a direct commnnication with the centre apartment. The doors rise in an elliptic arch to the height of eighteen feet—above which are eight large elliptic windows, with the intervention of a cornice, and an Arabic inscription in black marble characters, that surrounds the room. Around each door also there is a beautiful inscription descending to the floor.

The tombs of Shah Jehân and his consort Momtauz-e-Zemauna stand in the middle of the room, surrounded by a marble railing of net-work nearly nine feet high, and of exquisite beauty. To say that these tombs are of the most lovely white marble is but slight praise, where marble, and that of the most transcendent kind, is the least costly article of which the building is composed.

These monuments boast far other beauties;—but justly to describe these, or give an adequate idea of this paragon of beauty, is an undertaking far beyond the limited powers of my feeble pen.

I shall, therefore, only observe generally, that whether we regard the beauty of the various inscriptions, the delicacy of the luxuriant bouquets of flowers rising in bold relief from the white marble vases that adorn the walls, or contemplate the rich glow, the glare of brilliancy, the happy effect exhibited by the rich gems that enter into the composition of the beautiful flowers and other ornaments that decorate the tombs, the fine marble net-work that surrounds them and various other parts of the building, we are equally left in astonishment at the dignity of mind that planned, and the merit that executed, so wonderful a task.

The extreme delicacy of the Arabic inscriptions on the tombs, of the radiated circles and rich wreaths of flowers composed of the most beautiful agate, onyx, cornelian, various-coloured jasper, and lapis-lazuli, that shine in rich profusion over the lovely surface of these delightful monuments of regal splendour, no pen can describe, no mind conceive.

These tombs are properly cenotaphs, the bodies being correspondently interred in a subterraneous apartment, and enclosed in monuments of the whitest marble I ever saw. The evening sun, entering only by the doorway, displays as you descend, their excessive beauty to the greatest advantage. These tombs are richly decorated. The glory or radiated circle of gems, on the tomb of Shah Jehan, and the Arabic inscription on the other, are delicate beyond conception of the most ardent imagination.

Softened by the sad reflection of the instability of human happiness, the mind retires from the contemplation of this rich scene, impressed with regrct, on casting an eye on the certain seeds of future dissolution, scattered over the fair surface of this grand edifice, where trees, and other vegetable productions, menace with certain fate its fine architectural and *devoted* beauties.* Thus, like the human frame, cherishing in its unconcious bosom the fatal seeds that urge it to destruction,—

> " As man perhaps, the moment of his breath,
> Receives the lurking principle of death ;—
> The young disease—that must subdue at length,—
> Grows with his growth, and strengthens with his strength !"

---

* Since the Taj Mah'l came into the possession of the Honourable East India Company, a sum has been annually allowed for keeping it in proper repair, and all the incipient vegetation has been eradicated.

Having, at the close of my last day's journey, left the traveller in the garden of the Taj Mah'l, preparing perhaps to inspect some drawings by a native artist, of the Taj and its ornaments, I now claim his attention to other objects of estimation, and shall as briefly as possible relate what I have seen.

Being desirous of visiting the buildings in the fort, the Governor's permission was accordingly obtained; and, at seven o'clock in the morning, accompanied by the Dewan, I approached the outer gate, through fifty file of armed men. On a signal given, the opposing iron chains were lowered for our admittance; and, attended by three servants, who had previously lodged their offensive weapons with the guard, I entered the fort.

The first object that attracted attention was a large piece of ordnance lying on the ground. It was of fine bronze, of a high polish, and exhibited a freshness of appearance as if recent from the foundery, though a Persian inscription referred its origin to the period of the great Acbar, who died in 1605, and who declared its weight to be 1,150 maunds (123,000lb.) thus exceeding by twelve ton the weight of the gun at Dacca, as stated by Rennell. The gun at Agra is fourteen feet long, four feet in diameter at the muzzle, and twenty-three inches calibre.

After gratifying my fancy by diving into the bosom of this enormous piece, I proceeded to the *Dewan-e-Aum*, or public hall, where the sovereign usually gave audience to his splendid court. This hall is sixty yards by twenty, open on three sides, and supported by rows of stone pillars. It has an appearance lofty, grand, and airy. The *Dewan-e-Khass*, or private hall, next presented itself, being a large room of white marble, seventeen yards by seven, and joining by an arched colonnade an open gallery of equal extent. The walls are ornamented with white marble vases and flowers in relief, but infinitely inferior in beauty to the work at the Taj.

Passed thence to the Zenânah apartments, of white marble, elaborately adorned with flowers in festoons, and other ornaments, carved, painted, or gilt, and covering the walls and ceilings in extravagant profusion. Near this is the Hummaum, consisting of several apartments for bathing, the walls and floors whereof are adorned with mosaic-work of various coloured marbles, and semi-pellucid gems. The floors are extremely beautiful, and from a fountain in the middle of one of them, the water, rising from a hundred springs, falls in soft showers into a central bath. A large black marble slab, raised two feet from the floor, was shown as the throne whereon the emperor usually sat, in private conference with his ministers; its length is about eleven feet by seven, and it has Arabic inscriptions on the outer edge or depth of the stone, in elegant relief. This fine slab is cracked right across, towards one extreme, which is said to have been miraculously occasioned by the impure foot of the impious Jewan Sing, son of Soorij Mull, late chief of the Jauts. The conscious stone, accustomed only to the foot of majesty, thus manifesting its displeasure at being ascended without the sanction of that divine behest, by which kings assume the sceptre of authority over God's chosen people. Had this been a vestige of Hindoo superstition, and under the protecting care of guardian divinities, I should not have wondered at the tale; but we every where find superstition stepping in to the aid of popular prejudice, for purposes which the human mind is often at a loss to develope.

Two brilliant apartments, with marble floors and fountains, compose the mansion called *Sheesha Mahul*. The walls and ceilings are ornamented throughout with *talc*, and small mirrors, formed into various pretty patterns; and being intended as night apartments, illumination must produce a fine effect. This must greatly be heightened by the play of the fountains, as the reflected rays, passing through the descending showers, would produce infinite corruscations, from the multiplicity and varied positions of the reflecting surfaces; and it is with this view, I judge, that one of the fountains is placed within a covered recess at the extremity of the room.

On ascending a flight of rough red free-stone steps, whose shabby appearance, and dilapidated balustrade, raised no favourable expectation in the mind, a sudden turn to the left discovers to the view the most beautiful object in the fort,—the *Mootee Musjid*. At the extremity of a square court, paved with large white marble flags, and surrounded by a beautiful gallery and colonnade of the same material, rises this delightful mosque, comprising a single room, fifty-four yards by twenty, supported by rows of pillars, and crowned with three lovely domes, and several well-proportioned pavilions;—the whole of marble of the purest white. Of all that I have seen in this neighbourhood, the delicate appearance, the just proportions, the simple majesty, and *tout ensemble*, of this building, pleased me most; free from the aid of foreign ornament, its fair resplendent face shines with a lustre that I think unrivalled. The impartial eye, endeavouring to trace defects, marks some new charm at each succeeding view; and you reluctantly retire, satisfied of the justness of its claim to the appellation of the *Pearl Mosque*, which the name implies.

Though I was not above an hour in the fort, my cicerone, the Dewan, seemed to wish the business over, and *looked impatience* with so plain a face, that I unwillingly shortened my visit, after a transient view of the apartments in which Shah Jehân passed the last eight years of his life, imprisoned by his son Aurungzebe, who had usurped the throne. These apartments look into the

Dooâb, and command a fine view of the river and the Taj, and rise directly from an extensive garden, the only open space in the fort I could get a sight of, the view being obstructed by the high walls of the Zenânah and other buildings; and I found myself not at liberty to range about, owing, I presume, to the circumstance of the late celebrated Ishmael Beg being then a prisoner in the fort; to this, also, I attribute their objection to my passing between the fort and the Jumna, as his apartments probably overlooked the river. The fort on that side is nearly a right line—perhaps 800 yards in length; the ditch is narrow, and the fort has two walls, the inner rising more than thirty feet above the outer, which is full forty feet. I have heard the extent of the fort rated at two miles; my computation falls far short of this estimate, but I may obviously be mistaken, not having circumscribed it.

There are still some good buildings in the town of Agra, and the streets are paved with stone, having a drain in the middle. In general they are narrow, except the main street, occupied by merchants, which is broader than in the generality of Indian towns: but if this be an advantage on the side of beauty, it is fully counterbalanced on the score of convenience, for, as business is usually transacted in the middle of the day, the heat is extremely oppressive where the streets are wide, and the houses low; whereas, narrow streets and high houses, oppose excellent barriers to the fervour of the solar influence, and leave the shaded inhabitants cool in the hottest weather. This I have often experienced at Benares, where I have frequently rambled about to pick up curiosities in the shops, or scraps of mythologic knowledge in the temples. I am the more solicitous to establish this observation, because Mr. H——, in his book of Indian travels, deduces an opposite conclusion from the same cause; alledging that—" the height of the houses, and narrowness of the streets, by causing double and treble reflections of the sun's rays, must make the heat intolerable." Let us examine this a little. To produce these reflections, it seems necessary that the reflecting surface be regular, white, and highly polished,—none of these requisites, however, are yielded by the walls in question; they are either of brick or stone, and it being the nature of all opaque bodies to absorb the rays of light, no reflection whatever is here absolutely produced; for the upper stories meeting the solar rays, either absorb them altogether, or variously disperse them over the irregularities of their rough surface. But experience is superior to all reasoning, and enables me, with due submission, to assert that Mr. H—— is mistaken in the fact.

I feel a gratification on this occasion, in citing a passage from Tacitus, in the life of Nero. Speaking of the new streets of Rome after the conflagration, he says,—"Yet some there were who believed the ancient form and structure more conducive to health, as, from the narrowness of the streets, and the height of the buildings, the rays of the sun were hardly felt or admitted, whereas, now, so spacious was the breadth of the streets, and so utterly destitute of all shade, that the heat scorched with unabated rage."

On the road to Secundra, and about three miles from Agra, you pass through a handsome gate, which connects two large portions of a wall that once enclosed the city of Agra, and is said to have comprised a space of twelve coss (twenty-four miles) in circuit. Beyond this, and reaching to Secundra, the eye is presented with one rude extended view of ruined buildings, squares, mosques, gates, pavilions, and extensive gardens, which sufficiently evince the grandeur of this once splendid paradise of Indian opulence—now, alas! a dreary waste, save where "the moping owl doth to the moon complain,"—or midnight robber take his usual stand. Impressed with the sad solemnity of the scene, which invites the mind to serious meditation, you insensibly approach the great gate that leads to the mausoleum of the renowned Acbar—and here let me sit down, that you may at leisure contemplate the magnificence of the scene before you.

A print of the gate most people have seen; and you will find the splendid mausoleum in the centre of a grove, nearly two miles in circuit. The whole is upon a grand scale. The buildings, the gates, the fountains, the broad stone walls, dividing the garden into four great sections, each equal in extent to the square of the Berhampore cantonments. I question not but you will be much gratified; if, however, contrary to all probability, it should prove otherwise, I shall at least have the consolation of not having imposed much trouble, by having brought you half-a-dozen miles to breakfast in one of the twenty-two apartments of this grand edifice—for which purpose you will find the upper room large enough, (you will, however, find it more convenient to breakfast below, and will thence receive fresh gratification from a visit to the summit) being thirty yards square, including its gallery, of white marble throughout, partly open at the top, and having its arches filled up (as at Yihtimâd ood Dowla's tomb) with delicate lattice work cut through the solid slab. Although this monument (which is chiefly of red stone) rises perhaps 120 feet from a base 120 yards square, has numerous turrets, and an arcaded open gallery round each decreasing story of the pyramid, and terminates above in four small marble turrets, that rise from the angles of the supernal marble room; yet the building is not altogether to my taste,—nor yet the gate. While, therefore, you are at breakfast, or amusing yourself with the Arabic inscriptions on the marble walls, and the highly adorned cenotaph in the middle of the room, I shall make an excursion, of fourteen coss, to Futteh-poor-Sicri, (whither, if you possess one spark of curiosity, you will directly follow me) to view the superb gate of the charming square, the lovely shrine of the celebrated Saint Shah Selim Chishtee. You will thence, I am persuaded, accompany me to Delhi, to view one of the wonders of the East, the Jumma Musjid, whose celebrity has so justly placed it in the foremost rank of Indian curiosities. Long may it remain, a just monument of the taste and splendour of its royal founder, Shah Jehân. No monarch can boast of having raised such models of perfection as *this*,—the temple in the fort of Agra,—and the Taj Mah'l in its neighbourhood.

This mosque stands on an eminence in the centre of the town. A noble stone stair of nearly forty steps, leads up to a terrace above a hundred yards square, paved with red freestone, and having a large reservoir of water in the middle. The temple occupies the measure of one side, and the converging rays of beauty from its splendid face, salute the ravished eye on entering the eastern gate. And here for a moment I shall leave you, entranced in admiration of the charming structures that now surround you;—nor shall I deprive you of the pleasure of giving a description of the scene. You have seen a print of this superb mosque, highly executed, by the Daniels—but, though manifestly beautiful, it falls far short of the original. No man can do it justice, either with pencil or with pen. Though I had come with expectations highly raised of the surpassing beauty of this temple, above all others of the kind in Hindostan, I consider it a just tribute, to declare myself fully gratified on inspection. To compare it with the temple in the Fort of Agra—it displays a degree of masculine beauty, that interferes not with the delicacy and lovely chaste appearance of the other, which, in these points, must ever stand unrivalled. Here, the scene presents a bold sublimity of aspect, contributed by its splendid spires and great extent. The Mootee Musjid, on the contrary, is perfect beauty on a scale more delicate.

Besides the Jumma Musjid, you will find numerous objects at Delhi, either to challenge admiration, or gratify curiosity—such as the Gardens of Shalimar, and of Nizam ood-deen; the Mausoleum of Humâioon, and that of Sufdur Jung, grandfather to the present Nawaub of Oude; the Observatory, the staff of Feroze Shah, similar to the pillar of Allahabad; the Fort of Delhi, and Shah Jehanabad; and the Kootub-Minar, or round tower, rising about 240 feet from a base fifty yards in circuit,—had its colour been uniform, and the fluting continued to the top, this magnificent tower might justly be styled beautiful.

But I must particularly attract your attention to the mausoleum of Sufdur Jung, which I think the handsomest edifice of the kind about Delhi. This, and the buildings around it in the garden, afford accommodation to the largest party; there are several neat apartments in the second story of the monument, and a large circular room within the body of the dome. As this situation is nearly equidistant from every place worthy of observation about the capital, a few days' residence might here be made with infinite advantage and accommodation to the traveller. While you are engaged within the town, you should reside at Sufdar Jung's palace, or obtain permission to sojourn in the delightful gardens of Shah Nizam ood Deen, in the suburbs of the capital. But as you will come provided with a letter from the Resident with Scindia, to the native agent at Delhi, he will facilitate all matters, and will procure you, if desirable, an audience of his majesty. This will cost you some money, in nuzzers to his majesty, to Acbar Shah, the heir apparent, and to the sulateen, or junior branches of the family, who are usually present on such occasions. I shall not here presume to prescribe the measure of your liberality —what others of your own rank may have given, will serve you as a guide, and the native agent will instruct you in the due proportions of the gifts. I have heard of a great man presenting 101 gold mohurs to the king, forty-one, I think, to Acbar Shah, and thirty or forty in a purse to be distributed among the sulateen. To the nuzzers might be added rich Indian muslins, and articles of European manufacture,—such as superfine broadcloth, velvets, satins, silks, &c.; and air-guns and pistols to the prince, to whom, also, a telescope or two would be extremely acceptable;—but, alas! the horrid act of the infamous Gholaum Kauder, who obscured the light of heaven from the unfortunate Shah Allum, has rendered this, otherwise desirable article, of no utility to his majesty, to whose longing eyes, "that roll in vain to find the piercing ray," no longer returns day, or—

> "The sweet approach of eve or morn,
> Or aught of vernal bloom, or summer rose;
> Or flocks or herds, or human face divine;—
> But clouds instead—and ever during dark
> Surrounds him"——

Should his majesty honour you with a title, the fees of office will somewhat exceed an hundred rupees.

You may easily obtain permission to visit the fort, without an introduction to the royal presence—and I would recommend your reading Capt. F—'s description of the buildings, in his "History of Shah Allum."

The people of these provinces are chiefly of the tribes of Jauts, and you will in general find much security in travelling through their districts; they are, however, extremely warlike, and very numerous beyond Delhi. Every village abounds with soldiers, and so martial is their turn, from the frequency of predatory incursions into their country by the Seiks and Mahrattas, that, if left undisturbed for one season, they would, as is said, arm against each other on the next. They fight very desperately, and, if they have time to assemble, they unite for the common cause; but, if a village yields on the first assault, or is taken by a *coup de main*, the conquerer may safely sit down, and collect the customs and rent;—but failing in the first attempt, the invader usually retires, as the war signals soon invite the neighbouring hosts to the scene of action.

About four days' journey to the west of Delhi stands a Jaut village called Bordonney, which has ever been successful against the hostility of attack: like a second Gibraltar, it has become the touchstone of their valour, and it seems a point of honour to defend it at all hazards. It has neither walls nor bastions, but is guarded by men who risk their lives at the cannon's mouth in its defence: hence, cannon and large armies, I have heard, have in vain appeared against it. The capture of this place would give a mortal wound to their reputation, and destroy that ardour of exertion, which is here brought to an irresistible focus. These are generally the people who, under the denomination of Mewattees, are employed as escorts by travellers, and by the merchants of the upper provinces. They are Hindoos, and are properly denominated Bridje Baassy, from the name of their original country; Bridje being the district around Muttra sacred to Chrisna, the shepherd god. The Mewattees are Mussulmen, and come from a province south of Delhi—and it seems they came first to be employed on such occasions, from having been long notorious for their exactions upon travellers; it was at length judged prudent thus to purchase their protection. The name of Mewattee and public robber, had long been synononomous, hence all adventurers of this nature fell under this denomination; very few, however, of real Mewattees now come down to be employed—they have given place, perhaps, to better men—for the Jauts are trusty servants, very vigilant and active. They are extremely impatient of abuse, which, indeed, is characteristic of the Indian, especially of the upper provinces, and this equally applies to the Mussulman as to the Hindoo. Gentlemen who travel amongst them, should be aware of this circumstance, and hence constantly guard against the impulse of irascibility:—neither the Patan nor Rajpoot will tamely suffer their abuse, and 'tis well if they confine themselves to a bare return of the compliment, without directly appealing in the first instance to the sword.

Within the limits of our own districts, the natives are more subservient to our humours, and the dread of punishment might influence them to bear with our abuse; but in those provinces not subject to our authority, the spirit of independence fully manifests itself in our progress ;—hence, the European who unguardedly gives the reins to his passion, will meet a spirit of resistance he may find it difficult to controul. When gentlemen, whether native or European, stop in the vicinity of any considerable town or village, in the Nawaub's portion of the Dooâb, the Cutwal, or other public officer, usually sends a supply of earthen vessels and fire-wood, for culinary purposes, and frequently milk, straw, kids, &c. for the accommodation of the party. This is the expiring remnant of that ancient hospitality, established by Shere Shah throughout Hindostan. From Bengal to the Indus, wells were dug, and serauees (public buildings for travellers) erected, at convenient distances, for the accommodation of the traveller, who was furnished with lodging and refreshment at the expense of the state :—but, alas ! most of the wells are now dry or out of repair, and the serauees dilapidated,—the funds for their support having long ceased to exist. One cannot contemplate the present state of these once populous towns, extensive serauees, grand reservoirs of water, mosques, and other splendid edifices, now in ruins, without the tribute of a sigh at the shrine of fallen greatness, when one reflects on the surpassing splendour of these rich provinces in the happy days of Acbar and Jehangeer ;—but, unhappily, what the cruel hand of the first rapacious invaders had left unfinished, has more recently been completed by the arms of Abdalla, who tore up the fruitful tree of abundance by the roots, and left it to wither in solitude on these deserted plains.

* * * * *

I am now again on a visit to Agra, after an interval of seven years. I find most things much improved since I first came here. Alas! what can escape the ravages of time? The Mootee Musjid has lost much of its brilliancy. When first I saw it, seven years ago, it was as white as snow; it has since suffered extremely from the weather and want of care; and a great portion of the marble, both of the court and temple, is dirty and discoloured. Some of the pavilions have received a shock from the concussion occasioned by the fire from General Perron's batteries, when he attacked the fort some years ago, which has rendered it necessary to fill them up with masonry, to guard against their tumbling to the ground. Several cannon-balls have struck the marble buildings in other parts of the fort, and the Taj, though so distant, has somewhat suffered, from the violent agitation of the air, during that unhappy contest between the subjects of the Maha Rajah. The interior works of the Taj, however, are still in good order; and I must confess, that, notwithstanding the usual effect produced by the novelty of a first view, I again saw them with increased pleasure. In things of common beauty, admiration is lessened at each succeeding view, but here, I think the effect is different, I can at least answer for my own feelings;—the more I contemplated the lovely shrine, the railing, and the tombs in the subterranean chambers, the more I admired them.

The weight of the great gun in the fort, much exceeds what I formerly stated, I then depended on the information of others; at present I can, from personal inspection, venture to declare, that the weight mentioned in the inscription, is 1464 maunds and $6\frac{1}{4}$ punserees, (nearly 34 seers) which, at twenty-eight maunds to the ton, of only eighty sicca-weight to the seer, gives above thirty-two tons as the weight of this enormous piece. Another inscription states, that Jehangeer having with this gun conquered the Deccan, placed it here. He was successor to the great Acbar, in whose reign this piece was cast. The inscriptions which state the weight of the gun, and its having been cast in the reign of Acbar, appear to have been stamped while the composition was yet warm; all the others having been subsequently engraved.

On my way hither, I stepped aside in search of the caves fabled to be at Muttra, and the giants they are said to contain; but the only thing of this description I could discover, was a small cell, scarce six feet square, about twelve feet beneath the surface of the temple at But-Isser Maha Deo. It contains only a rude stone-seated statue, about two feet high, of Patal Devi, the goddess of the shades; the entrance into the *Sacellum* being scarce seventeen inches by twenty-two. I was obliged to creep into the apartment, where I found just room enough to stand upright. In visiting the goddess, it is necessary to take down a light, as that of day never enters this gloomy cell. In none of the temples at Muttra that I visited, could I discover any resemblance to the cross, as stated in "Maurice's Indian Antiquities." The temple of Rajah Maun Sing, at Bindrabun, six miles from Muttra, is the only one I have yet met with in India, that can come under this description. Whoever visits the temples and ghauts at Muttra, should possess either a good stock of patience, or plenty of cash, and due inclination to disburse it: such a host of Brahmins and Byragees vociferate for his bounty, crowd about him, and raise such a clamour in his ears, that if he can listen with indifference, and assume the listless gravity of patient philosophy, I pronounce him much better calculated for a traveller than I am;—the incessant vociferation of that class of encomiasts called Bhât, is peculiarly distressing, especially if you happen to be in the vein of seeking knowledge from the more enlightened of the assembly; and unless you satisfy their wants, you are frequently provoked to repulse them with rude language, unless you depar from the place to get rid of their importunity.

I have often wondered that none of the gentlemen of the Asiatic Society, conversant in Sanscrit literature, have taken the pains to favour the public with a translation of the "Incarnation of Vishnoo;" a work that I am persuaded would tend to develope the mysteries of the Hindoo religious code, and furnish a vast field for the labours of learned commentators.—Were a proposal to appear for such a publication by subscription, it could not fail of being very liberally supported, as well in Europe as in India, and in the execution of the work, I would recommend the translator to confine himself literally to the text, leaving the public to form their own opinions on any casual coincidence, either with the mysteries of the Christian religion, or the ample code of Grecian mythology. To render such a work more entertaining to the public, it should exhibit the history of the principal actors in each avatar; this would considerably swell the work, but would render it more complete; and if to this were added a translation of the *Chundy Poot*, I am confident it would exhibit, under the form of a mythological romance, as complete a system of moral allegory, as the world has ever produced.

On passing through Secundra, I stopped at Acbar's mausoleum, but could not discover on the tomb the inscription mentioned by Hodges. The tomb, which is of plain white marble, stands in a large central room, on the ground floor; this room has but one entrance, by a long, dark, narrow passage; well calculated to keep the mind in unison with that degree of religious awe inspired by the occasion.

On subsequently entering the Agra gate, I was much incommoded by the quantity of loose bricks scattered upon the road,* for five miles to the Taj. My elephant and horse were both lamed in their progress, and the bearers every moment in danger of tumbling with the palankeen. An expense of ten rupees a month would obviate this inconvenience; but as the Mahratta state would derive no benefit from the measure, it is accordingly neglected. I hinted the matter to the commanding officer at Agra, who, I am persuaded, will obtain the Maha Rajah's permission for the removal of this nuisance. I know nothing that tends more to the credit of a state than good public roads, and places of accommodation. I trust the civil officers in the ceded districts, sensible of this truth, will recommend it to the attention of Government; and that we shall accordingly soon hear of their ordering the serais to be repaired, the wells cleaned, the tanks (now almost dry) to be sufficiently deepened, and good roads made throughout the provinces. Commercial and military intercourse will thus be facilitated, and the grateful thanks of the merchant, the soldier, and the traveller, will

* The roads have since been made good, and at least twenty-four feet in breadth.

resound throughout the country, in due praise of their new masters.

As it seems the province of a traveller to notice such occurrences out of the common line as present themselves to view, I therefore beg leave to give a short account of the recent festival of the Churruck Poojah, which terminated yesterday, on the appearance of the new moon. About five o'clock in the afternoon, five candidates for the favour of the divinity made their appearance on the great road near the Byta Khanneh: each candidate had a large iron hook struck through the flesh on each side of the back bone; these hooks were compressed with a twisted cloth tied firmly at the breast, which served to guard against undue laceration of the flesh. A large pole, about thirty feet high, stood fixed in the middle of the road, on the summit of which was fastened a transverse beam, having a suspended rope at either end: to one of these the candidate was attached by the hook ropes at the back,—and all being thus ready, ten or twelve men bearing npon the other rope, the actor rose into the air, and was swung round, for above five minutes, with great velocity: during his aerial progress, he highly gratified the crowd by liberating among them some pigeons he had carried up in a bag; as, also, a store of plantains and pomegranates, which were eagerly scrambled for by the pious votaries of Hindoo faith. On a signal from the actor, the swing ceased; he gently descended into the arms of his servitors, and was directly succeeded by another candidate. Of the five who ascended, two performed the task to admiration,—the first, with cool unimpassioned aspect, and a decorum suited to the solemnity of the occasion; but to the third it seemed mere pastime. He was dressed in a white linen vest, blue trowsers, and a cap; and, while the crowd stood, with outstretched hands, ready to receive the proffered plantain, he frequently disappointed them by eating it himself. Gay and facetious, he often pulled off his cap to salute the company, and at length descended amidst the applause of the multitude. Notwithstanding the pressure of the cloth, the weight of the body, and the velocity of the motion, appeared to draw the flesh at least four inches from the back, and some drops of blood trickled from the wound.

This festival lasts several days, and each has its peculiar ceremony. On that preceding the swing, I met several groups parading the streets with drums and cymbals, and other instruments, cheering the spirits of the deluded actors; many of whom appeared with long iron rods thrust through their tongues, and long bamboo slips, or pointed scions of a mango branch, borne on the occasion, which gave the party the appearance of one smoking an hookah. Many of these rods were half an inch in diameter, as used by the adult and aged, (those for boys of twelve and fourteen years old, were slighter) and above seven feet long, fastened to the middle, through the tongue, and held fast by the teeth—the boys thus danced about without apparent pain. Some boys appeared with an arrow stuck through the flesh on either side, near the short rib; these arrows united in front, and, attached to a small torch, were held by the young votary, who, jocund, danced about in unison with his brother actors. I was present with one group, during the operation of fixing these arrows, and was astonished at the little sense of pain manifested on the occasion; the youngest, about twelve years old, scarce seemed to feel it. Some of the more robust appeared accoutred in a manner that conveyed a strong sense of pain to the spectator. Two slips of bamboo, about half an inch broad, and twenty feet long, being passed through the flesh on either side, were united at the ends, and held in full tension by a man at each extreme, while the actor moved backward and forward, the lines passing through his flesh. The friction thus occasioned, must have been severe and painful, though, to check its influence, a man stood ready with some ghee* to keep the lines well lubricated.

I was present on a former day during the exhibition of a fire oblation, in which one of my own servants was the principal actor. Suspended by the heels from a transverse beam supported by two

* Clarified butter, made of buffalo's milk.

posts, his flowing hair brushed at every swing a large fire placed on the ground, till having at length scattered the fire with his hands, he descended and joined his party, who directly commenced a dance with naked feet on the live coals; and taking some in their hands, they thus kept moving until the fire was completely extinguished, and reduced to ashes—dancing and singing all the while to the loud dissonance of Indian minstrelsy.

The rites are said to be consecrated to Seeva, who is thus propitiated, by those who wish for offspring, the smiles of fortune, or pardon for their transgressions.

If some gentleman more conversant with the subject, possessing more leisure, and more correct sources of information, than an itinerant stranger, would favour the public with an ampler detail, and elucidation of the rites, ceremonies, and origin of this festival, I could at least insure him the thanks of— A TRAVELLER.

### EXTEMPORE LINES ON SEEING THE TAJ MAH'L.

Oh thou! whose great imperial mind could raise
This splendid trophy to a woman's praise:
If joy or grief inspired the bold design,
No mortal joy or sorrow equalled thine!
Sleep on secure—this monument shall stand
When desolation's wing spreads o'er the land,
By Time and Death in one vast ruin hurl'd,
The last triumphant wonder of the world!

## AN ODE.

[WRITTEN ON THE OCCASION OF THE RETREAT OF THE FRENCH OUT OF RUSSIA.]

HUMBLED and low see hapless Europe lie!
See patriots plead in vain their holy cause;
Lo! Valour, hopeless—forc'd the field to fly,
And Wisdom e'en, forswear her wonted laws!

A tyrant reigns—all nature seems appall'd,—
Freedom aghast, prepares to quit the world;
Fury and Terror on the earth have scope
In dire array:—and o'er each nation's hope
See Slav'ry's flag unfurl'd!

But shall the patriot's zeal be vain,
And Valour's force for e'er withstood?
Nor Wisdom's power the hand restrain,
Which bathes its palm in Europe's blood!

Forbid it Heav'n! And hark! th' inspiring sound
From Moscow's ancient walls which speeds along;
Exulting nations spread the tidings round,
And chaunt with general joy
Of Liberty the song.

No more the tyrant rears aloft in pride,
His blood-stained banner, and his eagle crest;
Rent by the Russian bear, and scatter'd wide,
Th' unhallow'd fragments to the dust are press'd.
See the wild Cossack furious charge his rear,
And urge with direful thrust, his never failing spear!

Now Havoc summons to her dreadful car,
Each scheme of vengeance, and each arm of war!
  Gleams the red thunder through his thronged ranks,
    And scatters wild dismay and death around;
  Ten thousand glitt'ring swords assail his flanks,
    And strike their trembling victims to the ground.

  From Moscow's smoking walls to Smolensk's tow'rs,
    Mark the wide ruin which around him grows;
  Thick and more thick the Russian tempest low'rs,
    And pours hot vengeance on these ruthless foes.

  From Smolensk's tow'rs to Krasnoy's fatal plain,
  See the wild Cossack press his rear again:
  There on that plain, he meets the deathful blow,
  Which venges Europe's rights, and lays his glory low.
  Now panic seizes on his scatter'd host,
  Whose eager flight portends that all is lost!

But mark where yonder they again make stand
Close by the river's side, a desperate band!
    Fourscore thousand warrior men,
      The wreck of all their vast array,—
    Met—but ne'er to meet again,
      Nor homeward bend their willing way.

  For two long days the rapid stream to pass,
    In vain each effort and each art they try;
  Opposing hosts their utmost skill surpass,
    And on the blood-stained shore they sink and die.
Now breaks the morn which seals at length their fate,
And dawns on Europe's hopes a brighter sun, though late!

Lo; the fierce Cossacks near,
  Again the rear assail,
Again spread death and fear,
  And e'en o'er hope prevail;
Till struck by wild affright,
Safety they seek in flight,
  And cast their arms aside;
While Berezyna's flood
Of many a Frenchman's blood
  Receives the reeking tide!

The song of joy now raise—
  Who most shall triumph now?
Who chaunt the victor's praise?
      Oh! England,—thou!

'Tis thine of all the nation's round
  To swell the notes of liberty;
And gladd'ning in the sound,
  To dare thyself be free.

Thine 'tis o'er ev'ry suff'ring land,
  To spread thy wide protecting shield;
And rouse the slumb'ring patriot band,
  The sword in Freedom's cause to wield.

Thine 'tis to bid pale sorrow's cheek,
  In mantling smiles again be dress'd;
To make the drooping mourner speak,
    And pour the tide of joy
    Through ev'ry aching breast!

In ev'ry clime—through ev'ry age,
Thy pitying hand bestows
The balm which other's griefs assuage,
The solace for their woes.

E'en now while o'er thy deadly foe,
Fell wars, dread horrors low'r;
The orphan's cry—the widow's woe,
Each truly British heart shall know,
And feel soft pity's power!

## TO FORTITUDE.

Teach me, stern Fortitude, each shock to bear,
That wayward Fortune on my brow may heap;
To thee I'll breathe a silent fervent pray'r,
Nor scarce allow myself in woe to weep.

May thy firm arm uphold my shrinking frame,
Shield me from pallid fear and wild alarm;
Thy steady, kind protection I will claim,
And let thine influence each sorrow calm.

Though stern thy mien, most friendly is thine heart,
Thy frown Despair appals and makes him flee;
To my weak soul thy courage blest impart,
And I will offer up each prayer to thee.

Thine aid will save,—Misfortune's dart must fail,
For Truth and Fortitude will e'er prevail.

[The following Lines were written on the occasion of the death of Senior-Captain Charles Lionel Showers, of the 19th Regiment Bengal Infantry, who, at the assault of the fortified heights of Mallown, on the 15th April 1815, led one of the principal columns to a separate attack, in the most gallant style, and gloriously fell at its head, just when, in personal conflict, he had, with his own hand, slain the chief of the enemy.]

---

ON Alpine heights a daring foe
His flag in stern defiance wav'd:
Proudly he viewed the bands below,
And long with scorn their valour brav'd.

To check that foe's insulting pride,
Those lofty heights in triumph gain,
The march of war with skill to guide,
Nor prove his country's summons vain,—

To Showers was given;—a chosen band
His dauntless spirit led to fight,
Up the rough cliffs now waves his brand,
Now on the mountain's rugged height.

And there unmov'd his standard flies,
While round him roars the storm of war,—
And there the gallant hero dies,
Far from his home—from friends afar!

Weep for the brave whose sun is set,—
Weep for the friend whom all deplore;
Danger and death he fearless met,
And comes to glad our eyes no more!

In glory's bed his manes rest,
In honour's breast his name's enshrined;
His Christian spirit speaks him blest,
Who join'd to faith a virtuous mind.

Hark! from his grave a warning voice,
Like him it bids us stand prepar'd;
Angels o'er him in heaven rejoice,
For whom on earth they greatly car'd.

And fir'd by his inspiring course,
Shall many a youthful hero rise,
And many a Christian learn the source,
Whence springs the bliss beyond the skies.

## LINES.

[OCCASIONED BY READING THE "ADDRESS TO LOVE."]

Is Love or Fiend or Angel?—Ask the heart
Which glows with its impassion'd, fiercest throbs,
And it will tell thee—'tis a frenzy dire,
That makes the breast to ache with keenest pangs.
The mind is tost 'twixt Hope, and Doubt, and Fear:
For now Suspicion's deadly fangs assail,—
Then chased by Hope's bright visionary gleam,
The soul is cheer'd, and looks to sweetest bliss;
When comes Suspense to overcloud the morn,
And leaves the mind again to Doubt a prey!

The agitated mind, thus whirl'd in storms,
Resigns to Passion ev'ry finer sense,
The soul's best impulse deaden'd,—soon of Love
Each trace is lost; and *self* alone prevails!
Ah! then—if cold disdain, or rival blest,
Meets the neglected lover's jaundiced view—
Farewell each softer passion; for his breast's
Insulted selfishness claims deep revenge!

Can this be Love?
Yes—but 'tis Love of earth—born kind, who oft
With sullied wings flits brooding o'er the world,
And changes man to demon.
But yonder see a beauteous form approach,
Heaven's offspring, who with gentlest feelings speaks,
And pours soft balm into the wounded heart;
See, playful Innocence and Purity, fair maids,
Attend his footsteps, and diffuse fresh charms
O'er ev'ry glowing feature, beaming bright,
And in resistless modesty array'd!

Blest pow'r! I'll woo thee, and enshrine my heart
Beneath thy gentle and alluring sway:
For kind beneficence, and social ties,
From thee derive new charms, and make the soul
To sympathize with jocund nature round,
Whose joyous voice proclaims thy genial reign.

Each humble plant and beauteous flow'r that blows,
The winged insect, and the cheerful lark,
That carols forth the first gay note of morn;
The varied songsters of the spicy grove,
And scaly tribe that cleave the liquid wave,
With ev'ry animal that life enjoys,

Display the kind beneficence divine,
Which sheds o'er earth blest influence of Love!
But most on man the pure effulgence falls,
And blends the whole to harmony supreme.

Thou gracious pow'r! whose genial warmth inspires
Each gen'rous sentiment in man to man:
Guides calm benevolence, and fills the breast
With warmth of feeling t'wards the friends we love.
But oh! most sweet—when soft affections meet,
And soul communes with soul without disguise.
The open brow, with candour beaming bright,
And pleasing smiles, full confidence bestows,
Nor has a thought it e'er can wish to hide.
Away Suspicion! and each meaner art—
True Love disdains them all:—its tender balm
Can heal the sick'ning mind, where rudest pain,
And grief, have sought to fix their dire abode.
Nor can Misfortune's darkest frown relax
The steady pow'r of Love—whose mighty arm
Can snatch from wild Despair its keenest barb,
Soothe the deep murm'ring of the stricken heart,
And charm severest woe!—
Yes—this is Love—ecstatic, heav'nly Love,
That raises man to angel!

# TRANSLATION OF A SONNET OF DESBARREAUX'.

"Grand Dieu, tes jugemens sont remplis d'équité."

Great God, thy judgments are with wisdom fill'd,
  And still to mercy is thy soul inclin'd;
But I have sinn'd, that though thy goodness will'd,
  Thy justice conld not aught of pardon find.

Yes, Lord, the measure of my crime so great,
  But choice of vengeance to thy pow'r it leaves,—
Thy interest's self forbids a happier fate,
  And e'en thy pity of all hope bereaves.

Then wreak thy wrath,—thy glories thus require,—
  Nor heed the tears that from my eyes will flow;—
Strike—speed thy bolt—consume with lightning's fire;
  And though I perish, I'll adore the blow.

But on what part can thy dread thunder fall,—
Does not a Saviour's blood bedew, redeem them all?

## ON THE DEATH OF B. W. MARSH, Esq.

### (OF RUNGPORE.)

When Marsh, the favour'd child of Nature, died,
Nature herself, in grief retiring, sigh'd:
"Who'll now transcribe my calendar of Spring,
My buds in embryo, or the varied wing
Of birds, that haunt the unfrequented wood,
Or lave their painted plumage in the flood?
Who now will tread the desert's dangerous way,
Where Flora shuns th' irradiate blaze of day,
And blooms untouch'd,—but by the spicy breeze
That whispering fans through undiscover'd trees;
A fragrant tribe, that to the viewless sky
Now blush unnoticed—unregarded die!"

A Muse replied—"Not grieved alone thy breast!
True, none like him could scan thy painted vest,
Could mark the laws, the varied ways pursue
Of all that walk'd, that swam, that crept, that flew;
Or plunging downward to thy midmost earth,
Trace matter's form through every chymic birth;
Yet these alone not fill'd his spacious mind,
Long is the train of science still behind;
Far as the realms of Knowledge spread around,
Thy favoured son in foremost rank was found;
And if aught solace Sympathy's fond tear,
Each Muse, each Grace, with thee shall weep o'er
Marsh's bier."

## MY HOOKAH.

---

When thunders crash, or lightning rends,
When angry Jove in storms descends,
My mind from terror what defends?
My Hookah!

Yes—tho' the god descend in showers,
Or tho' the sky with threatening low'rs,
Thou canst beguile the tedious hours—
My Hookah!

On every hand when woes appear,
To raise the sigh, or claim the tear,—
What then my pensive heart can cheer?—
My Hookah!

When thoughts of home came o'er my mind,—
Of distant friends I've left behind,
In what can I then comfort find?—
My Hookah!

When absent from my lovely fair,
Or doom'd by her to nurse despair,
What then alleviates my care?—
My Hookah!

Alone, without a friend to warm,
Without a book my thoughts to calm,
What gives to solitude a charm?—
My Hookah!

When sober mirth in wine is drown'd,
And noisy Folly roars around,
In what for me is refuge found?—
My Hookah!

Or when thro' business toils I wade,
Those toils by profit scarce repaid,
Thou lend'st thy sweet refreshing aid—
My Hookah!

Or languid with the noonday's heat,
When scarce my heart and pulse can beat,
Oh! then I find thee doubly sweet—
My Hookah!

Some seek the fair to banish woes,
With friends and wine some seek repose,
But thou art better far than those—
My Hookah!

The fair deceive,—no friends are true,—
Who trusts to wine may sadly rue;—
But never he who trusts to you—
My Hookah!

Yes, loved companion, in thy praise,
My grateful voice I'll ever raise;
And thou'lt reward me for my lays—
My Hookah!

# MONODY

## ON THE DEATH OF COL. ALEX. MACLEOD, H.M. 59TH REGT.

---

Hark! the deep muffled drum's low sadd'ning sound,
The soldier's heavy foot-fall wends this way;
With martial pomp they seek the sacred ground
Where they their honour'd burthen soon must lay.

Halt! soldiers, halt! let the dull earth receive
The cold remains of one beloved and brave;
With trem'lous hands, and hearts that inly grieve,
They fire the volley o'er the soldier's grave.

What virtue graced not thy heroic mind?
In duty just, in friendship most sincere;
Thy name shall leave a soothing charm behind,
To check the tears that friends shed o'er thy bier.

Son of the valiant! though no more we view
Thy manly form,—yet shall thy honour'd name
Live in the mem'ry of the brave and true,
And dark Cornelis' fight record thy fame!

Glory shall bind a wreath in days to come,
And "Brave Macleod" be sculptur'd on thy tomb!

## ANECDOTE.

DURING the administration of Lord Clive, when fashion was in its extreme of richness, there came out a letter from the Court of Directors, positively prohibiting their servants from wearing any *gold* or *silver* lace on their clothes. Immediately after the receipt of this, Mr. Hosea appeared in the council-room in a dress rather repugnant to the order; his lordship perceiving this, and pointing to the gold binding of his coat, asked him how he reconciled it with the late injunction. Mr. Hosea immediately replied—"this article of dress, my lord, is in no way affected by the Court's letter,—for it is notorious, and your lordship must know, that the Company's orders are not *binding*."

"FAREWELL, a long farewell, to all my greatness!
——————— I have ventured,
Like little wanton boys that swim on bladders,
But far beyond my depth."

SHAKSPEARE.

FINIS.

LONDON:
RICHARDS, PRINTER, ST. MARTIN'S LANE, CHARING CROSS.

939712

Printed in Great Britain by
Amazon.co.uk, Ltd.,
Marston Gate.